THIRTY YEARS OF
MATTEL
FASHION DOLLS

Identification & Value Guide

1967

through

1997

J. Michael Augustyniak

COLLECTOR BOOKS

A Division of Schroeder Publishing Co., Inc.

The current values in this book should be used only as a guide. They are not intended to set prices, which vary from one section of the country to another. Auction prices as well as dealer prices vary greatly and are affected by condition as well as demand. Neither the Author nor the Publisher assumes responsibility for any losses that might be incurred as a result of consulting this guide.

Searching for a Publisher?

We are always looking for knowledgeable people considered to be experts within their fields. If you feel that there is a real need for a book on your collectible subject and have a large comprehensive collection, contact Collector Books.

Cover design: Beth Summers
Book design: Sherry Kraus

COLLECTOR BOOKS
P.O. Box 3009
Paducah, Kentucky 42002–3009

Copyright © 1998 by J. Michael Augustyniak

Printed in the U.S.A. by Image Graphics, Paducah, KY

Contents

Preface

What is your favorite childhood toy? Ask a hundred people, and you'll likely get a hundred different answers. Even if the favorite toy is a mainstay of toy departments like Barbie doll, each response will still be different since every Barbie doll is unique in her owner's eyes. Adult doll collectors can describe in the most minute detail the features of their favorite doll — hair, eyes, lips, nose, body, clothes — even blemishes and wear caused by many happy hours of play, including the all-too-frequent haircuts by budding beauticians. And all too often, that childhood favorite has been thrown out, given away, or lost.

One of the great joys of doll collecting is reliving those precious childhood memories by rebuying the dolls owned as children. Mattel has touched millions of lives in the last 53 years by offering children a wide range of dolls appealing to nearly every girl. For today's under 40 doll collector population, Small Talk refers not to idle chatter people make but rather to Mattel's series of talking dolls. When we mention Rock Flowers or Rosebud, we're not referring to the garden. Dolittle refers to the Doctor, not to our job performance. We'd rather collect the latest Hot Looks than wear them. The only Starr we look for is not in the sky. And having a perfect family means completing our Sunshine Family or Heart Family collections!

These dolls and so many more, including fan-favorite Barbie, lie in the pages ahead. It is the author's hope that a special childhood memory of a long-forgotten doll will be rekindled.

Introduction

Thirty Years of Mattel Fashion Dolls features the complete lines of such widely collected series as The Heart Family, Disney Classics dolls, The Sunshine Family, and celebrity dolls, along with a three-decade overview of perennial favorite Barbie. An entire spectrum of Mattel fashion dolls is included, ranging from 1960s favorites like Story Book Small Talk dolls, Buffy and Mrs. Beasley, and Twiggy, to 1970s classics like the Rock Flowers, Miss America, Honey Hill Bunch, and Donny and Marie, to 1980s Starr, Dazzle, Princess of Power, and Hot Looks, to 1990s Jazzie, Shani, Beverly Hills, 90210, and Elvis.

The Disney Classics section contains entire doll lines from such notable series as Cinderella, Snow White, Aladdin, and Beauty and the Beast.

The Celebrity/Character section features every Mattel personality produced from 1967 to the present.

Many more doll lines are included, from the popular to the unusual and rare. Store exclusives and foreign editions round out the book. A zoo full of animals — horses, Pixietails, dogs, and cats — are also shown.

Stock numbers are given with every entry. Variations and never-released prototype items are also pictured. Vivid close-ups and body markings will aid in the easy identification of out-of-box dolls.

A special section, Barbie Dolls on Parade, is a pictorial 30-year look at Barbie doll's many looks and innovations since 1967. A much-needed Barbie Doll's Family Tree shows every friend and family member of the Barbie doll family from 1959 to 1998.

One of the most fascinating things about many of the dolls featured in *Thirty Years of Mattel Fashion Dolls* is the relationship among dolls. Barbie doll's tiny sister Tutti provided body molds for the Pretty Pairs dolls. 1980s 4½" Dazzle doll uses Barbie doll's actual head mold in a reduced form. Starr's friend Kelley provided the head mold for Mrs. Heart of The Heart Family, whose babies were made from Rosebud molds. Virtually all adult Disney dolls use Barbie and Ken dolls' bodies, and most celebrity dolls use either Barbie doll family bodies or The Sunshine Family bodies. There are many more shared head/body uses, all identified in this book.

Above all else, *Thirty Years of Mattel Fashion Dolls* provides readers a glimpse at many doll series not featured elsewhere.

History

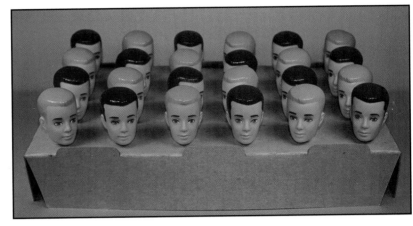

Mattel Toys used to supply toy stores and doll hospitals with replacement parts such as heads and limbs for dolls. Shown here is a factory shipping carton of 24 painted-hair Ken heads. The carton is dated 1963. A tray in which the necks of each Ken head can be inserted allows all 24 heads to face upright.

In the 1970s Mattel packaged All is Not Lost parts booklets with many of their toys, offering such items as jewelry and boa for SuperStar Barbie and individual Sunshine Family replacement dolls at a small cost. More recently, instead of offering replacement parts, Mattel usually finds it more cost effective to simply replace damaged toys covered by warranty. Mattel no longer offers replacement parts, but on occasion sends out replacements for certain items, such as 1990s Winter Fantasy Barbie doll's head; the doll's blue earrings caused her ears to discolor, so Mattel mailed out these replacement heads with silvery earrings in plastic bags. In 1997 Mattel offered to replace Poodle Parade Barbie doll's head to consumers unhappy with her hairstyle. This indicates Mattel is concerned with keeping customers satisfied. Judging from the company's growth, they are keeping *many* customers satisfied.

5

1945 – Mattel is founded, primarily producing dollhouse furniture in the early years.
1955 – The introduction of a new toy gun and unprecedented weekly advertising on the *Mickey Mouse Club* helps Mattel flourish.
1959 – Mattel unveils Barbie doll at Toy Fair.
1960 – Chatty Cathy dolls are introduced. Mattel offers public stock.
1963 – Midge, Barbie doll's friend, is released, creating the now common practice of having friend dolls use the same body for shared wardrobes.
1967 – Barbie doll's newly redesigned face is introduced with a trade-in offer.
1968 – Mattel launches its popular Hot Wheels line.
1970 – Mattel's factory in Mexico burns down.
1974 – The Sunshine Family, a wholesome, craft-themed line, is introduced.
1975 – Company founders, Elliot and Ruth Handler, leave Mattel.
1985 – The Heart Family, a contemporary version of The Sunshine Family, is introduced.
1991 – Mattel begins producing dolls based on Disney animated features.
1993 – Mattel acquires Fisher-Price Toys.
1997 – Mattel adds Tyco Toys to its holdings.

Pricing

Values in this book are for NEVER REMOVED FROM BOX (NRFB) toys. An item removed from the box and then replaced in like-new condition is MINT-IN-BOX (MIB) and is worth 25% less than an NRFB example. MINT toys without boxes, but complete with all accessories, are worth half of the same NRFB toys. INCOMPLETE and played-with toys are valued at the seller's discretion.

Terminology

Terms used by toy dealers and collectors are listed below with a brief definition. Doll collectors may not be familiar with some terms more often used to describe action figures.

ACTION FIGURE – a doll by another name, usually only a few inches tall featuring some action feature.

BLISTER OR BUBBLE CARD/PACKAGE – refers to items sold on an illustrated flat piece of cardboard with a clear plastic dome, or bubble securing the toy to the package.

BUBBLE DENT/DING – damage to the clear plastic dome covering a toy secured to cardboard.

C 1 to C 10 – a rating system used more extensively by toy and action figure collectors than by doll collectors; C 1 to C 10 is a range of conditions with C 1 being the worst and C 10 being the best.

MIB – mint in box, perfect toy in the original box; although it may have been removed and replaced.

MOC – mint on card, item is mint on its original cardboard packaging.

NRFB – never removed from box

NRFC – never removed from card

NRFP – never removed from package

SHELF WEAR – box appears slightly mishandled, as often happens to toys sitting on toy store shelves for an extended time.

STORE STOCK – term used by dealers to describe a boxed toy that appears to have just been placed out for sale on a store shelf.

WRIST TAG – an identifying foil or paper tag attached to a doll's wrist stating the doll's identity, country of origin, and copyright information. Collectors prize intact wrist tags used on many dolls primarily from 1961 – 1973. Shown here are the celebrity wrist tags bearing the dolls' names.

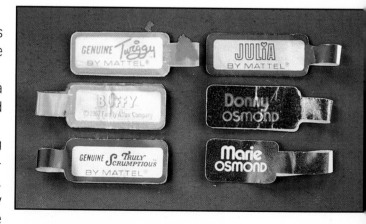

Celebrity and Character Dolls

The Monkees

The Monkees musical group featured four entertainers who quickly rose to fame with such hit songs as *Daydream Believer* and *I'm a Believer* and starred in *The Monkees* television show from 1966 to 1968. Mattel produced a hand puppet featuring all four band members in 1967.

1967 TV'S THE MONKEES TALKING HAND PUPPET #5373 features superb likenesses of Mickey Dolenz, Davy Jones, Mike "Woolhat" Nesmith, and Peter Tork. This was advertised as "the world's first 4-headed hand puppet," which plays the voices of the performers when the talking pull string is pulled. Among the sentences The Monkees say are "Hi! I'm Mickey Monkee! Aw, shut up!" "C'mon guys, quit monkeying around!" Are you ready for this song? No!" and "I think I'm falling In love. Not again!" MARKINGS: QUALITY ORIGINALS BY MATTEL/MONKEES c 1966 Raybert Productions, Inc. Trademark of Screen Gems, Inc. **$300.00.**

Twiggy

Twiggy, Leslie Hornby, was London's top teen model in the late 1960s, and the clothing she modeled became all the rage both in England and the U.S. Her style and appearance were decidedly fresh and different, ushering in the Mod or modern look in women's fashion. This Mod look was quickly adapted by Mattel onto Barbie doll's Modern cousin Francie in 1966, who was both shorter and had a smaller bust to complement the fashions of the day. In 1967 Mattel acquired the license to produce a doll version of Twiggy, who became Barbie doll's first celebrity friend. During the production period from 1967 to 1968, the Twiggy doll, four exclusive Twiggy fashions, and several vinyl Twiggy accessories were produced by Mattel.

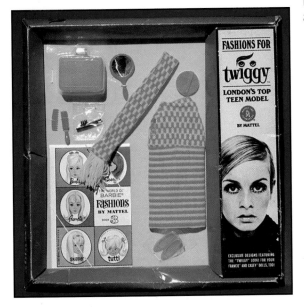

1968 TWIGSTER #1727 contains an orange and yellow dress with matching scarf and shoes, along with an orange cosmetic case, powder puff, mirror, eyelash brush, pencil, brush, and comb. The little accessories in this ensemble are often missing from out-of-box outfits, making this set the most valuable of the four Twiggy fashions. **$235.00.**

1967 TWIST 'N TURN CASEY #1180 with blonde hair is shown here for comparison with Twiggy. **$275.00.**

1967 TWIGGY #1185 is Mattel's first fashion doll modeled after a living celebrity. Twiggy uses the head mold of Francie doll's friend Casey, also introduced in 1967, and the body of Francie doll. Twiggy doll stands 11¼" tall and has rooted eyelashes, heavy eye makeup, and the new Twist 'N Turn waist design debuted on Barbie, Francie, and Casey dolls in 1967. Twiggy wears a yellow, blue, and green striped dress with panties and yellow boots. She has bendable legs and a silver and orange wrist tag. A clear plastic posin' stand is included. Twiggy doll has heavier lower painted eyelashes than Casey and no earrings, while Casey doll has longer hair than Twiggy and a single golden triangular earring in her left ear. MARKINGS: Rear: c 1966/ MATTEL, INC./ U.S. PATENTED/ U.S. PAT. PEND./ MADE IN/ JAPAN. **$495.00.**

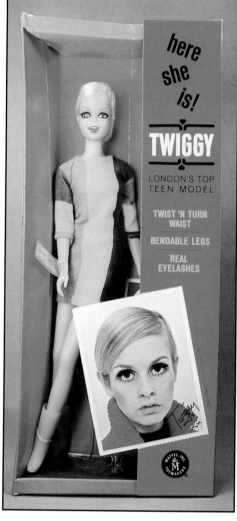

1968 TWIGGY-DOS #1725 is a short yellow dress with green stripes and matching yellow socks, shoes, purse, and necklace. The suggested price for these outfits in the World of Barbie Fashion booklet is $2.75 each. **$200.00.**

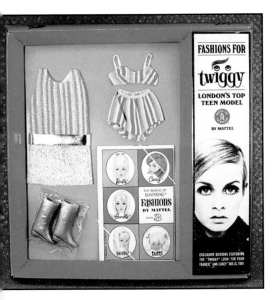

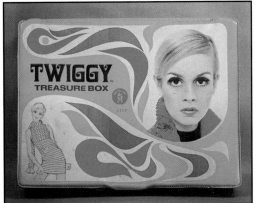

1968 TWIGGY TREASURE BOX #5106 is a small trinket box with lock and key. The interior is turquoise. Twiggy's photo from the doll's box is featured prominently on the Treasure box, along with artwork of Twiggy wearing Twigster. **$120.00.**

1968 TWIGGY TURNOUTS #1726 is a sparkly, silvery one-piece dress with belt, bra, panties, and boots. **$200.00.**

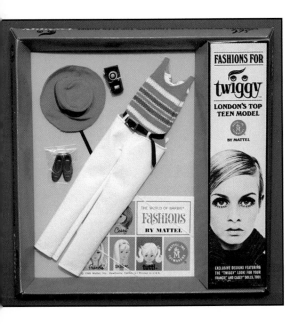

1968 TWIGGY MINI-PURSE #5105. This Mini-purse, the Treasure box, and the Fashion-Tote were made in yellow and white versions. **$95.00.**

1968 TWIGGY GEAR #1728 features a tank top with white pants, belt, hat, shoes, and camera. **$200.00.**

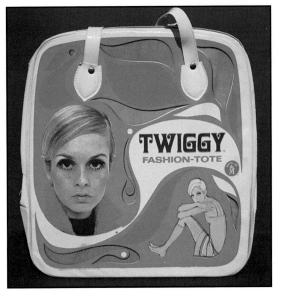

1968 TWIGGY FASHION-TOTE #5102 is 12" long, 12" tall, and 4½" deep (at the bottom). The photo of Twiggy is the same as that used on the doll's box. The drawn picture features Twiggy modeling Twiggy-Dos. While hard to find today, the Twiggy Fashion-Tote (and Barbie doll fashion cases in general) lacks the popularity of the fashions. **$130.00.**

Buffy and Mrs. Beasely

A popular CBS television show from 1966 – 1971, *Family Affair*, featured adorable twins Buffy and Jody, their older sister, widowed father (played by Brian Keith), and English housekeeper, Mr. French. Buffy, portrayed by Anissa Jones, frequently played with her stuffed doll named Mrs. Beasley. Mattel acquired the rights to produce doll versions of both Buffy and Mrs. Beasley, which were well received. The Mrs. Beasley doll, produced in various versions, remained in production through 1973. Buffy was produced in two size versions — a smaller 6¼" tall bendable, poseable doll and a 10" Small Talk doll.

1968 BUFFY AND MRS. BEASLEY #3577 contains freckle-faced Buffy holding her stuffed companion doll, Mrs. Beasley. Buffy uses the one-piece poseable body (made of vinyl over wires) of Barbie doll's tiny sister Tutti, introduced in 1966. Buffy wears a one-piece red and white dress with white socks and red shoes — the same outfit first worn by Tutti in the **1966 Walking My Dolly set #3552**. Buffy has a green and silver wrist tag. Mrs. Beasley has curly yellow hair, glasses, and an original blue and yellow outfit with skirt and cape. Mrs. Beasley's glasses and cape are frequently missing from out-of-box sets. MARKINGS: Buffy's neck rim: c MATTEL INC JAPAN; Buffy's back: c 1965/ MATTEL, INC/ JAPAN/ 23. Mrs. Beasley's back of head: MATTEL; Mrs. Beasley's cloth tag: Mrs. Beasley R/ c 1967 FAMILY/ AFFAIR CO./ c 1967 MATTEL,/ INC.-JAPAN. **$225.00.**

1969 TALKING MRS. BEASLEY #5307 was sold individually in the same size as the doll featured on *Family Affair* — 22" tall. She was advertised as big, soft, and lovable, and she said one of ten phrases when her talking ring was pulled: "You may call me Mrs. Beasley. Would you like to play?"; "Long ago I was a little girl just like you."; "Would you like to try on my glasses? You may if you wish."; "Do you want to hear a secret? I know one."; "Gracious me, you're getting to be such a big girl."; "If you were a little smaller, I could rock you to sleep."; "It would be such fun to play jump rope, don't you think?"; "If you could have three wishes, what would you wish for?"; "Speak a little louder, dear, so Mrs. Beasley can hear you."; "I do think you're the nicest little friend I ever had." Although sold through 1973, she is difficult to find in the original box today. **$600.00.**

1968 TV'S TALKING BUFFY AND MRS. BEASLEY #3107 features a 10" Buffy using Mattel's regular-line Small Talk molds with a large Mrs. Beasley doll. Buffy's outfit is similar to the red and white dress that the smaller bendable, poseable doll wears. When her talking ring at the back of her neck is pulled, Buffy says one of eight phrases. These phrases are: "Hi, my name is Buffy."; "I'm always asking questions."; "Let's play with Mrs. Beasley."; "Count my freckles, Ha! Ha!"; "Did you know I'm a twin?"; "I like to meet new friends."; "How old is a grown-up?"; and "Tell Mrs. Beasley your secrets." MARKINGS: Buffy's neck rim: c MATTEL INC 1967 HONG KONG; Buffy's back: c 1967 MATTEL INC./ U.S. & FOR./ PATS. PEND./ MEXICO. **$350.00.**

Doctor Dolittle

The Doctor Dolittle Mattel toy series is based on the popular 1967 musical motion picture **Doctor Dolittle**, featuring a man, Doctor Dolittle, who actually talks and communicates with animals. Doctor Dolittle was played by Rex Harrison, whose likeness was perfectly captured by Mattel's designers in a series of dolls featuring that character. Except for Rex Harrison's Doctor Dolittle, most of the other Mattel celebrity dolls of this period use existing head molds painted to resemble the celebrity. Mattel created a number of Doctor Dolittle items, ranging from the dolls and animals to Music Box Ge-Tars and a jack-in-the-box giraffe.

1968 DOCTOR DOLITTLE & POLYNESIA THE PARROT #3575 introduces Doctor Dolittle wearing his black coat jacket, tie, and top hat along with his parrot, Polynesia, with moving eyes. This Doctor Dolittle doll is only 6¼" tall and therefore not in scale for the Barbie doll family, although his body is basically the same as that used for both Barbie doll's tiny sister Tutti and the small Buffy doll. MARKINGS: Doctor Dolittle's back: c 1967/ MATTEL,INC/ JAPAN. **$60.00.**

11

1968 DOCTOR DOLITTLE AND HIS PUSHMI-PULLYU #3579 pairs the Doctor Dolittle doll (with Polynesia the Parrot sewn to his coat arm) and the two-headed Pushmi-Pullyu llama-type creature. MARKINGS: Pushmi-Pullyu's tag: Quality Originals by Mattel R/ PUSHMI-PULLYU. **$95.00.**

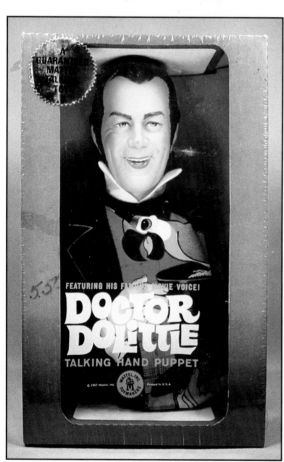

1968 DOCTOR DOLITTLE PRESENTS THE TALKING PUSHMI-PULLYU #5225 features the two-headed creature with the pull-string talking feature in a large 13" x 9" size. **$160.00.**

1968 DOCTOR DOLITTLE TALKING HAND PUPPET #5365 uses the head of the 24" **Talking Doctor Dolittle #5349** with a cloth print body illustrating his coat jacket, vest, collar, top hat, and Polynesia the parrot. A pull string at his lower left side allows the hand puppet to speak in Rex Harrison's voice. **$150.00.**

1968 DOCTOR DOLITTLE'S MARVELOUS MOVIE PET PUSHMI-PULLYU #3578 contains only the small two-headed Pushmi-Pullyu. **$65.00.**

1968 DOCTOR DOLITTLE TALKING PUDDLEBY COTTAGE #5125 is the vinyl home for Doctor Dolittle. The cottage was sold with a hang tag and has a carry handle at the top. **$130.00.**

1968 TALKING DOCTOR DOLITTLE #5349 is marketed as your movie & story-book friend who talks to animals and people too! Standing 24" tall (to the top of his hat), this doll is outstanding. Wearing his tan plaid pants, red vest, black tie, and black felt coat with flocked black top hat, Doctor Dolittle's most incredible feature is his exact likeness to actor Rex Harrison. The doll is soft bodied with a vinyl head. MARKINGS: Tag at waist: Quality Originals By/ MATTEL R/ DOCTOR DOLITTLE/ c MCMLXVII Twentieth/ Century-Fox/ Film Corporation/ and Apjac/ Productions, Inc./ All Rights Reserved./ c 1967 Mattel, Inc. **$175.00.**

He says the following ten phrases: "How do you do? I'm Dr. Doolittle."; "As a people doctor, I was a total failure."; "Did you know that every animal has its own language?"; "I've talked with animals all over the world."; "I study elephant and eagle, buffalo and beagle."; "Think what fun we'd have asking crocodiles for tea."; "Dab Dab says I'm very untidy. She's probably right."; "If asked to sing in hippopotamus, I'd say 'why notamous.'"; "Imagine talking to a tiger, chatting with a cheetah."; "You have to pet both ends of a Pushmi-Pullyu or they get jealous." Note: The Doctor Dolittle Talking Hand Puppet, the Talking Puddleby Cottage, and Talking Doctor Dolittle all have indentical phrases.

13

Julia

Julia, an NBC television program debuting in 1968 and running until 1971, featured Diahann Carroll as nurse Julia Baker, who works in a medical clinic and is the widowed mother of a six-year-old, Corey. Mattel produced Julia dolls using Barbie doll's body molds in two different versions in 1969 — a Twist 'n Turn waist doll wearing a two-piece nurse's uniform and a talking doll wearing a gold and silver jumpsuit. Both versions of the Julia doll were produced again in 1970 with some minor changes and remained on the market until 1972. Four exclusive fashions for Julia were sold in 1969; these fashions feature the old Mattel logo — a starburst with a large M on which a boy wearing a crown (company mascot Mattie Mattel) rests under the words MATTEL, INC. The second year the fashions were in production, 1970, Mattel adopted its current gear symbol logo with only the name MATTEL across the graphic. The four Julia fashions of 1969 have the older Mattel logo; the same fashions made in 1970 have the new Mattel logo and might have some variations in the fabric material. Mattel used the 1968 Christie doll head mold to create the Julia doll (Christie is Barbie doll's first African-American friend, introduced in 1968). The rarest Julia item is the Sears exclusive 1970 gift set Simply Wow, featuring a Talking Julia doll with an extra original fashion. Today many Julia dolls' hair has lost its original color, or oxidized, to a lighter color ranging from medium brown to bright orange, although the hair color does not affect the doll's value.

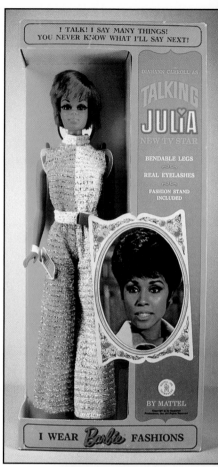

1969 JULIA #1127 is described on the doll's box as a new TV star with bendable legs, Twist 'N Turn waist, and real eyelashes. This first version of Julia wears a two-piece nurse's uniform — a skirt and a jacket — along with a white nurse's cap with a black stripe and white shoes. A posin' stand is included. Julia wears a wrist tag. MARKINGS: All Julia dolls' heads are marked: c 1968 MATTEL INC JAPAN; Rear: c 1966/ MATTEL, INC./ U.S. PATENT-ED/ U.S. PAT. PEND./ MADE IN/ JAPAN. **$225.00.**

1969 TALKING JULIA #1128 wears a one-piece jumpsuit that is gold on one side and silver on the other, with a silver belt buckle and clear color shoes. Her wrist tag and hairstyle are identical to the #1127 Julia. She also has a posin' stand. A cut-away section on the box back allows the doll's talking ring to be pulled without opening the package, but most talking dolls of the 1960s and 1970s are now mute. Collectors of NRFB dolls generally prefer that the doll remain undisturbed and mute inside the box rather than open it for repair, even though most mute talkers can be repaired. She says "Hi! My name is Julia." "Would you like to be an actress?" "We sure have a lot of fun!" "What should I wear on my show?" "Nursing is great fun." and "I love the new dress styles." MARKINGS: Rear: c 1967/ MATTEL, INC./ U.S. & FOREIGN/ PATS. PEND/ MEXICO. **$195.00.**

1969 BRRR-FURRR #1752 offers Julia an aqua fur-trimmed coat and matching hat and belt with a one-piece dress and shoes. The box boasts, the look of now! Custom designed for your Talking and Twist 'N Turn waist Julia dolls. Julia fashions feature finest quality fabrics and dressmaker detailing. Brrr-Furrr, although custom designed for Julia, was also sold for Barbie doll in a red version. **$165.00.**

970 JULIA #1127 wears a edesigned nurse's uniform in 970 — a one-piece outfit with horter sleeves than 1969's wo-piece version. The box, rist tag, body markings, and airstyle remain the same as he 1969 edition. **$175.00.**

1969 CANDLELIGHT CAPERS #1753 is a yellow and orange dress with matching cape and hat with fur trim and shoes. **$165.00.**

1969 LEATHER WEATHER #1751 contains a pink top and plaid skirt with a red coat, purse, and shoes. **$165.00.**

1969 PINK FANTASY #1754 is a sheer pink peignoir set with shoes. **$175.00.**

1970 TALKING JULIA #1128 was sold in a brown shipping carton through several catalog stores. The sticker on the box top lists STOCK No. 1128/ 849-6679/ 921-2234/ MADE AND PRINTED IN HONG KONG. Her wrist tag is identical to the Mexico-made Talking Julia with the exception that this doll's wrist tag states, Made in Hong Kong and her rear markings are identical except for the HONG KONG instead of MEXICO reference. A fire destroyed Mattel's Mexico factory in 1970, so this Julia doll is among the first to be produced in Mattel's Hong Kong facilities. The doll is secured to a white cardboard liner and wears the Talking Julia fashion, although the doll shown here has an unusually dark skin tone, probably due to the new country of origin. **$210.00.**

1971 TALKING JULIA #1128 received a new hairstyle after being on the market since 1969 with the same hairdo. This edition has a curly, afro hairstyle, and her skin is darker. Her markings reflect the new country of origin, Hong Kong, but her box and outfit remain the same as when first introduced. **$220.00.**

I TALK! I SAY MANY THINGS! YOU NEVER KNOW WHAT I'LL SAY NEXT!

DIAHANN CARROLL AS

TALKING JULIA

NEW TV STAR

BENDABLE LEGS

REAL EYELASHES

FASHION STAND INCLUDED

BY MATTEL

I WEAR *Barbie* FASHIONS

1970 TALKING JULIA SIMPLY WOW Gift Set #1594 features the Talking Julia doll in her gold and silver jumpsuit repackaged with an exclusive fashion — a blue skirt with white bodice and golden collar and waist bands, a blue jacket with gold trim, and matching blue shoes. This set was a Sears exclusive and is very rare today. MARKINGS: Julia label sewn in jacket. **$1,200.00.**

Chitty Chitty Bang Bang

A popular family motion picture of 1968, *Chitty Chitty Bang Bang*, featured a fantastic car named Chitty Chitty Bang Bang that amazingly adapted itself to whatever situations it encountered, whether driving, flying, or floating. Dick Van Dyke starred as Mr. Potts, father of two young children. Truly Scrumptious, played by Sally Ann Howes was Mr. Pott's love interest. Mattel created doll versions of Mr. Potts, Truly Scrumptious, and the two children, and a Chitty Chitty Bang Bang car as well. The Truly Scrumptious dolls, created with Barbie doll bodies and Francie doll head molds, are the most sought after of these collectibles today.

1969 CHITTY CHITTY BANG BANG MIRACULOUS MOVIE CAR #6150 contains molded plastic passengers depicting Mr. Potts, Truly Scrumptious, and the two children. The car rolls on flat surfaces and has an inflatable raft for floating on water. **$175.00.**

1969 TALKING MR. POTTS #5235 is a soft, huggable 24" plush doll wearing the likeness of Dick Van Dyke. Talking Mr. Potts wears a tan corduroy jacket with metal buttons over his shirt collar, paisley tie, blue slacks, and black boots, all of which are non-removable. A pull string is located on the doll's left side. When pulled, the doll speaks in Dick Van Dyke's voice. **TALKING MR. POTTS** says the following ten phrases, accompanied by sounds from Chitty Chitty Bang Bang: "I'm Mr. Potts, but you can call me Caractacus."; "I'm a specialist in scientific instruments and contrivances."; "Would you like to help me with my inventions?"; "Listen to Chitty Chitty Bang Bang talk."; "I'm going to invent the candy that whistles."; "Hiccup! Sounds like old Chitty has the hiccups."; "You're just in time to go on a trip with us."; "What kind of adventure shall we go on today?"; "Wouldn't it be fun to go to the seaside?"; "I'm a nurse maid, private tutor, chief cook, and bottle washer." MARKINGS: Label sewn to jacket: Quality Originals by/ MATTEL R/ MR. POTTS TM/ c 1968 GLIDROSE/ PRODUCTIONS, LTD./ and WARFIELD/ PRODUCTIONS, LTD,/ c 1968 Mattel, Inc./ Hawthorne, Calif./ Made in Mexico. **$150.00.**

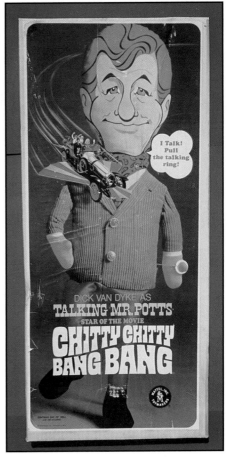

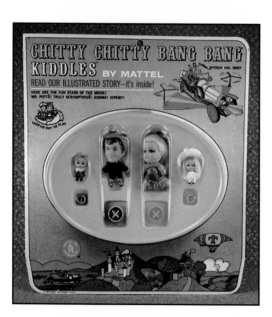

1969 TALKING TRULY SCRUMPTIOUS #1107 stands 11½" tall and uses Barbie doll's body with Francie doll's head. She has rooted eyelashes and bendable legs. Truly wears a lavender gown with black dotted net overlay and pink bodice, along with a feathered hat. Roses adorn her hat and the hem of her gown. She wears a wrist tag. The doll's talking ring, found at the back of her neck, may be pulled through the opening at the back of the box. She

says "Truly Scrumptious." "Follow your dreams." "Do you invent things?" "Let's go for a drive." "What a nice friend." and "I love ruffles and lace." A posin' stand is included. MARKINGS: Neck rim: c 1965 MATTEL, INC/ JAPAN; Rear: c 1967/ MATTEL, INC./ U.S. & FOREIGN/ PATS. PEND/ MEXICO; Dress label: Truly Scrumptious R/ c 1968 GLIDROSE PRODUCTIONS, LTD./ AND WARFIELD PRODUCTIONS, LTD./ MADE IN JAPAN/ c 1968 MATTEL, INC. **$600.00.**

1969 TRULY SCRUMPTIOUS #1108 is typically referred to as Standard Truly Scrumptious since she uses the Standard Barbie doll body with non-twisting waist and non-bending straight legs. Unlike Talking Truly Scrumptious, this standard version has painted fingernails and toenails. She wears a pale pink taffeta gown with net overlay. Roses adorn her waist ribbons and her feathered hat. MARKINGS: Neck and dress markings are the same as #1107; Rear: Midge/ c 1963/ Barbie R/ c 1958/ By/ MATTEL INC./ PATENTED. **$525.00.**

1969 CHITTY CHITTY BANG BANG KIDDLES #3597 features tiny doll versions of Mr. Potts, Truly Scrumptious, and the two children. The adults stand about 2½" high, and the children are 1" tall. **$325.00.**

Miss America

The annual Miss America Pageant has become part of our culture. Contenders from all 50 states compete before an audience of millions to determine who is the most worthy of the Miss America title. Beauty and talent are both essential elements for successful contestants. Mattel, in conjunction with the Miss America Pageant, began producing 11½" Miss America dolls in 1972. Miss America dolls underwent changes in both hair color and costume in the six years Mattel produced them. Three Walking Miss America fashions sold in 1972 – 1973 are the rarest and most valuable Miss America collectibles. The Kellogg's Company offered the Miss America doll as a premium beginning in 1972.

1972 WALKING MISS AMERICA #3200 is part of the Walk Lively series of dolls that includes Walk Lively Barbie, Walk Lively Ken, and Walk Lively Steffie. When pushed along on their walk 'n turn stands, these dolls' legs and arms move back and forth as their head turns left to right. Walking Miss America's box states, "I walk! I turn! I hold my head high! My head 'n arms move! People smile as I go by!" Walking Miss America has bendable legs and real eyelashes. Her head mold is the same as Walk Lively Steffie's, and her body is the Barbie doll body. She wears a textured gold lamé top, white satin gown with sheer overskirt, Miss America banner, red cape with fur trim, silvery textured crown, and white shoes. Her accessories include three red cloth roses tied in a red ribbon and a golden scepter. She has a silver wrist tag that simply says Taiwan. MARKINGS: Neck rim: c 1971 MATTEL INC. TAIWAN; Rear: c 1967 MATTEL, INC./ U.S. PAT. PEND./ TAIWAN. **$275.00.**

1972 ROYAL VELVET #3215 is a red velvet gown with fur collar, matching fur muff, slip, and red shoes. **$575 .00.**

1972 WALKING MISS AMERICA PROTOTYPE DOLL has silver-blonde hair and brown eyes. The doll released on the market has brown hair and blue eyes. Photo courtesy Martha Armstrong-Hand.

1972 REGAL RED #3217 has a gold lamé top with red dress, fur-trimmed cape, yellow gloves, purse and red shoes. **$575.00.**

1972 MAJESTIC BLUE #3216 is one of three fashions created for Walking Miss America. Majestic Blue is an aqua blue gown with fur wrap and white gloves, along with a Miss America banner, rose bouquet, and blue shoes. **$575.00.**

1972 MISS AMERICA #3194-9991, a special mail-away offer from the Kellogg's Company, is attached to a white cardboard liner inside a brown mailing box. For three dollars and two box tops from either Kellogg's Corn Flakes or Frosted Mini Wheats, Kellogg's sent out this Walking Miss America doll, minus her walk 'n turn stand. This mail away doll and the regular Walking Miss America are virtually identical — the mail away doll still functions as a walking doll even without the special stand. Laurie Lea Schaefer, Miss America of 1972, helped Kellogg's promote this offer. MARKINGS: All head and rear markings identical to #3200. **$175.00.**

1974 MISS AMERICA #9194-4, offerred by the Kellogg's Company for three dollars and two cereal box tops, differs from the Walking Miss America promotional doll sent in 1972 and 1973. Kellogg's now sent out Quick Curl Miss America dolls, either brunette or blonde, secured to white cardboard liners inside brown mailer boxes. Mattel changed the color of the Miss America doll's hair to blonde in 1974, so recipients of the Kellogg's Miss America received either the older brunette Quick Curl doll or the new blonde version. The outfit remained unchanged except for the gown's bodice, now made of gold lamé instead of the earlier textured gold material. An instructional sheet titled No Setting! No Wetting! No Waiting! gives directions for using the curler and lists the accessories included. Terry Anne Meeuwsen, 1973's Miss America, helped promote this doll. MARKINGS: Same as 1973 Quick Curl Miss America. **$150.00.**

1974 BARBIE DOLL'S MISS AMERICA BEAUTY CENTER #7893 is a rare Sears exclusive — the side of the box states, "Designed especially for Sears," and Sears' catalog number 4913804 is printed on the box. This is the only instance of Barbie doll herself being identified as Miss America; in the Walk Lively and Quick Curl lines, Miss America and Barbie are two distinctly different dolls with different head molds. In this set, the large 1972 Barbie Beauty Center head, modeled after 1967's Twist 'N Turn Barbie, is used for Miss America. The head is 6" tall and stands 11" tall when attached to the neck base. The box says to Make Barbie pretty for the Miss America Pageant. She has Growin' Pretty hair — a ponytail section can be pulled out long and then shortened with a pull ring at the back of the head. Beauty accessories include a compact with blue and green eyeshadow, cheek blusher, lipstick, eyebrow pencil, sponge applicators, and false eyelashes. Three barrettes, three ribbons, a brush, comb, twelve bobby pins, and four rollers are included. Of course, Barbie doll gets the silvery crown and Miss America medallion! MARKINGS: Back of head: c 1971 MATTEL INC./ MEXICO; base: c 1971 MATTEL, INC./ U.S. PATENT PENDING/ MEXICO. **$150.00.**

1973 QUICK CURL MISS AMERICA #8697 is part of the Quick Curl series of dolls that includes Quick Curl Barbie, Quick Curl Kelley, Quick Curl Francie, and Quick Curl Skipper. Quick Curl Miss America wears the same outfit as Walking Miss America, but Quick Curl Miss America has painted, not rooted eyelashes, her body is no longer equipped with walk 'n turn features, a white posin' stand replaces her white walk 'n turn stand, and Quick Curl Miss America has new Quick Curl hair. This Quick Curl hair has tiny wires rooted with the strands of hair for easier styling, so there is No setting! No wetting! No waiting! Extra hair accesories are included — a brush, comb, curler, four ribbons, four rubberbands, and three bobby pins. MARKINGS: Neck rim: c 1971 MATTEL INC. TAIWAN; Rear: c 1966/ MATTEL, INC./ U.S. & FOREIGN/ PATENTED/ OTHER PATS/ PENDING/ MADE IN/ TAIWAN. **$195.00.**

21

1975 QUICK CURL MISS AMERICA #8697 is shown here in a special catalog box with catalog numbers from four different catalog retailers printed on the front. This should not be confused with the Kellogg's promotional Miss America. The numbers 49-30019 identify Quick Curl Miss America in the Sears catalog; the other three sets of catalog numbers pertain to the Alden's, Ward's, and Spiegel's catalog numbers for Quick Curl Miss America. This is a transitional doll because she has the textured gold bodice, cloth rose bouquet, and silver Taiwan wrist tag of the earlier Quick Curl Miss America dolls, but she has a new thin, shiny, silver crown. She is packaged with a Quick Curl Instructions sheet. MARKINGS: Same as 1973 Quick Curl Miss America. **$125.00.**

1974 QUICK CURL MISS AMERICA #8697, now available only with blonde hair in a slightly different box than the 1973 edition, wears the same outfit as her 1973 counterpart. This box has illustrated graphics on the two sides of the doll's bubble window packaging, while the 1973 version uses actual photographs. MARKINGS: Same as 1973 Quick Curl Miss America. **$145.00.**

1976 QUICK CURL MISS AMERICA #8697 is packaged in a pale pink box with a 10" window opening and cardboard flap extending the box front an extra 4". Her box is dated 1972, the year Quick Curl Miss America was first manufactured, even though this pink-box version was only sold from 1976 to 1979. She has the new thin, shiny, silver crown and gold lamé bodice, but her rose bouquet is made of plastic rather than cloth. She is the first Quick Curl Miss America not to have a wrist tag. MARKINGS: Head: same; Rear: c MATTEL, INC./ 1966/ TAIWAN. **$95.00.**

1976 QUICK CURL MISS AMERICA #8697 has been found with several interesting variations. This version has a silver lamé top, and her fur-trimmed cape is missing the black spots found on all earlier Miss America capes. MARKINGS: Same as regular 1976 version. **$120.00.**

22

Space: 1999

Even before **Star Wars** forever changed public perceptions about outer space, a television series called **Space: 1999**, airing from 1975 to 1977, was about humans stranded on the moon dealing with the mysteries of space from their Moon Base Alpha headquarters in the year 1999. Mattel produced 9" dolls of the three leading characters from the show, as well as a playset for them, Moon Base Alpha, and the large plastic Eagle 1 spaceship containing 3" versions of these characters.

1976 COMMANDER KOENIG #9542, played by Martin Landau, stands 9" tall, using the Steve Sunshine Family body. He wears a yellow uniform with shoes. Each of the 9" dolls has a stun gun, holster, and a communicator-computer, which clips to their belts. MARKINGS: Back of head: c 1975 ATV LICENSING LTD. TAIWAN; Back: c 1973/ MATTEL, INC/ TAIWAN. **$60.00.**

1976 MOON BASE ALPHA #9592 features a vinyl play area for the 9" dolls that measures 18" x 30" x 11". Moon Base Alpha contains the control room and launch monitor center with the plastic Starflash computer that lights up. Two chairs and a table are included. MARKINGS: Base of computer: c MATTEL, INC. 1976. **$75.00.**

1976 DOCTOR RUSSELL #9544, played by Barbara Bain, wears an orange uniform with shoes. She uses the body of Stephie from the Sunshine Family. MARKINGS: Back of head: c 1975 A.T.V. LICENSING LTD. TAIWAN; Back: c 1973/ MATTEL, INC./ TAIWAN. **$60.00.**

1976 MOON BASE ALPHA DELUXE SET #9593 includes all three 9" dolls and is very rare. **$300.00.**

1976 PROFESSOR BERGMAN #9543, played by Barry Morse, wears a brown uniform with shoes. MARKINGS: same as Koenig. **$60.00.**

1976 EAGLE 1 SPACE SHIP #9548 is 2½ feet long with living quarters and detachable command and engine modules. The module hatch opens and seats two. Side panels swing open to reveal the living quarters with two chairs, a weapons rack, and space crane. The ship is complete with three 3" tall plastic characters of Commander Koenig, Doctor Russell, and Professor Bergman wearing orange space suits. Helmets, four stun guns, and a laser rifle are included. MARKINGS: Bottom of ship: ATV LICENSING LIMITED/ c 1976 U.S.A.; Bottom of escape hatch: c MATTEL, INC. 1976 U.S.A. 9548-2; Leg of 3" figures: c 1975 ATV LICENSING LTD. **$165.00.**

Donny and Marie Osmond

Donny and Marie Osmond, teenage brother and sister singers and entertainers, hosted a popular variety television show from 1975 to 1978. A little bit country and a little bit rock and roll, the show had a wide audience appeal and featured the Osmond Brothers, including youngest brother Jimmy. Mattel produced doll versions of Donny, Marie, and Jimmy, along with a T.V. studio playset, doll carry case, and over two dozen fashions from 1977 to 1978.

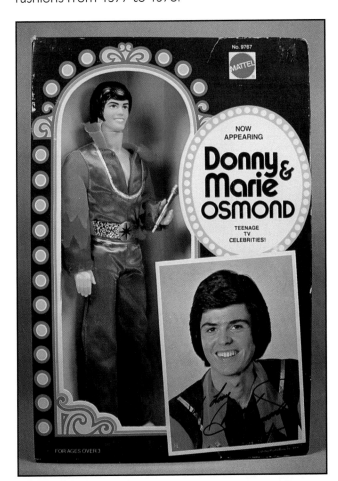

1977 DONNY OSMOND #9767 wears a purple jumpsuit with layered chiffon sleeves and collar and trademark purple socks and white shoes. Donny stands 12" tall and uses the Ken doll torso and legs, with the modification of one arm to a permanently bent position for holding his microphone, which fits in a hole in his left hand. The first edition of Donny Osmond has a U shaped silver stripe across his chest. The lower left corner of his box states, FOR AGES OVER 3; the second edition of his box adds, CONTAINS DONNY OSMOND DOLL/ FOR AGES OVER 3. Apparently, some consumers may have been confused by the box fronts stating Donny & Marie Osmond when only Donny is included in the box. It is interesting to note that the autographed photos of Donny, Marie, and Jimmy show the celebrities wearing the same outfits their dolls wear. MARKINGS: Neck rim: c Osbro Prod. 1976 HONG KONG; Back: 1088-0500 4/ c MATTEL/ INC. 1968/ HONG KONG. **$45.00.**

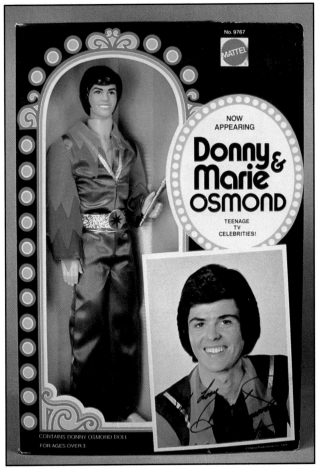

1977 DONNY OSMOND #9767 second edition is shown here. Note the CONTAINS DONNY OSMOND DOLL line added to the lower left corner of the box and the V-shaped silver stripe on Donny's top. MARKINGS: Head: same; Back: 1088-0500 2/ c MATTEL/ INC 1968/ HONG KONG. **$45.00.**

1977 MARIE OSMOND #9768 wears a tiered chiffon dress with satin bodice, belt buckle with six rhinestones, and purple shoes. The earlier Marie Osmond box lacks the CONTAINS MARIE OSMOND DOLL line on the box front, and no posin' stand is included. The doll shown is the second version with a pink posin' stand. Marie stands 11½" tall and uses the Barbie doll torso with one permanently bent right arm with a hole in the hand for her microphone and one straight arm. Although the doll is a perfect likeness of Marie Osmond, her hairstyle differs from the box photo. Strands of brown thread go through Marie's head behind her ears and around the back of her head to keep her hair in place. MARKINGS: Neck rim: c OSBRO PROD 1976 KOREA; Rear: c MATTEL INC/ 1966/ 14 KOREA. **$50.00.**

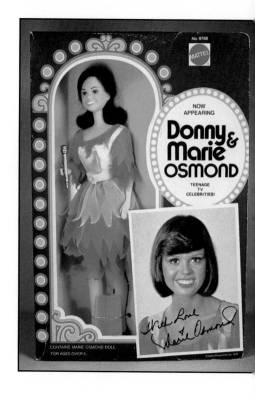

1977 DONNY & MARIE OSMOND #9769 second edition shown here. Donny Osmond's outfit now has the V shape silver collar band, and Marie Osmond's wrist tag now ha Marie Osmond on the front and MADE IN KOREA on the back A pink posin' stand for Marie, not included in the first editio two-doll set, is now packaged in this set. MARKINGS: Donny head: same; back: c MATTEL/INC. 1968/HONG KONG. Marie neck rim: same; rear: c MATTEL INC/ 1966/14 KOREA. **$140.00**

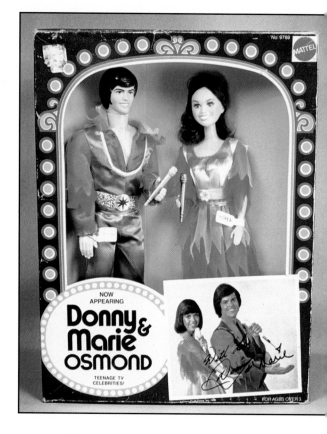

1977 DONNY & MARIE OSMOND #9769 pairs both Donny Osmond and Marie Osmond in one box. Especially noteworthy about this set are the wrist tags on the dolls' arms, since Mattel discontinued the use of wrist tags in late 1974. Donny's wrist tag has Donny Osmond on the front and MADE IN HONG KONG on the back; Marie's wrist tag has only KOREA on it. The dolls' outfits are the same as found on the first-edition individually-boxed dolls, but this box features a new autographed photo of the duo. MARKINGS: Donny's head: same as #9767; back: 1088 0500 4/ c MATTEL/ INC. 1968/ HONG KONG. Marie: neck rim: c OSBRO PROD 1976 KOREA; rear: c MATTEL INC./1966/ 8 KOREA. **$150.00.**

Note the differences in the facial paint of the **Marie Osmond #9768** and the **Marie Osmond from the #9769 set**, particularly the shape of the eyebrows.

1977 MARIE OSMOND MODELING DOLL #9826 is a hard to find 30" tall Marie mannequin doll wearing a long pink satin gown with sparkly top and sheer sleeves with white shoes. The box invites children to share Marie Osmond's favorite hobby by learning to sew on her mannequin. A large beige plastic stand bearing the Marie Osmond name is included, along with five basic patterns. The box photos show the 30" Marie Osmond doll modeling some of the outfits that can be made using the patterns. The doll has a twisting waist, but her legs are not movable. She has molded on flesh tone floral-design undergarments. MARKINGS: Back of head: c OSBRO PROD. 1976; back of neck: c OSBRO PROD./ 1976/ U.S.A. **$95.00.**

1977 DEEPEST PURPLE #9813 for Donny features a white suit with shimmery purple vest. All of the Donny fashions include purple socks, regardless of the outfit color, a Donny Osmond tradition. **$25.00.**

1977 DEEPEST PURPLE #9817 for Marie features a tiered, ribbed white dress with shimmery purple bodice and purple trim. **$25.00.**

1977 FIRE ON ICE #9822 for Marie is Marie's hot pink ice skating costume with pink hose and white fur muffs and ice skates. **$25.00.**

1977 SATIN 'N SHINE #9824 for Marie contains pink gaucho pants, sparkly pink top, jacket, and boots. **$25.00.**

1977 SILVER SHIMMER #9815 for Donny is a blue jumpsuit with silver belt and trim. **$25.00.**

1977 SILVER SHIMMER #9819 for Marie is a blue gown with white sleeves and collar. A matching non-functional umbrella is included. **$25.00.**

1977 SOFT SUMMER NIGHT #9823 for Marie is a fuchsia gown with gold panels. **$25.00.**

1977 SOUTH 'O THE BORDER #9814 for Donny contains blue satin pants and matching vest with a yellow satin shirt. **$25.00.**

1977 SOUTH 'O THE BORDER #9818 for Marie features a five-tiered gown of yellow, orange, pink, green, and blue layers with a blue bodice and yellow shoes. **$25.00.**

1977 STARLIGHT NIGHT #9816 for Donny is a yellow and black tuxedo. **$25.00.**

1977 STARLIGHT NIGHT #9820 for Marie is a yellow dress with layered chiffon overlay and black and silver trim. **$25.00.**

1977 WARM WRAP-UP #9821 for Marie is a belted white full-length fur coat. **$30.00.**

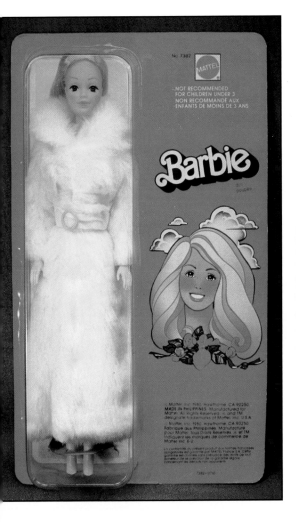

1981 BARBIE #7382 is an inexpensive foreign-market doll wearing Marie's Warm Wrap-Up coat. Apparently, Mattel used up remaining inventories of discontinued fashions on these dolls. **$50.00.**

1977 SEARS EXCLUSIVE DONNY #2078 features brown pants with matching vest and purple shirt. **$45.00.**

1977 SEARS EXCLUSIVE MARIE #2074 features a brown skirt with matching vest and white blouse with boots. **$50.00.**

1977 SEARS EXCLUSIVE DONNY #2079 contains blue pants, a Purple Whiz tee-shirt, and purple cap. **$45.00.**

1977 SEARS EXCLUSIVE MARIE #2075 contains blue gauchos with matching jacket, purple shirt, and red boots. **$50.00.**

**1977 SEARS EXCLUSIV[E]
MARIE #2076** is a pin[k]
jumpsuit with a belte[d]
print top. **$50.00.**

**1977 SEARS EXCLUSIV[E]
MARIE #2077** contain[s]
beige pants, orange to[p]
and a M logo scarf. **$50.00**

1977 DONNY & MARIE OSMOND T.V. SHOW PLAYSET #9830
promises all the razzle-dazzle of their real T.V. show set! The playset opens to nearly three feet long and folds back into a carrying
case. Some of the features of the T.V. Show Playset include separate furnished dressing rooms for Donny and Marie, different
backgrounds for country and rock 'n roll shows, a stage equipped with a camera, spotlight, guitar, piano, and cue
card holder with cue cards of dialogue for Donny and Marie. Two autographed pictures of the stars and a real
record featuring the new song *We're Gettin' Together* also come with the set. The set was redesigned in 1986 as
Barbie and the Rockers stage playset. MARKINGS: Bottom of stage: c MATTEL INC. 1976/ U.S.A./ 9830-2049 C.
$85.00.

32

1978 DONNY & MARIE OSMOND DELUXE TV FASHIONS are four pairs of boxed, not carded, high quality fashions with shoes. Each fashion includes a microphone and shoes. Many collectors are unaware that boxed Donny & Marie fashions even exist; these are much harder to find than the regular 12 carded Donny & Marie Osmond T.V. Fashions.

1978 COUNTRY HOEDOWN #2455 for Donny features purple overalls, shirt, and cap. **$30.00.**

1978 COUNTRY HOEDOWN #2452 for Marie features a short white dress with polka dot underskirt, hose, and hair ribbon. **$30.00.**

978 PEASANT SENSATION #2492 for Marie as a long black skirt with pink trim, matching ape, and sheer pink blouse with green vest. **30.00.**

1978 GLIMMER 'O GOLD #2453 for Donny is a blue satin jumpsuit with golden vest and matching blue cape. **$30.00.**

1978 GLIMMER 'O GOLD #2450 for Marie is a blue satin gown with gold lamé bodice, sheer blue overskirt, gold lamé purse, and gold lamé cap. **$35.00.**

Not shown: **1978 PEASANT SENSA-TION #2493** for Donny has black slacks, green vest with gold trim, and gold jacket with black lapels. **$30.00.**

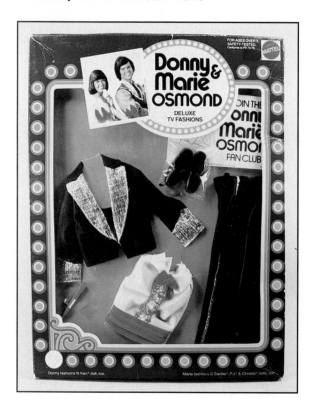

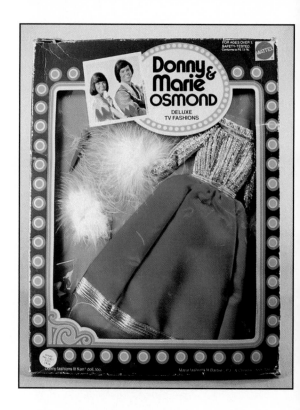

1978 SILVER 'N SHINE #2454 for Donny is a black tuxedo with silver lapels and cuffs and red bowtie and cummerbund. **$30.00.**

1978 SILVER 'N SHINE #2451 for Marie is a re satin gown with textured silver top and marabo trim with a silver cap with marabou feather $35.00.

1978 DONNY & MARIE OSMOND DOUBLE DOLL CASE #2331 has compartments for two dolls, a storage bin with two doors, and a vinyl pouch for storing small accessories. The illustration on the front of the case shows Donny and Marie wearing the Deepest Purple fashions of 1977. **$50.00.**

1977 MARIE'S MAKEUP CENTER #9957 is mad in the style of Barbie's Miss America Beauty Cer ter with a large-size Marie head on a plastic bas with a compact, comb, brush, and hair acces sories included. **$65.00.**

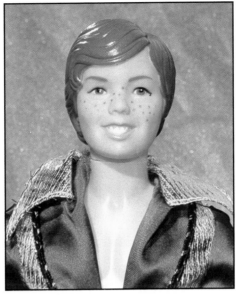

1978 JIMMY OSMOND #2200 represents the youngest brother of Donny and Marie Osmond who occasionally appeared on their television show. The doll is 10" tall and has a permanently bent left arm with a hole in the center of his hand for holding his microphone. He has painted freckles on his face. His textured silver lamé jumpsuit has purple sleeves and a J logo belt buckle, and he wears black shoes. MARKINGS: Back: 2200-2109 2/ c MATTEL, INC/ 1968/ TAIWAN. **$60.00.**

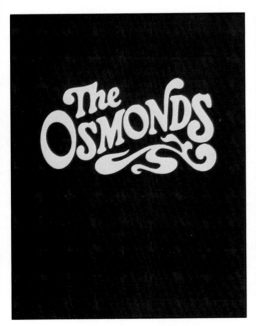

1980 THE OSMONDS official fan club kit is shown here. Every Donny and Marie doll and fashion contains a form for joining the club, yet these fan club kits are hard to find. This kit contains a brown The Osmonds folder, poster of Donny and Marie, golden Osmond International Fan Club certificate, membership card, welcome letter, eight wallet-size photos, a poster of the Osmond family, vital statistics sheets featuring each of the Osmonds, Backstage newsletter, and Fan Fair catalog with Os Buck. Of particular interest to doll collectors, this Fan Fair announced that the entire inventory of the 30" Marie Osmond Modeling Doll had been purchased by them and was now being offered at half price — only $15.95. It also stated that the Fan Club might be offering clothes for the 30" dolls. **$40.00.**

Welcome Back, Kotter

A popular ABC comedy television series from 1975 to 1979, *Welcome Back, Kotter* starred Gabe Kaplan as a high school teacher returning to teach at the high school from which he graduated. His students are Sweathogs, each with his own distinctive personality. Mattel produced five 9" Welcome Back, Kotter dolls using the Steve Sunshine Family body, as well as a vinyl classroom playset, and a motorcycle.

MARKINGS: Each doll is marked on the back of head: c WOLPER/KOMACK; Back: c 1973/ MATTEL INC/ TAIWAN.

1977 BARBARINO #9772 the Sweathog preoccupied with his appearance. John Travolta played Barbarino and went on to motion picture stardom, so this doll the most desirable of the series. Barbarino wear brown pants with an orange shirt, leather jacket, an shoes. His ever-present comb is included. Each c the Sweathogs dolls wears Sweathogs patch on h shirt or jacket. **$50.00.**

1977 EPSTEIN #9774, played by Robert Hegyes, is the trouble-maker who forges his mother's notes. He wears cuffed jeans and vest with a blue denim shirt, belt, gym shoes, and red bandana. **$35.00.**

1977 HORSHACK #9771, played by Ron Palillo, is the student always raising his hand, hoping to be called upon. He wears jeans with a wine-colored tank top, pea green jacket, striped scarf, and black shoes. He has a molded on blue cap and carries a lunchbox. **$35.00.**

1977 MR. KOTTER #9770, por-rayed by Gabe Kaplan, is the only eacher who relates to the weathogs. He wears brown lacks, white shirt with wide reen tie, brown shoes, and rown jacket. His accessory is an ttache case. **$35.00.**

1977 WELCOME BACK, KOTTER SWEAT HOGS BIKE #9880, is a ⅛ scale motorcycle. This is very hard to find. **$150.00.**

1977 WELCOME BACK, KOTTER CLASSROOM #9854 is a vinyl case that unfolds into a schoolroom measuring 17" by 20½" with two walls and functional door. Classroom furnishings include four student desks, teacher's desk, a coat rack, globe with stand, four notebooks, and a piece of chalk to use with the blackboard. A 33⅓ record features the voices of the cast including the memorable, up your nose with a rubber hose, spoken by John Travolta. **$150.00.**

1977 WASHINGTON #9773, played by Larry Hilton-Jacobs, is the suave basketball player. He wears jeans, white shirt, shoes, and letterman jacket. A basketball is included. **$35.00.**

A RARE CLASSROOM DELUXE SET #9882 includes all five dolls. **$300.00.**

Grizzly Adams

The Life and Times of Grizzly Adams, a popular NBC television show of 1978, featured a rugged outdoorsman named Grizzly Adams, played by animal trainer/actor Dan Haggerty, and his adventures with a playful 600-pound grizzly bear, Ben. Nakoma, played by Don Shanks, is the Native American friend of Grizzly Adams and Ben. Mattel produced dolls of Grizzly Adams and Nakoma, as well as a bear toy of Ben.

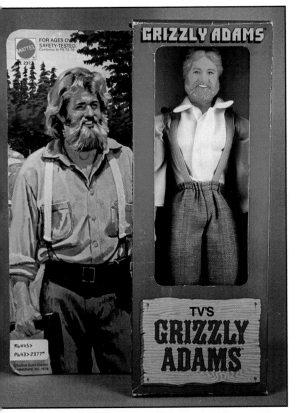

1978 GRIZZLY ADAMS #2377 is 10" tall and wears brown pants with suspenders, a beige shirt, and boots. He uses the Big Jim body (Big Jim is Mattel's action adventure figure introduced in 1972) with bendable arms, jointed wrists, gripping hands, twisting waist, bendable knees, and jointed ankles. Pressing the button in Grizzly Adam's back makes the doll's right arm swing up and down for use with his ax. MARKINGS: Inside neck: c SCHICK SUNN 1978 HONG KONG; Back: c 1971 MATTEL, INC./ U.S. & FOREIGN PATENTED/ HONG KONG. **$50.00.**

978 NAKOMA #2381 is identified on the box as staunch Indian riend of Grizzly Adams and his friend, Ben. Nakoma wears eather-like pants, vest, and noccasins, along with silver rm bands. His hair is parted n the center and two front ections are braided and tied. Nakoma has three white tripes of paint on his cheeks. plastic knife and spear are ncluded. Nakoma has the ame 10" body as Grizzly Adams with moving arm ction. MARKINGS: Back of ead: c 1976 MATTEL INC; Back: same as Grizzly Adams. 60.00.

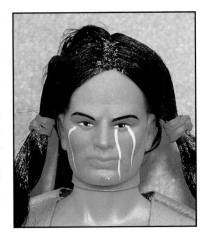

Not pictured: **1978 GRIZZLY ADAMS & BEN SET #2378** contains the regular Grizzly Adams doll packaged with Ben, the 600-pound grizzly bear. **$120.00.**

How the West Was Won

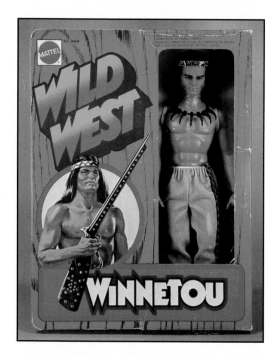

How the West Was Won was a popular ABC television series of 1978. The storyline involved Zeb Macahan, a rough-cut mountain man on his prairie schooner journey from Virginia to Oregon. The series was filmed in scenic Kanab. Mattel produced 10" tall versions of Zeb Macahan and his Indian friend Lone Wolf, as well as Zeb's horse Dakota. Zeb Macahan was played by James Arness, and Ivan Naranjo played Lone Wolf.

1978 LONE WOLF #2369 wears beige pants with fringe, moccasins, bear claw necklace, and headband. He also has a rifle and a knife, although Lone Wolf is one of Zeb Macahan's friends. Lone Wolf has the same arm action feature as Zeb. MARKINGS: Back of head: c 1976 MATTEL INC HONG KONG; Back: same as Zeb. **$65.00.**

1977 NSCHO-TSCHI #2173 from France's Karl May series is an unusual and rare doll. This Indian maiden wears a lovely fringed outfit with fur-trimmed boots; the blue and red material on her bodice, purse, boots, and headband matches the side panels of Lone Wolf's pants. Nscho-Tschi could have been included in the U.S. How the West Was Won line since Zeb Macahan had many Indian friends, but she was only produced for the foreign market. She uses the Stephie body from the Sunshine Family line. MARKINGS: Neck rim: c MATTEL, INC. 1977 TAIWAN; Back of head: c MATTEL INC. 1977; Back: c 1973 / MATTEL, INC./ TAIWAN. **$110.00.**

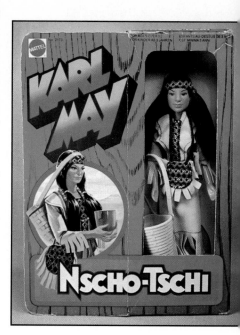

1976 WINNETOU #9404 is from Canada's Wild West series. Winnetou is identical to Lone Wolf from *How the West Was Won*, including his markings. **$70.00.**

1978 ZEB MACAHAN #2367 wears a brown buckskin jacket with yellow bandana and brown pants. He has a belt with a handgun and a rifle, and he also comes with boots and a hat. Zeb Macahan uses the 10" Big Jim body with a button in the back to activate his right arm's movement. MARKINGS: Back of head: c MATTEL INC 1975 HONG KONG; Back: c 1971 MATTEL, INC./ U. S. & FOREIGN PATENTED/ HONG KONG. **$55.00.**

1978 ZEB MACAHAN & DAKOTA SET #2371 packages Zeb Macahan in the same box with his horse Dakota. **$110.00.**

TV's Star Women

A popular ABC television show from 1976 to 1981, *Charlie's Angels*, featured Kate Jackson and Cheryl Ladd as beautiful detectives who often found themselves in danger. Hasbro produced 9" versions of their characters in 1977, but Mattel made 11½" dolls of the two actresses in 1978. Kate Jackson and Cheryl Ladd, along with stuntwoman Kitty O'Neil, form a series named TV's Star Women, which is complemented by six TV's Star Women fashions. All three dolls' faces are excellent likenesses.

1978 CHERYL LADD #2494 wears red slacks under a pleated red skirt, with black and gold braid tied at her waist and across her bodice. She uses the 11½" Barbie doll body, and she has a beauty mark on her face. Her character on *Charlie's Angels*, Kris Monroe, replaced Farrah Fawcett-Majors. MARKINGS: Back of head: c MATTEL INC. 1978; Inside neck rim: c MATTEL INC. 1978 KOREA; Rear: c MATTEL, INC./ 1966/ KOREA. **$55.00.**

1978 KATE JACKSON #2495 wears a long white gown with sheer pleated overskirt and a red print bodice with golden collar and waist band. Even though the box doesn't mention *Charlie's Angels*, the box front states, "She's a beauty with brains"; an indirect reference to Jackson's character on *Charlie's Angels*, Sabrina Duncan, who was especially smart. Kate Jackson is very hard to find. MARKINGS: Back of head: c MATTEL INC. 1978; Inside neck rim: c MATTEL INC. 1978 KOREA; Rear: c MATTEL INC/ 1966/ KOREA. **$95.00.**

1978 KITTY O'NEIL #2247 wears a yellow racing suit with a red cape, scarf, belt, boots, and helmet bearing her name logo. Her jumpsuit has a real working zipper. She uses the SuperStar Barbie body, except she has no ring hole in her hand. The first version box has an orange sticker covering the words Includes "Kitty O'Neil story," and this box contains no story booklet. Later dolls have the booklet. MARKINGS: Inside neck rim: c ROCKET KAT 1978 TAIWAN; Back: c Mattel, Inc. 1966/ TAIWAN. **$65.00.**

1978 INTERVIEW AT HOME #2483 is one of six hard to find TV's Star Women Fashions. Each box shows a photo of Kate Jackson, Cheryl Ladd, and Kitty O'Neil. Notice the top illustration on the right — it depicts Kitty, Cheryl, and Kate walking arm in arm. This outfit is a long red gown with a zig-zag striped top and shoes. **$35.00.**

1978 PRODUCER'S PARTY #2498 is a red strapless gown with shimmering stripes adorning the skirt. A flower worn at the neck and shoes are included. **$35.00.**

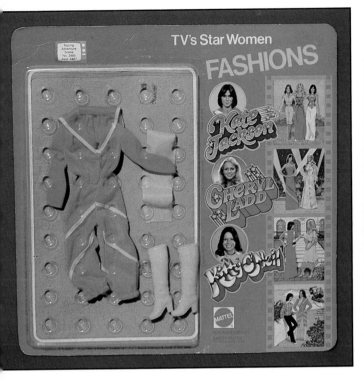

1978 RACING ADVENTURE SCENE #2485 contains an orange jumpsuit with yellow scarf and boots. **$35.00.**

1978 REHEARSAL TIME #2499 has jeans, a red and white plaid shirt, white scarf, and shoes. **$35.00.**

1978 SEASON PREMIERE PARTY #2486 is a short yellow gown with orange floral trim, matching cape, and shoes. **$35.00.**

1978 TV AWARDS NIGHT #2484 features an ice blue gown with silver lamé panel and a sheer blue wrap with silvery fringe and shoes. **$35.00.**

Debby Boone

Not technically one of TV's Star Women, Debby Boone nonetheless became a celebrity in her own right in 1978 as a recording star. Her hit single, *You Light Up My Life* sold millions of records, and the lyrics to the song are still well known today. She is the daughter of entertainer Pat Boone.

1979 DEBBY BOONE

#2843 wears a blue satin jumpsuit with sparkly pink and blue jacket, pink scarf, and blue shoe. She uses the 11½" SuperStar Barbie body except she has no ring. A microphone is included. MARKINGS: Back of head: c RESI, INC. 1978 TAIWAN; Back: c Mattel, Inc. 1966/ TAIWAN. **$65.00.**

Kristy McNichol

Kristy McNichol played Buddy, a young teenage girl, on the hit ABC TV show *Family*, which aired from 1976 to 1979. The realistic drama portrayed the ups and downs of modern family life. Mattel produced a Kristy McNichol as Buddy doll in 1979. MEGO Toys also produced their own version of a Kristy McNichol doll.

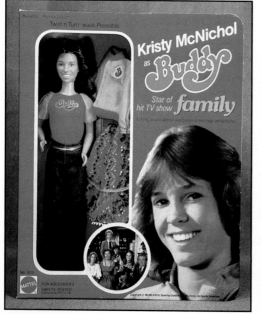

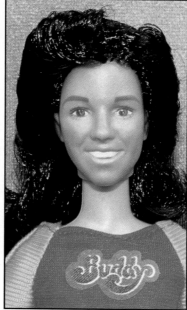

1979 KRISTY MCNICHOL AS BUDDY

#1013 wears jeans, a Buddy logo shirt and gym shoes, and she comes with an extra red floral print skirt, yellow Buddy logo sports jacket, cap, and sandals. She uses the 10" tall body of Super Teen Skipper. This Kristy McNichol doll is not easy to find, so her price should rise to reflect her scarcity. MARKINGS: Back of head: c 1978 Spelling-Goldberg prod.; Back: c Mattel, Inc. 1978; Rear: c MATTEL, INC. 1967/ PHILIPPINES. **$45.00.**

Chantal Goya

Just as the United States had Debby Boone as its top recording star in 1979, France was enthralled with singer Chantal Goya. In the same manner that Mattel U. S. released an 11½" tall version of Debby Boone, Mattel France produced an 11½" tall doll of Chantal Goya. Mattel France also issued a line of four Chantal Goya fashions. Many celebrity doll collectors in the U.S. are still unaware of the Chantal Goya doll and fashions.

1980 CHANTAL GOYA #8935-63 stands 11½" tall with the Barbie doll body with a permanently bent right arm for holding her microphone and a straight left arm. The first edition of Chantal Goya wears a wine-colored floral print gown with lace collar, white socks, and red tie-on shoes. A SuperStar Barbie star-shaped posing stand is included. A full-length photo of the real Chantal Goya wearing the same dress as her doll is shown on the box back. MARKINGS: Back of head: c C. GOYA 1979 TAIWAN; Rear: c MATTEL INC/ 1966/ TAIWAN. **$95.00.**

1980 CHANTAL GOYA #8935-63 also appeared dressed in a white gown with a pink ribbon at the waist. This fashion, named Sarouel, is also available as one of Chantal Goya's boxed fashions. The same box was used for both versions of the Chantal Goya dolls. MARKINGS: same. **$110.00.**

1980 CAMPAGNE #8938 is a blue floral-print jumpsuit with orange fringed belt and shoes. **$50.00.**

Celebrity and Character Dolls

1980 ROMANTIQUE #8937 is a two-piece yellow floral-print gown with red ribbon at the waist and shoes. **$50.00.**

1980 SAROUEL #8936 is a white dress with overskirt and lace-trimmed collar, tied at the waist with a pink ribbon, and shoes. **$50.00.**

1980 WEEK-END #8939 is casual outfit featuring blac pants with suspenders, whit shirt, belt, and shoes. **$50.00.**

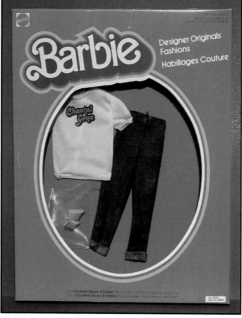

1981 DESIGNER ORIGI NALS #8233 contain jeans, sandals, and tee-shirt bearing th Chantal Goya nam logo. This is rare **$55.00.**

1981 DESIGNER ORIGINALS #8937 is a repackaged Romantique Chantal Goya fashion. **$40.00.**

Mork & Mindy

A popular television comedy of 1978 – 1982 *Mork & Mindy* featured Mork, a human-looking alien from the planet Ork, who was sent to Earth to learn about humans. Settling in Denver, Mork met Mindy, who helped teach him about Earthlings as they shared many zany adventures. Mattel produced 9" tall dolls of Mork and Mindy in 1980, as well as a large Mork talking rag doll, a jeep for the 9" dolls, and a 4" action figure of Mork packaged with his egg-shaped spaceship.

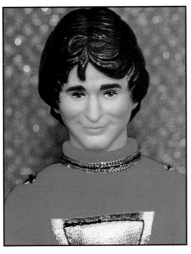

1980 MORK WITH TALKING SPACEPACK #1276 is a 9" tall doll in a red spacesuit packaged upside down in his box. His face is an excellent likeness of actor Robin Williams, who played Mork on the TV show. Mork uses the Steve body from the Sunshine Family. When the talking ring on Mork's plastic spacepack is pulled, one of eight phrases is played, including, "Na-no, Na-no" and "Shazbot," two phrases used on Ork, along with "Don't look at me like that"; "Aaargh—aargh—aargh—aargh—aargh—aargh"; "Oh, that was a joke. Ha, ha"; "Don't ever go to Pluto; it's a Mickey Mouse planet"; "Mork signing off"; and "Time for a dodo, dumb dumb." MARKINGS: Back of head: c 1979 PPC TAIWAN; Back: c 1973/ MATTEL INC/ TAIWAN; Backpack: c 1972 MATTEL INC./ HONG KONG/ U.S. & FOREIGN PATD. **$45.00.**

980 MINDY #1277 is dressed n jeans with a red turtleneck hirt. Mindy's face is molded fter actress Pam Dawber, vho played Mindy on the TV how. She uses the Stephie ody from the Sunshine amily. MARKINGS: Back of ead: c 1979 PPC TAIWAN; 3ack: c 1973/ MATTEL INC./ AIWAN. **$45.00.**

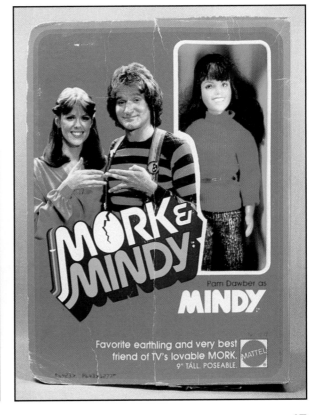

1980 MORK & MINDY 4-WHEEL DRIVE #1543 is an 18" long blue high-rider with white interior made for the 9" dolls. A winch with hand crank and hook is at the front of the vehicle, which has roll bars, an antenna with flag, and two gas cans. This is the same vehicle body as used with the Sunshine Family's Van & Piggyback Shack. MARKINGS: Bottom of vehicle: c 1973 MATTEL, INC./ U.S.A. **$70.00.**

1980 MORK FROM ORK #1275 features a 4" tall action figure of Mork in his red spacesuit packaged on a blister card with his egg-shaped spaceship. **$35.00.**

1980 MORK TALKING RAG DOLL #127 is a 16" tall stuffed doll made in Robi Williams' likeness. He wears non removable blue pants, sneakers striped shirt, and suspenders. Whe the talking ring on his lower left side i pulled, he says one of seven phrase including "Na-no, na-no." MARKINGS Label at rear: A Quality Original by MATTEL/ Copyright c 1979/ Paramour Pictures/ Corporation/ Mattel, Inc. Hawthorne, CA 90250/ MADE IN TA WAN/ ALL NEW MATERIALS. **$35.00.**

Wayne Gretzky

Wayne Gretzky is a famous hockey player. Born in 1961, he joined ~~~e Edmonton Oilers hockey team in 1979 and won the Hart Trophy for ~~ost Valuable Player in the NHL in 1979, 1980, 1981, and 1982. In 1983 ~~attel Canada produced a 12" doll of the famous Canadian hockey play-~~. The doll was sold mainly in Canada. Since Gretzky is still a great hock-~~ player in 1998, his doll continues to increase in value and desirability.

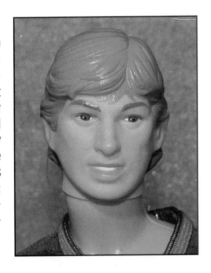

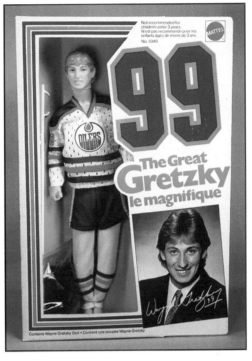

~983 THE GREAT GRETZKY #5949 ~~ears an Edmonton Oilers home uni-~~rm, and he has a hockey stick, hock-~~y gloves, and ice skates. The Great ~~retzky uses the 12" Ken doll body ~~ith bent fingers, bendable arms, and ~~all-jointed waist — the same body ~~sed with 1982's All Star Ken. The ~~acial sculpting masterfully re-creates ~~he look of Wayne Gretzky. MARKINGS: ~~nside neck rim: c Mattel, Inc. 1982 TAI-~~VAN; Rear: c MATTEL, INC. 1968/ TAI-~~VAN. **$125.00.**

~982 THE GREAT GRETZKY JOG-~~GING SUIT #4174 contains sweat-pants, sweat shorts, and a ~~weatshirt with gymshoes. **$100.00.**

1982 THE GREAT GRETZKY AWAY UNIFORM #4107 is one of three extremely rare fashions produced by Mattel Canada for the Wayne Gretzky doll. **$100.00.**

1982 THE GREAT GRETZKY TUXE-DO #4175, $100.00.

Beverly Hills, 90210

More than a decade after making their last character dolls, Mork and Mindy, Mattel U.S. produced five Barbie and Ken doll-sized versions of the most popular characters from the hit Fox television show *Beverly Hills, 90210*, a drama about twins Brandon and Brenda Walsh, Minnesota teenagers adjusting to a new life in Beverly Hills, California. Dylan McKay, Donna Martin, and Kelly Taylor are their new friends and classmates in Beverly Hills. The television series debuted in 1990 and continues in 1998. During this time, the gang graduated both high school and college. The Brenda and Dylan characters have since been written out of the show. Mattel produced 11½" dolls of Brenda, Donna, and Kelly, and 12" versions of Brandon and Dylan. All of these dolls have specially designed faces that greatly resemble the characters they represent. Besides the five individual dolls, Mattel released a three-doll gift set containing Brandon, Brenda, and her boyfriend Dylan. A Peach Pit playset and a vehicle were made for use with the dolls, along with a set of fashions.

1992 BRANDON WALSH #1573 is described on the box as handsome and thoughtful. In his struggle to fit into the fast-paced lifestyle of West Beverly Hills High, Brandon meets one challenge after another, but manages to hold on to his Midwestern values the box text continues.

Brandon Walsh, played by Jason Priestly, wears jeans, a pea green shirt with necklace, gymshoes, and brown suede jacket. A pair of plaid beach shorts and a display stand are included, along with a cardboard car key and photo (all of the 90210 dolls have a cardboard insert with their photo and appropriate cardboard accessory). MARKINGS: Back of neck: c 1991 TORAND; Back: c Mattel Inc. 1968/ MALAYSIA. **$30.00.**

1992 BRANDON WALSH #1573 was produced in China late in production with one notable change. The facial paint on the China-made doll is much more vivid than the Malaysian-made doll, and their hair paint is visibly different as well. MARKINGS: same except back says CHINA instead of MALAYSIA. **$35.00.**

1992 BRENDA WALSH #1577 wears tan shorts with a striped white shirt, paisley vest, purple tie, belt, boots, and hat. Brenda Walsh, played by Shannen Doherty, is impetuous and passionate. She is packaged with a blue two-piece swimsuit and a posing stand. The SuperStar Barbie body is used for the girls in this series. MARKINGS: Back of head: c 1991 TORAND; Back: c MATTEL, INC 1966/ CHINA. **$30.00.**

992 DONNA MARTIN #1575 is described on the box as trendy, thoughtful, dependable, and good friend. Donna Martin, played by Tori Spelling, wears a black floral-print dress with headband, black panties, purse, and shoes. A two-piece floral-print swimsuit, display stand, and cardboard Bacy shopping bag are included. MARKINGS: same as Brenda. **$30.00.**

is described the box as only han some but al serious an intelligen Rebellious the outsi and trouble on the insid he shuns h family's mega-wealthy status. Dylan McKay, played by Luke Per wears jeans, a black tee-shirt, belt, red corduroy jacket, and gy shoes. Black swimming trunks and a posing stand are include The Dylan McKay doll wears a gold earring in his left earlobe popular style among teenage males in 1992, yet this doll receive none of the negative publicity aimed at the controversial Earrin Magic Ken of 1992. MARKINGS: Back of neck: c 1991 TORAN Back: c Mattel Inc. 1968/ MALAYSIA. **$30.00.**

1992 DYLAN MCKAY #1574 was produced in China late in produ tion with much more vivid facial paint than the Malaysian-mac doll. MARKINGS: same as **#1574** except back says CHINA instead MALAYSIA. **$35.00.**

1992 KELLY TAYLOR #1576 is the hardest to find individual 90210 doll. She wears a short black dress with purple jacket, silver purse, black panties, and shoes. Kelly Taylor, played by Jenny Garth, is very fashion conscious. She is packaged with a yellow swimsuit, display stand, and cardboard Vazara fashion magazine. MARKINGS: same as Brenda. **$40.00.**

1992 BRANDON FASHION #2531 features Brandon's Peach Pit server's uniform with apron. **$18.00.**

1992 BEVERLY HILLS 90210 GIFT SET #2562 packages China-made versions of Brandon Walsh and Dylan McKay with Brenda Walsh in one box. The 90210 girls were made only in China, so there are not facial paint differences among them as there are with the boys, who were produced in both Malaysia and China. This gift set is hard to find. MARKINGS: same as individual dolls above. **$120.00.**

1992 DONNA FASHION #2540 contains peach pants, crop top, belt, floral headband and matching purse, and gymshoes. **$18.00.**

1992 BRENDA FASHION #2532 is a pair of belted jeans with purple velour top, necklace, and shoes. **$20.00.**

1992 BEVERLY HILLS 90210 4 X 4 CRUISER #7210 is the vehicle of choice for the Beverly Hills, 90210 dolls. MARKINGS: Underside ARCO c Mattel, Inc. 1987 CHINA. **$125.00.**

1992 KELLY FASHION #2535 is a short fringed denim skirt, rose print top, belt, denim purse with silver heart decorations, and shoes. **$20.00.**

1992 PEACH PIT SNACK SHOP #7207 re-creates the popular Beverly Hills diner hangout with counter, two stools, table, two chairs, juke boxes, soda machine, cash register, table service, and food. This is hard to find. **$100.00.**

1992 DYLAN FASHION #2534 is long sleeve striped shirt with beig pants and shoes. This outfit wa not produced.

M. C. Hammer

M. C. Hammer, a rap singer, enjoyed great success with ̇s song *U Can't Touch This*. 1991 was certainly Hammer ̇ne as the performer's catchy music and unique fashion ̇ok reigned. Mattel made a M. C. Hammer doll, available in ̇o different outfits, and three M. C. Hammer fashions. J. Penney also offered a unique combination of the doll, ̇om box, and cassette tape in one box.

̇92 M. C. HAMMER & BOOM BOX #1089 features the per-̇rmer wearing gold lamé baggy pants and matching jacket ̇th gold glasses and black shoes. A microphone and a silver ̇om box that makes rap sounds are included. M. C. Ham-̇er uses the Ken doll body, but his head was specially creat-̇d in M. C. Hammer's likeness, including the intricate hairstyle ̇ the back of his head. The holographic stickers on the ̇om box are blue in this set. MARKINGS: Back of neck: c ̇91 BUSTIN'; Back: c Mattel, Inc. 1968/ MALAYSIA. **$40.00.**

̇92 M. C. HAMMER & BOOM BOX #1089 ̇vas offered through the 1992 J. C. Penney's ̇hristmas catalog as an exclusive packaged ̇vith a cassette tape containing the songs *U ̇an't Touch This* and *Dancin' Machine*, ̇long with a message from M. C. Hammer. ̇his cassette is from the **M. C. Hammer & ̇xclusive Cassette Tape set #1090**, so the ̇only way to get the doll in the gold lamé ̇utfit with boom box and cassette tape all in ̇ne box was through J. C. Penney's catalog. ̇he holographic stickers on the boom box in ̇his set are red. MARKINGS: same. **$50.00.**

1992 M. C. HAMMER & EXCLUSIVE CASSETTE TAPE #1090 contains the M. C. Hammer doll wearing purple lamé pants, a purple lamé jacket, a sheer black tank top decorated with stars, glasses, and black shoes. The cassette tape included features the songs *U Can't Touch This* and *Dancin' Machine* and a message to kids from M. C. Hammer. MARKINGS: same as #1089. **$30.00.**

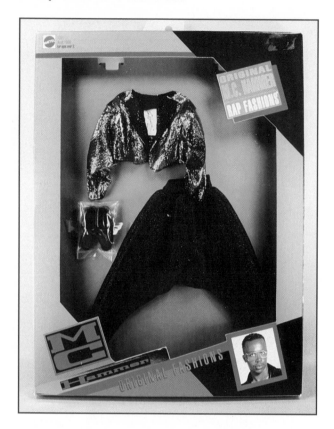

1992 M. C. HAMMER ORIGINAL FASHIONS #1091 contains black baggy pants, a multicolored lamé jacket, and black shoes. Each of the M. C. Hammer fashions has a label at the collar with M. C. Hammer's signature followed by TM BY MATTEL. **$15.00.**

1992 M. C. HAMMER ORIGINAL FASHIONS #1093 features sparkly blue pants with matching jacket, a purple lamé cummerbund, and black shoes. **$15.00.**

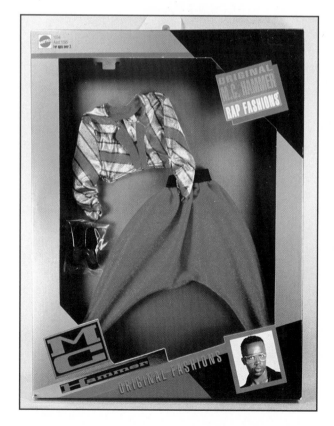

1992 M. C. HAMMER ORIGINAL FASH-IONS #1094 has sparkly red baggy pants with a red, pink, and purple lamé jacket, and black shoes. **$15.00.**

Johnny Hallyday

In 1995 Mattel France immortalized popular French singer Johnny Hallyday on the 35th anniversary of his career with a 12" doll using existing Ken doll body molds with a newly designed head to capture the musician's features. Since his debut in 1960, he has sold 80 million records, released 50 albums, and performed at 400 concerts for 15 million fans. Like the 1980 Chantal Goya doll made by Mattel France, Johnny Hallyday is not well known by American audiences and celebrity doll collectors.

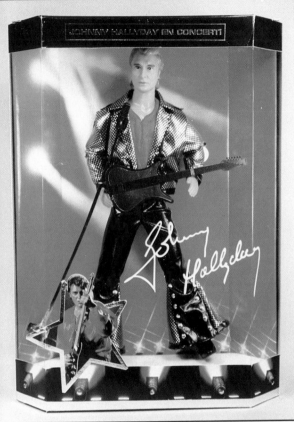

1995 JOHNNY HALLYDAY EN CONCERT #14069 features the singer wearing black leather pants, red shirt, silver lamé jacket, and golden earring. A stage microphone, guitar, and numbered certificate of authenticity are included. MARKINGS: Back of head: c 1994 MATTEL INC; Back: c Mattel, Inc. 1968/ CHINA. **$120.00.**

1995 JOHNNY HALLYDAY EN CONCERT Gift Set #62210 features the doll packaged with a special CD collection of Johnny Hallyday's songs. This set is harder to find. **$150.00.**

Nancy Kerrigan

Nancy Kerrigan, one of the best known figure skaters in the world, was a top contender for the 1994 United States National Figure Skating Championships. Her quest for the title gained national attention when she was attacked on the ice rink and had her leg beaten. Her injury kept her out of that competition, but she earned a silver medal at the 1994 Winter Olympics. Mattel did not release the Nancy Kerrigan doll, which was shown in a photograph in the widely distributed Barbie doll fashion brochures (shown below) that year.

1995 HOT SKATIN' NANCY KERRIGAN #13393 wears a blue sparkly body suit with blue overskirt, leg warmers, knee pads, helmet, and ice skates. An extra pair of roller skates and a brush were to be included with the doll. The prototype doll uses the 1994 Gymanst Barbie bend and move body with a specially designed head in the exact likeness of Nancy Kerrigan. When the Nancy Kerrigan endorsement was cancelled, Hot Skatin' Midge, using a regular head mold, was released in the same outfit that was designed for Nancy.

Clueless

A successful motion picture comedy called *Clueless* was made into a weekly television series by the same name, although the original cast changed. *Clueless* is about the chicest teen trio in Beverly Hills — Cher played by Rachel Blanchard; Amber played by Elisa Donovan, and Dionne played by Stacey Dash. The term clueless is slang for someone who doesn't have a clue as to what is going on. Mattel produced 11½" dolls of the three major characters from the *Clueless* TV show, four Clueless fashions, and a vehicle for the dolls.

1997 CHER #17036 is shown in the photo on the back of her box with a different head mold than was actually used for the Cher doll. The head appears to belong to the new Teen Skipper and doesn't resemble the actress who portrayed Cher on the television show. This Skipper head also appears on the Clueless car and fashions, so the Cher head resculpting must have been a last minute change. The Clueless dolls all use the 11½" Barbie body with B logo white painted on panties. Cher wears a blue skirt with vest, jacket, hat, stockings, white shoes, and a blue animal backpack that can be worn by a child as a bracelet. She also has a feather pen, a blue child-size ring, and of course, a telephone. MARKINGS: Back of head: c 1996 Par. Pic.; Back: c MATTEL INC 1966/ CHINA. **$20.00.**

1997 AMBER #17038 wears leathery pink pants, a sweater, jacket, headband, sunglasses, yellow shoes, and a yellow animal backpack containing a pink ring for the child. She also has a telephone for calling Cher and Dionne. MARKINGS: same as Cher. **$20.00.**

1997 DIONNE #17037 wears a lavender skirt and jacket, white blouse, hat, stockings, and lilac shoes. She carries a feather pen and has a telephone. Her white animal backpack contains a purple ring for the child. Dionne's hair is outstanding. MARKINGS: same as Cher. **$30.00.**

1997 CLUELESS FASHIONS #17103 is part of the Clueless Fashions assortment #17102; each of the four fashions has identical outer boxes with Asst. 17102 on them; the individual outfit's stock numbers can be found on the inner box liners on which the fashions are sewn. The box back states, "Fashion victims? As if!...Collect their totally designer-inspired outfits and create a fashion sensation." Clueless Fashions #17103 is a green and white plaid mini skirt with matching jacket, pink top, socks, hat, purse, and pink shoes. The most endearing part of these fashion ensembles are the newly-designed shoes, which duplicate Italian styling and retro design in the first truly different Barbie-doll size footwear in years. MARKINGS: Sewn label: Genuine Barbie B (all four fashions have this label, which may confuse future collectors of out of box fashions who think this is a Barbie fashion). **$14.00.**

1997 CLUELESS FASHIONS #17104 contains floral print blue pants with a sparkly lavender top and sweater, along with glasses, purse, and shoes. **$14.00.**

1997 CLUELESS FASHIONS #17105 is a sparkly blue two-piece top and skirt ensemble with white net pantyhose, white satin hat with iridescent ribbbon, purse, glasses, and blue platform shoes. **$14.00.**

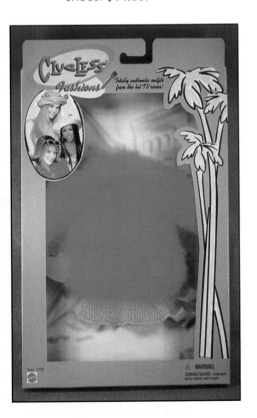

1997 CLUELESS FASHIONS #17106 is the most desirable of these fashions, as it contains a fun fur coat, along with a pink dress, purse, and platform shoes. **$14.00.**

1997 CLUELESS SUPER COOL 4 WHEELER #67579 is a white vehicle with California CHER license plate, speakers, hand-held pretend cellular phone for the child, doll-size cellular phone, music player with earphones, and a Clueless logo shopping bag. This is the same style vehicle made for the Beverly Hills 90210 dolls. MARKINGS: Underside: ARCO c Mattel, Inc. 1987 CHINA; Child-size phone: c MATTEL, INC. 1996/ CHINA. **$30.00.**

Elvis Presley

Elvis Presley, the king of rock & roll, was born in 1935. In 1953 he signed with Sun Records and had five number one singles and two number one albums by 1956. His first gold record was *Heartbreak Hotel*, his first gold album was the self-titled *Elvis Presley*, and his first motion picture was *Love Me Tender*. While a number of other doll companies have produced authorized doll versions of Elvis over the years, Mattel's first Elvis doll is packaged with Barbie doll in a sensational set called Barbie Loves Elvis Gift Set. (Since all Hollywood Legends dolls are Barbie as and Ken as…they are not included in this book.)

1997 BARBIE LOVES ELVIS GIFT SET #17450 fictionalizes a encounter Barbie doll might have had with Elvis Presley; a a 1957 Tupelo, Mississippi, concert, Elvis notices Barbie i the audience and asks her to join him on the stage, wher he sings to her. This gift set features that event, with Bar bie doll wearing a pink sweater, black velvet skirt featurin both her and Elvis' name amidst rhinestones, crinolin scarf, pearl necklace, socks, and saddle shoes. She carries photo of Elvis, with her lipstick print, which Barbie hope to have autographed. Elvis wears a gold lamé jacket wit silver cuffs and lapels, black satin shirt, and black slack socks, and shoes. He carries a handsome brown guitar wit strings and carry strap and a microphone. Two doll stand are included. Barbie doll's head is made from the origina 1958 molds with contemporary painting. Elvis uses th 1976 Young Sweethearts Michael doll's slender, poseabl body. MARKINGS: Barbie's head: c MATTEL INC. 1958; back: MATTEL, INC. 1966/ CHINA. Elvis' back of neck: c EPE.; back c 1975 MATTEL, INC./ CHINA. **$90.00.**

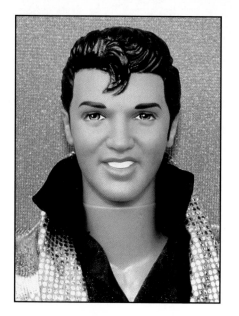

Barbie is so excited! It's 1957 and Elv

The Archies

Based on the popular, long-running comic book character, Mattel's The Archies features four of the best-known characters from the series, along with a jalopy. Mattel's dolls have vinyl heads created in each character's likeness with cloth bodies.

1978 THE ARCHIES ARCHIE #2308, JUGHEAD #2311, and **VERONICA #2310, $30.00 each.**

SABRINA #2309, $75.00.

THE ARCHIES JALOPY #2335, $85.00.

Lucille Ball

1997 I LOVE LUCY STARRING LUCILLE BALL AS LUCY RICARDO #17645 features a specifically-designed likeness of Lucille Ball as featured in episode 30 of the *I Love Lucy* television show, first airing May 5, 1952, where Lucy is cast as the "Vitameatavegamin Girl" in a commercial. Lucy wears a black and white dress, pantyhose, hat, and faux pearls; she has rooted eyelashes, red painted fingernails, spoon, a bottle of Vitameatavegamin, shoes, and a doll stand. MARKINGS: Back of head: c 1996 Desilu,too, LLC. **$50.00.**

Children's Line

Small-Talk Dolls

In 1968 Mattel released the first of many popular Small-Talk dolls. At 10" tall, the dolls stood apart from the larger, life-size baby dolls and more petite teenage fashion dolls. With adorable toothy smiles and realistic poseability, the Small-Talk doll molds are found on several lines between 1968 and 1976. Most desirable of these series are the Storybook Small-Talk dolls of 1969 and the Buffy & Mrs. Beasley character doll (see Celebrity/Character section for Buffy). As their name implies, these are talking dolls, but today most are mute because of the deterioration of the talking mechanism over time.

MARKINGS: All 10" Small Talk dolls made before 1971 have these markings: Back of head: c 1967 MATTEL, INC JAPAN; Back: c 1967 MATTEL, INC./ U.S. & FOR./PATS. PEND./U.S.A.

1968 BABY SMALL-TALK #3010 is described as the tiny, tiny talker by Mattel, who says lots of little things. The Small-Talk dolls have a pull string at the back of their neck, which when pulled produces random, recorded phrases. Their boxes have cut-away sections in the back so one could hear the dolls before purchase. **$60.00.**

1968 SISTER SMALL-TALK #3011, Baby Small-Talk's older sister, wears a mod ensemble with go-go boots. The green material in her shirt is from the 1968 Talking Christie, the orange material is from the 1967 Twist 'N Turn Barbie, and the pink material is from the 1968 Talking Barbie. Mattel dolls of all types occasionally shared fabric lots, and it is fun to match one doll's material to another's. Sister Small-Talk is more valuable than Baby Small-Talk because her outfit is so typical of the period. **$75.00.**

1968 **BABY SMALL-WALK #3627** is a brown haired, blue-eyed Small-Walk doll that walks with a battery. She wears a white mini-skirt with orange top and yellow collar. Her white shoes and socks are molded on. MARKINGS: Back: c 1967 MATTEL, INC./ U.S. & FOREIGN PATENTED/ OTHER PATENTS PENDING/ U.S.A. **$55.00.**

1968 **BABY SMALL-TALK BABY PINK #3012** is a layette designed for Baby Small-Talk. This outfit is pink and white with white diaper and pink slippers. **$40.00.**

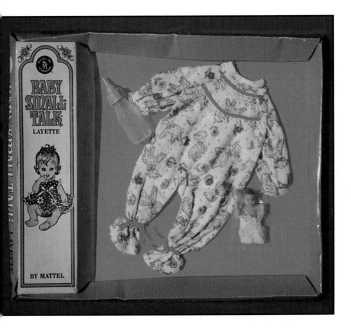

1968 **BABY SMALL-TALK SLEEPY-EYE BABY #3014** features a lamb-print romper with booties, bottle, and doll from Tutti's Walking My Dolly Set). **$45.00.**

1968 **BABY SMALL-TALK COZY BABY #3013** features a knit sweater for the baby with diaper and booties. **$40.00.**

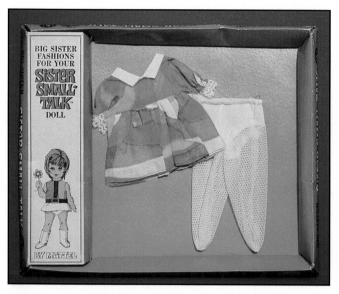

1968 SISTER SMALL-TALK SISTER'S SUITIES #3017 is an orange, yellow, and pink belted mini dress with matching panties and socks designed for Sister Small-Talk. **$40.00.**

1968 SISTER SMALL-TALK SISTER'S PLAYMATES #3015 features a sun dress with stockings. **$45.00.**

1968 SISTER SMALL-TALK SLEEPY SISTER #3016 features two-piece floral-print pajamas with slippers. **$40.00.**

1969 BABY SMALL-WALK WITH HER SCOOTABOUT 'N HAPPY HORSY #3114 is a set with a riding horse and scooter. **$55.00.**

1968 SMALL-TALK BEDDIE-BYE CASE #3004 is a vinyl carry case with space for one doll. The back of the case transforms into a bed when the fold-out headboard with pillow and a baseboard are raised. **$30.00.**

1969 TALKING CINDERELLA

3065 is the first and hardest to find Storybook Small-Talk doll. Each of these dolls represents a classic children's literary character. This gorgeous Talking Cinderella has auburn hair and a golden dress with chiffon panel and purple sleeves. She is based on the public domain heroine and not the Walt Disney cartoon version. An illustrated 16-page storybook is included with each of the first edition Storybook Small-Talk dolls, and a silver Made in Mexico wrist tag is on each doll's right hand. **$150.00.**

1969 TALKING GOLDILOCKS #3067 wears a green dress with floral print apron and collar and pantaloons. She says, "Hi, I'm Goldilocks."; "Do you like my curls?"; "Who lives in this house?"; "Hello, anybody home?"; "Do any bears live here?"; "Do you like bears?"; "This porridge is too cold."; and "I think I'll take a nap." **$125.00.**

1970 TALKING SNOW WHITE #3132, an addition to the Storybook Small-Talk line in 1970 says, "The magic mirror thinks I'm beautiful."; "The dwarfs are my friends."; "Hello my name is Snow White."; "I'm a princess."; "Am I the fairest one of all?"; "I found a cottage in the forest."; "I live in a castle." **$125.00.**

1969 TALKING LITTLE BO-PEEP #3066 is dressed in a blue and white shepherdess outfit with bonnet. She says, "Oh dear, oh dear."; "I've lost my sheep and don't know where to find them."; "Wherever have my sheep gone?"; and other phrases. **$125.00.**

1976 BABY SMALL-TALK #3010 is a reissue of the popular 1968 doll wearing a nearly identical outfit as the original in a new yellow box. The outfit's major difference is in the floral appliqués on the gown; the 1968 edition's flowers are simple pink circles with seven white petals; the 1976 edition has three tiny pink flowers amidst green leaves. MARKINGS: Back of head: c 1967 MATTEL INC HONG KONG; Back: c 1967 MATTEL, INC./ U.S. & FOR./ PATS. PEND./ HONG KONG. **$35.00.**

1976 TALKING GOLDILOCKS #3067 has several difference from the original 1969 doll. Her hair is now light blond while the original's is strawberry blonde. The reissue apron has far fewer flowers in its design, and her sho are white, while the original's shoes are pink. **$60.00.**

1976 TALKING SNOW WHITE #3132 is a reissue of the 1970 Storyboc Small Talk doll in a slim orange box. The storybooks and wrist tag were not included with the reissued Storybook Small-Talk dolls, an the fabrics differ slightly. The talking phrases remain the same. Th reissued Storybook dolls have these markings: Back: c 1967 MATTE INC./ U.S. & FOR./ PATS. PEND./ HONG KONG. **$60.00.**

Pretty Pairs

Little girls usually have one favorite toy that they love above all others. In 1970 Mattel released three such little girls, called Pretty Pairs, each with a cherished doll or teddy bear. The girls stand 6¼" tall, using Barbie doll's tiny sister Tutti's body mold. Their bendable, poseable body and arms allow each of them to clutch their precious toys.

1970 ANGIE 'N TANGIE #1135 contains an innocent-looking brown-haired girl with big blue eyes, Angie, clutching her yarn-haired doll, Tangie. The Pretty Pairs dolls are packaged on blister cards to which they are sewn; since the plastic bubble must be torn off the cardboard to remove the dolls, few of the dolls have their original packaging today. Each of the Pretty Pairs girls wears a silver foil Japan wrist tag on their left arms. Both Angie and Lori use the Liddle Kiddles' Biff Boodle/Lola Liddle head mold. MARKINGS: Angie's inside neck rim: c MATTEL, INC. JAPAN; Angie's back: c 1965/ MATTEL, INC./ JAPAN/ 25. **$250.00.**

1970 LORI 'N RORI #1133 contains an adorable blonde girl with big blue eyes, Lori, holding a fuzzy brown teddy bear with a yellow face and tummy, Rori. Lori 'N Rori is the hardest to find of this trio. Rori has a soft body with a vinyl head covered with a bear's ears hood. MARKINGS: Lori's inside neck rim: c MATTEL, INC. JAPAN; Back: c 1965/ MATTEL, INC./ JAPAN/ 26. Rori's Back of vinyl head: c M. I. **$275.00.**

1970 NAN 'N FRAN #1134 contains a sweet African-American girl, Na[n] ready for bed in her floral cotton nightgown, slippers, and cap, holdi[ng] her favorite soft-body doll, Fran. Fran's face and hair are so lifelike that [if] not for the cloth body, she would appear to be Nan's little sister. Nan us[es] the Tutti head mold. MARKINGS: Nan's inside neck rim: c MATTEL, IN[C.] JAPAN; back of head: SN 309; back of body: c 1965/ MATTEL, INC./ JAPA[N] 25; Fran's back of head: c M. I. **$240.00.**

Rock Flowers

The Rock Flowers are Mattel's answer to the groovy rock music counterculture which had made itself most visible at the Woodstock, New York, outdoor concert festival of 1969. Three 6½" girls wearing psychedelic wardrobes replete with bell bottoms, fringed shawls, and go go boots, form a band called the Rock Flowers. In 1971 Mattel produced the three members of the Rock Flowers, along with three coordinating fashion trio themed wardrobes for a total of nine fashions, two vinyl doll carry cases, and a gift set containing all three dolls. In 1972 the three girls were re-released in new packages, along with new band members Doug and Iris, nine new fashions, and one new gift set. By 1974 Mattel released leftover dolls in plastic bags with a Fashion Dolls cardboard header. The Rock Flowers dolls are invariably compared to the Topper Company's Dawn dolls, but unlike Dawn, the Rock Flowers have both bendable arms and legs thanks to their vinyl-over-wire bodies, and the Rock Flowers never strayed from the music concert theme.

1971 ROCK FLOWERS PRESENTING HEATHER #1166 packages the blonde, blue-eyed Heather wearing an orange top and yellow print bell bottom pants with matching fringed scarf and red sunglasses with a real orange 33⅓ record with stand for the doll to spin upon while the record is played. The record features Heather's solo *Sing My Song* on one side and *Sweet Times*, a group song, on the other. The back of her box shows the nine Rock Flowers fashions available in 1971. MARKINGS: Back of head: c MATTEL, INC. 1970 HONG KONG; Back: HONG KONG/ c 1970 MATTEL, INC./ U.S. & FOR. PAT'D./ PAT'D. IN CANADA. **$35.00.**

1971 ROCK FLOWERS LILAC #1167 contains the red-haired olive-green eyed Lilac wearing a multicolored top with flared arms, tights, sunglasses, and gold boots, along with a yellow 33⅓ record with stand. Lilac's record features her single, *Good Company* on one side and *Sweet Times* on the other. MARKINGS: same as Heather. **$35.00.** 1971 and 1972 boxes differ.

1971 LONG IN FRINGE #4050 is the first in the Fringe Trio yellow carded fashions. Long in Fringe features a bell-bottom body suit with fringed vest and blue shoes. For fashions that are almost 30 years old, the Rock Flowers fashions are very underpriced. **$15.00.**

1971 ROCK FLOWERS IN CONCERT #1173 is a special gift set containing Heather, Lilac, and Rosemary, and their three records. Each of the dolls has a Hong Kong wrist tag on their right arms; the dolls sold individually did not have wrist tags. This is a hard to find gift set. MARKINGS: same as individual dolls. **$100.00.**

1971 ROCK FLOWERS ROSEMARY #1168 offers the only African-American member of the group, Rosemary, wearing a blue print dress with red fringed shawl, go go boots, and sunglasses. Rosemary has an afro hairstyle, and her face resembles the 11½" Talking Christie doll. Her purple 33⅓ record features her single *Mixin' Matchin' Day* on one side and *Sweet Times* on the other. MARKINGS: Back of head: HONG KONG c MATTEL, INC. 1970. **$35.00.** 1971 and 1972 boxes shown.

71

1971 SKIRTED IN FRINGE #4051 features an orange body suit with olive green skirt with fringe, fringed purse, and orange shoes. **$15.00.**

1971 JEANS IN FRINGE #4052 features purple pants with fringe, orange top, purple vest, and orange shoes. **$15.00.**

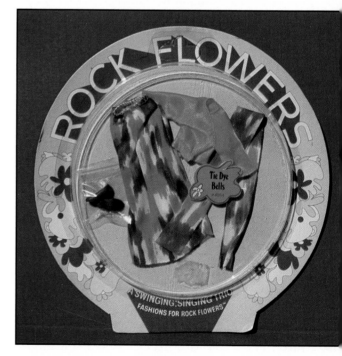

1971 TIE DYE MAXI #4053, first in the Tie Dye Trio pink carded fashions, features an orange and white maxi dress with yellow vest and brown shoes. **$15.00.**

1971 TIE DYE BELLS #4054 contains a hot pink blouse with blue, pink, and white tie dyed bell bottom pants and matching scarf, along with blue shoes. **$15.00.**

1971 TALL TIE DYE #4055 is a purple, pink, and white pantsuit with hot pink belted overskirt and pink shoes. **$15.00.**

1971 MINI LACE #4056 is the first in the Lace Trio green carded fashions. Mini Lace is a hot pink velvet skirt with sheer white top, gold lamé vest, and gold lamé boots. **$15.00.**

971 FLARES 'N LACE #4057 features flare-legged ange pants, yellow top with lace cuffs and blue belt, old lamé vest, and yellow shoes. **$15.00.**

1971 TOPPED IN LACE #4058 contains yellow satin pants, purple top with long lace cuffs, gold lamé belt, and yellow shoes. **$15.00.**

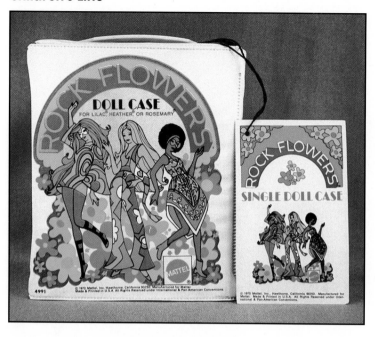

1971 ROCK FLOWERS DOLL CASE #4991 is a single vinyl doll case shown here with its original hang tag. The case front features artwork of Heather, Lilac, and Rosemary. Three yellow hangers are included. **$20.00.**

1972 ROCK FLOWERS HEATHER #1166 is a reiss of the 1971 doll in new packaging that now h Rock Flowers Heather above the doll's window; t 1971 box has Presenting Heather above the do window. The box back now shows one fashion fro each of the six fashion trios. The doll is the same the first year of issue. **$35.00.**

1972 ROCK FLOWERS PLATTER PARTY #1599 is a rare two-doll gift set containing the newest band members, Doug and Iris, and their records. MARKINGS: same as individual dolls. **$145.00.**

1971 ROCK FLOWERS ON STAGE CASE #4993 is a vinyl car case with compartments for three dolls. The front of th case depicts Lilac in Jeans in Fringe, Rosemary in Skirted Fringe, and Heather in Mini Lace. Included are three blu speakers, stage microphone, and a clip to hold the cas front upright when the base is being used as a stage. **$28.0**

74

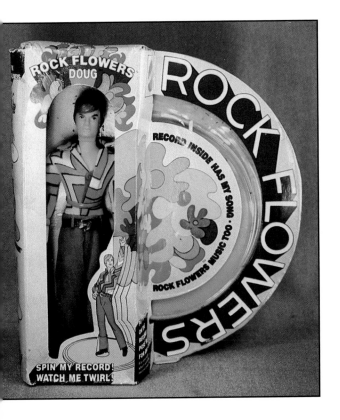

1972 ROCK FLOWERS DOUG #1177 has brown painted hair and blue eyes. He wears purple suede pants with belt, a multicolored shirt, and shoes. His 33⅓ green record contains his song *I Just Want to Make You Dance*, along with the group number *3 to Get Ready*. MARKINGS: Back: c 1970 MATTEL, INC/ HONG KONG/ U.S. & FOR. PAT'D/ PAT'D IN CANADA, 1970. **$40.00.**

1972 OVERALL GREEN #4067 combines green overalls, a red and orange shirt with yellow collar, and green shoes. **$15.00.**

1972 OVERALL BLUE #4066 features blue overalls with a red top with yellow cuffs and blue shoes. **$15.00.**

1972 OVERALL ORANGE #4065 is the first of the Overall Trio orange carded fashions. It offers orange overalls with a yellow top and orange shoes. **$15.00.**

75

1972 FRONTIER PATCHWORK #4068, first in the Frontier Trio of yellow carded fashions, features a blue, red, and white floral print dress, white shirt, red vest, apron, and red shoes. The Frontier Trio subset are the hardest Rock Flowers fashions to find. **$20.00.**

1972 FRONTIER GINGHAM #4069 features a blue, red and white dress, red and white top, apron, and red shoes. Both Frontier Patchwork and Frontier Gingham use 1972 Busy Barbie material. **$20.00.**

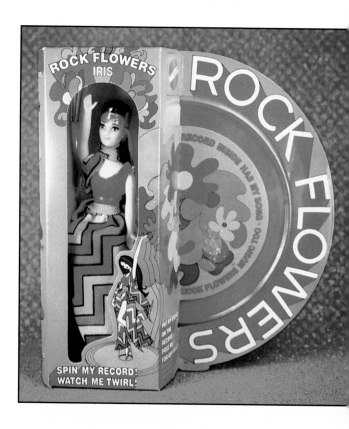

1972 FRONTIER FLOWERS #4070 contains a dark blue floral print dress with white floral-print sleeves, pink cinch belt, floral-design white apron, and blue shoes. This fashion is quite similar to the original fashion of 1972's, 11½" Busy Steffie doll. **$20.00.**

1972 ROCK FLOWERS IRIS #1176 has black hair with blue eyes. She wears a pink top, multicolored skirt, scarf, and pink shoes. Her pink record features her hit *Your Music 'N' My Music* and *3 to Get Ready*. MARKINGS: same as Heather. **$40.00.**

1974 FASHION DOLLS #1176 are left over Rock Flowers dolls sold in baggies with Fashion Dolls cardboard headers and Hong Kong wrist tags on their right arms. No shoes are included. **$35.00 each.**

972 INDIAN MIDI #4072 has a red top with a white, blue, yellow, and red skirt with fringe, yellow boots, and golden choker with a heart. **$17.00.**

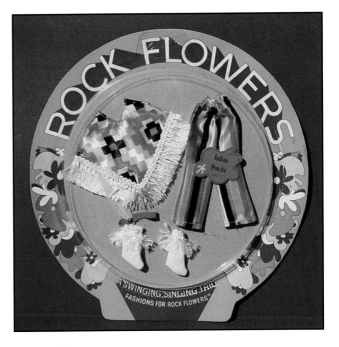

1972 INDIAN GAUCHOS #4073 contains a one-piece gaucho pantsuit with yellow top, gold ric-rac vest with black fringe, and black boots with gold trim. **$17.00.**

1972 INDIAN PONCHO #4071, first of the Indian Trio green carded fashions, features blue, yellow, and red striped satin pants, matching shawl with fringe, white boots, and headband with feather. **$17.00.**

Fashion Teeners

At only 4" tall, the Fashion Teeners dolls are among the smallest of Mattel's fashion dolls, and they certainly rank among the rarest. A set of four with rhyming names, each of the 4" dolls has movable arms, legs, and head with glued-on hair. Each wears a removable two-piece plastic swimsuit and has extra mix 'n match fashion pieces, two pairs of shoes, and a clear plastic stand. Packaged on blister cards, the dolls are viewed by some collectors as miniature Barbie dolls. In fact, their hands and bodies appear to be scaled-down versions of a Barbie doll body. (Note that their arms are similar to many Barbie dolls of the period, with hands turned to the side.) Fashion Teeners seem to literally be worth their weight in gold, as the dolls' rarity allows sellers to name their own prices, which have ranged from around $50.00 per doll (for the lucky buyer) to as much as $1,000.00 per set. MARKINGS: all four dolls are marked on the rear c 1971/ MATTEL/ INC HONG/ KONG.

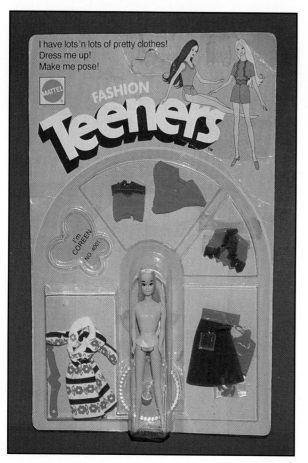

1972 COREEN #4001 is a blonde doll with black eyes wearing a yellow swimsuit. Her extra fashion pieces include a white coat with red flowers and purple stripes, red belt, red tank top with purple collar, red shirt, red vinyl vest with purple trim, purple shirt with red vinyl belt and pocket, red vinyl purse, and two pairs of red shoes. **$125.00.**

1972 DOREEN #4002 is shown here with a new warning label, NOT RECOMMENDED FOR CHILDREN UNDER 3, stuck on the doll's packaging. Dolls sold later in the year have this label, but the dolls and fashions are unchanged. **$125.00.**

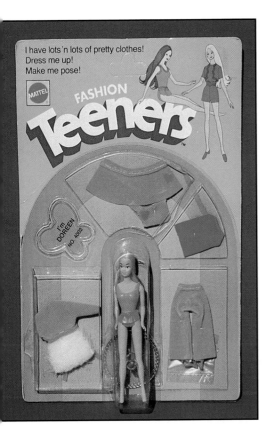

1972 DOREEN #4002 is a black-eyed blonde wearing a pink swimsuit. Her mix 'n match wardrobe includes a suede-top dress with white fur skirt, suede mini skirt with heart appliqué, hat, pink top, suede pants, and two pairs of tan shoes. **$125.00.**

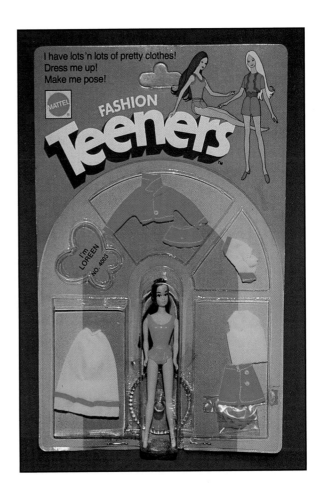

1972 LOREEN #4003 is a brunette doll with black eyes. She wears an orange swimsuit. A yellow skirt with red stripe, red jacket, red hat, yellow shorts, yellow top, red skirt, and two pairs of red shoes are included. Loreen is the hardest to find in this series. **$150.00.**

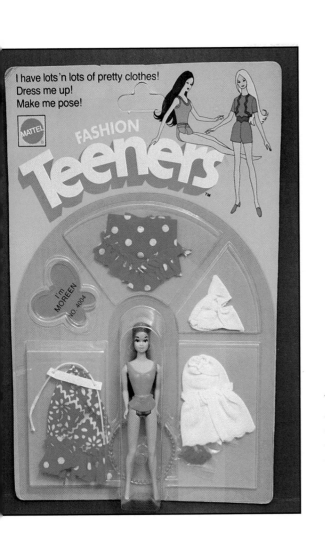

1972 MOREEN #4004, a redhead with black eyes, wears a green swimsuit. Her extra outfit pieces include a red dress with white polka dots and floral patterns, a red scarf with white polka dots, a red belt, red top, white skirt, and two pairs of shoes. **$125.00.**

Mod Models

Cool Cast allows children to make their own poseable 3½" fashion dolls. To make these dolls, a posing wire is first set into the plastic mold. After mixing hardening powder with RubberGoo, the mixture is then pressed into the mold. After 30 minutes, the dolls are ready to be dressed in instant Rub-Eze fashions. The Mod Models dolls are very similar in concept to the vinyl Tutti and Pretty Pairs dolls, which contain wires running through their bodies for super poseability, just as the Mod Models do.

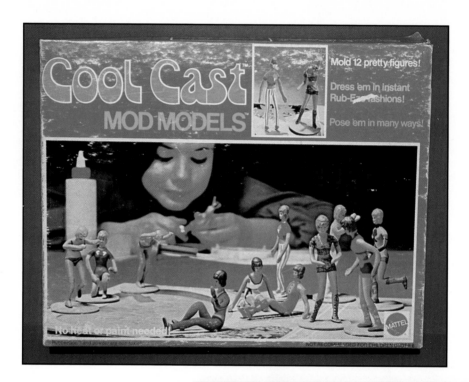

1972 COOL CAST MOD MODELS
#4729 contains materials for making 12 Mod Models fashion dolls, which can be posed in many standing, sitting, and bending positions. The Rub-Eze fashions feature all the latest trends, including lace-up boots, hot pants, and mini skirts; these 12 fashions are named Tennis Champ, Long 'N Cool, Short 'N Sweet, Beach Beauty, Merry Mini, Ballet Star, The Tree Top, Teeny Bikini, Wild Blue Yonder, Sleek Streaks, Rainbow Show, and Sunny Set. Cardboard posing stands and a swimming pool scene cardboard mat are included. MARKINGS: Mold: c 1971 MATTEL INC./ U.S.A./ 4729-051. **$45.00.**

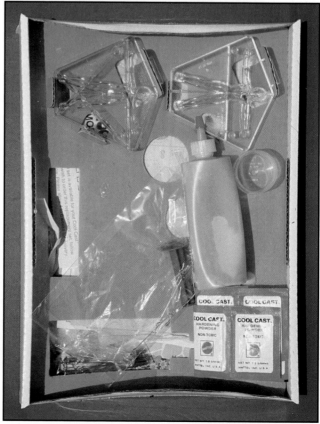

9" Fashion Dolls

Mattel makes a wonderful variety of dolls in all sizes, from the less than two inches tall Chitty Chitty Bang Bang Liddle Kiddle's children to the three foot tall My Size Barbie. Most popular seems to be 11½" fashion dolls, but the 19" Cynthia and Casey dolls of 1972 – 1974 have many fans who enjoy seeing fashion dolls in a larger than standard scale.

1974 QUICK CURL CASEY #8663 is a brunette doll using the Cynthia head and body molds, but instead of talking, Quick Curl Casey's special feature is her Quick Curl hair, which contains tiny wire strands rooted in her hair to provide extra styleability. This is the same type of hair introduced with Quick Curl Barbie and Quick Curl Miss America, both 11½" dolls. The name Casey is also from the Barbie doll family — Casey is Francie doll's friend. Quick Curl Casey wears a blue and white gingham gown with white collar and red trim, white panties, and white shoes. Extra hair accessories include a hairbrush, two barrettes, six bobby pins, a comb, four ribbons, and a curler. Quick Curl Casey is hard to find. MARKINGS: same as Cynthia. **$170.00.**

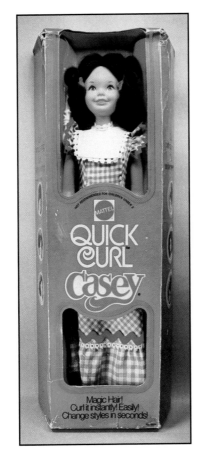

LIVELY FUN #3393

1972 CYNTHIA #3172 is a lovely blonde-haired blue-eyed talking doll who differs from Mattel's pull-string talkers: 2" records are inserted into a slot in the doll's left side. When the button on her back is pressed, Cynthia's record plays. Cynthia wears a pink dress with blue and white floral borders and cinch belt, white panties, and white heels. Extra boxed fashions for Cynthia were available. MARKINGS: Back of head: c 1971 MATTEL INC. HONG KONG; Back: c 1971 MATTEL, INC./ USA./ U. S. PATENT PENDING. **$150.00.**

1972 BEST FRIEND CYNTHIA
FASHION FUN #3394,

HAIR FUN #3389,

SCHOOL FUN #3392.

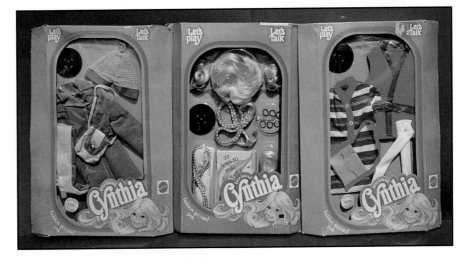

Fashion Record Paks each come with a double-sided talking record for use with Cynthia. **$45.00 each.**

The Sunshine Family

Nostalgia for the 1970s often involves fashion or music, but the 1970s also represent a simpler time when family meant father, mother, and children, all living in the same home. It was a decade of thrift, since the O.P.E.C. oil crisis led to rationing, and new concern for the environment, with the first Earth Day observed in 1970. The clothing label craze wouldn't arrive until the 1980s. Mattel's Sunshine Family dolls reflected this era beautifully, with father Steve, mother Stephie, and baby Sweets Sunshine. Whether sitting in a rocking chair at home, riding on the surrey cycle, visiting the grandparents, sewing their own clothing, or making crafts to sell from the back of their van, the Sunshine Family are so typically '70s flavored that it is hard to imagine them in any other time or place. Sold from 1974 to 1982, the Sunshine Family (and African-American Happy Family) found their way into the hands, and hearts, of many of us children who grew up during the 1970s. The values they represent are, hopefully, timeless.

1974 THE SUNSHINE FAMILY #7739 includes father Steve (9½" tall), mother Stephie (9" tall), and baby Sweets (3" tall), all with plastic eyes. Steve, who has brown hair and brown eyes, wears a wine-colored turtleneck with olive colored pants with pockets, brown belt with yellow

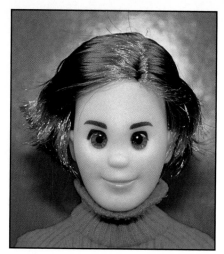

buckle, and brown boots. Stephie, who has blonde hair and blue eyes, wears a long dark blue floral print dress with white lace collar and cuffs, a long off-white apron with pockets, and sandals. Sweets, an adorable baby with fine blonde hair and blue eyes, wears a yellow romper with white collar. The box states the line's theme simply: Doing things together & with you. This first edition set features green wrist tags worn on each doll's arm. The pockets on Steve's pants and Stephie's apron are found on only the earliest dolls on the market. The first year's box is 5½" wide in front and 6¾" wide in back. MARKINGS: Steve's back of head: c 1973 MATTEL INC; Steve's back: c 1973/ MATTEL. INC./ TAIWAN. Stephie's back of head: c 1973 MATTEL INC; Stephie's back: c 1973 / MATTEL. INC./ TAIWAN. Sweet's back of head: c 1973 MATTEL INC; Sweet's back: c 1973/ MATTEL. INC./ TAIWAN. **$70.00.**

74 THE SUNSHINE FAMILY as originally envisioned by sculptor/designer Martha Armstrong-Hand. The original name for the dolls was The Good Earth Family.

photos on this page courtesy of Martha Armstrong-Hand.

The earliest presentation, Stephie has brown hair and the baby is bald except for one wisp of hair.

The second presentation shows the dolls more closely resembling the finished Sunshine Family.

A box sample showing the name The Good Earth Family is shown here.

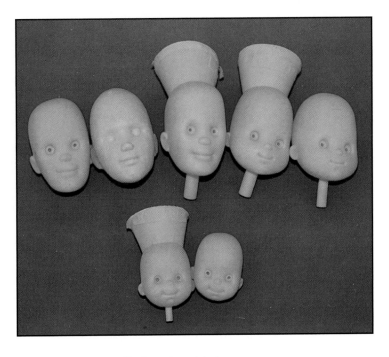

The family dog and cat prototypes with very different paint coloring than on the pets that reached the market.

Dolls' head molds in progress.

1974 THE SUNSHINE FAMILY #7739 are packaged wi▯ this Idea book of things to make. The introductory pag▯ states, "This is THE SUNSHINE FAMILY. They are like yo▯ family! The Mother and Father take care of the Ba▯ and play with it, just as your parents cared for you. Th▯ like to be out in the fresh air, because all growing thin▯ are so beautiful. They enjoy being home together, to▯ and like to make things for each other and for the▯ home. They want to share some craft ideas with you. ▯ this little book there are beds and chairs and tables ▯ things your family will need to get started. They will ▯ even more fun to play with when they have somethin▯ you have made especially for them...The SUNSHIN▯ FAMILY hopes you will share many happy times wi▯ them." Ideas found in the book include making a d▯ bed from a tissue box, a padded chair from a spray c▯ lid stuffed with cotton and then covered in fabric, and▯ table made from a milk carton.

1975 THE SUNSHINE FAMILY — LA FAMILLE BEAUSOLEIL #7739 by Mattel Canada are shown here as sold in Canada. **$50.00**

1977 THE SUNSHINE FAMILY WATCH 'EM GROW GREENHOUSE #7739 is a rare limited edition set combining the 1977 version of the Sunshine Family with a greenhouse craft kit and bean seeds. **$100.00**

1974 CAMPING CRAFT KIT #7790 is one of four craft kits available for The Sunshine Family in 1974. The Camping Craft Kit contains a shirt, sweater, apron, overalls, shorts and top, diaper, baby carrier, yarn 'n ribbon pack, lantern, baby dish, two pots with handles, two plates, frying pan, coffee pot, and stickers for decorating. Many of the plastic accessories in The Sunshine Family line, including the lantern and cookware from this set, are also used in the Barbie doll line. **$35.00.**

1974 GARDENING CRAFT KIT #7791 contains an apron, dress, hat, sun bonnet, panties, playsuit, basket with handle, hankie, yarn 'n ribbon pack, pruning shears, hedge shears, shovel, weeding fork, trowel, hoe, leaf rake, and a garden rake. **$35.00.**

1974 KITCHEN CRAFT KIT #7792 contains a stove, two mats, two aprons, diaper, towel, hankie, bib, hot mitt, pot holder, yarn 'n ribbon pack, casserole dish with lid, two pots with lids, pan, skillet, breadboard, fork, spoon, spatula, rolling pin, plate cutter, and utensil rack. **$35.00.**

1974 NURSERY CRAFT KIT #7793 includes an apron, hooded towel, nightie, diaper, washcloth, soap, blanket, rabbit, yarn 'n ribbon pack, tray, three cans, powder jar, baby bottle, tub, dish, duck, rattle, and baby carrier. **$35.00.**

1974 THE SUNSHINE FAMILY HOME #7801 is a four room home measuring 10" x 20" x 20" featuring a furnished kitchen, living room, bedroom, and patio. A bed, table, trunk, rocking chair, highchair, straight chair, cradle, curtain rod, and two shelves are included. Fun ideas found in the idea book include making an ice cream stick fence, a dresser out of cardboard matchboxes glued together, and a sofa made from a milk carton. The first box on the market has an illustration of Stephie, with her long-sleeved dress and apron with pockets, in the kitchen with Steve and Sweets. Later boxes used an actual photo of the trio in their home. **$65.00.**

1974 BARBIE BABY-SITS #7882, a Sears exclusive, uses the Baby Sweets doll — complete with The Sunshine Family wrist tag on her left arm — packaged in a brown catalog box also containing a pink and white checked apron for Barbie, bathtub, baby blanket, two bottles, baby dish, teddy bear, duckie, soap, baby dress with bonnet, bib, towel, pillow, diaper, tray, and Barbie's list of emergengy phone numbers. This doll establishes a link between Barbie and The Sunshine Family. This 1974 set in the cardboard mailing box is very hard to find. **$65.00.**

1975 THE SUNSHINE FAMILY #7739 is a reissue of the 1974 set with several differences. The box is now 5½" wide in both the front and the back. Steve's shirt has a tighter turtleneck, the woven bands in his shirt are wider, and his pants have no pockets. Stephie's dress is now short-sleeved, and her apron now has a rounded neck instead of the square cut on the 1974 edition, and this 1975 apron has no pockets and is 1" shorter. The artwork on the 1975 box front reflects these changes, as Stephie is shown with short sleeves and a short apron without pockets. Sweets has an elastic waist band which allows the bottom of the romper to be pulled down for changing diapers in the 1974 set; in the 1975 edition the elastic is gone so the baby's bottom cannot be seen without removing the entire outfit. MARKINGS: all same as 1974. **$55.00.**

975 LITTLE SWEETS #7258 features baby Sweets, now with curly red hair instead of blonde, wearing a yellow dress with white lace. Her idea book states, "You don't remember being a baby, now that you are an older person, but you know how babies love to be held and cuddled and played with, even very tiny ones. You will want to give this baby a bath in her own little tub, and put on her pretty little dress to go visiting." Included with Little Sweets are a high-chair, cradle, bathtub, two baby bottles, a baby dish, soap, duck, and teddy bear. This Little Sweets set appeared in the Mattel retailer catalog through 1982. The yellow outfit varied slightly over the years of production from a dark yellow satin to a light yellow cotton. MARKINGS: same as Sweets in the #7739 set. **$38.00.**

1975 THE HAPPY FAMILY #7279 are the African-American counterparts of The Sunshine Family. Father Hal has a black afro and brown eyes; he stands 9½" tall and wears blue jeans, a striped tank top, red belt, and black boots. Mother Hattie has curly black hair and brown eyes; she is 9" tall and wears a yellow top with blue trim, a green and red floral print skirt, and sandals. Baby Hon, at 3" tall with curly black hair and brown eyes, wears a one-piece play-suit with red bottom and white top. All three dolls have black versions of the Sunshine Family heads and bodies, and their markings are identical. The box back states that the Happy Family dolls share the same warm world as the Sunshine Family dolls. **$60.00.**

1975 MUSIC FUN CRAFT KIT #7257 is one of two new craft kits added to the four kits carried over from 1974. The Music Fun Craft Kit includes a dress, striped blanket, baby romper, music stand, guitar, tambourine, and keyboard. **$35.00.**

1975 RIVER TRIP CRAFT KIT #7258 contains an inflatable raft, paddles, two oxygen tanks, tackle box, fishing pole, three pairs of shorts, binoculars, and radio. **$35.00.**

1975 DRESS-UP KITS BEADS #7265 contains a blue Nehru shirt for Steve, a pink and red dress for Stephie, a pink playsuit for Sweets, and a pack of beads with which to decorate the outfits. **$16.00.**

1975 DRESS-UP KITS LACES #7266 contains a green jacket for Steve, a red cape for Stephie, orange bunting for Sweets, and laces for the clothing. **$16.00.**

1975 DRESS-UP KITS PATCHES #7267 includes a denim dress for Stephie, denim coveralls for Steve, denim playsuit for Sweets, and three pieces of print fabric to use as patches. **$16.00.**

1975 DRESS-UP KITS STENCILS #7268 offers a pink dress for Stephie, beige pants and green tank top for Steve, yellow playsuit for Sweets, and two stencils for use in decorating the clothes. **$16.00.**

1975 THE SUNSHINE FAMILY SURREY CYCLE #7237 is the Sunshine Family's tricycle built for three. The three wheels turn and the front handlebar moves. **$35.00.**

1976 THE SUNSHINE FAMILY PETS AND THEIR WORLD #9226 are important non-human members of the Sunshine Family. The set features a tan and white cat with green rhinestone eyes and a brown hound dog with white paws, tail, and nose and brown rhinestone eyes. A 10" tall pet house, dog cart, cat walk, bone, mouse, feeding dishes, and pet collars are included. MARKINGS: none. **$40.00.**

1976 THE SUNSHINE FAMILY #7739 underwent outfit change in 1976. Steve's turtleneck shirt now red, and he now wear denim jeans with a brown belt Stephie now wears a red an white vertically-striped dress with blue and green floral design; th same floral design is on the lac straps covering the red top o her bodysuit. Sweets' outfit is th same. The idea book is now calle the Sunshine Country Idea Book MARKINGS: all same as 1974 doll This 1976 edition is harder to fin than the dolls wearing the earlie outfits. **$65.00.**

1975 THE SUNSHINE FAMILY VAN WITH PIG GYBACK SHACK #7296 is a yellow vehicle with orange seats and black tires. A pressed wood shack rides piggyback to the countr fair. A Craft Fair sign with flags, vinyl materi als for making belts and purses, and plastic flower pots are included. The idea book sug gests making a cash box from a covered empty matchbox and milk carton tables with ice cream stick tops. MARKINGS: Bottom o van: 1973 c MATTEL INC. U.S.A. **$50.00.**

1976 THE SUNSHINE FAMILY GRANDPARENTS #9112 are the first extended family members of the Sunshine Family. Their idea book explains, "Grandpas and Grandmas are very nice to know. They have pockets with surprises in them, and stories about when your parents were children. They have hands to hold when you go for a walk and laps to sit on. Best of all, Grandmas and Grandpas have time to plant seeds or play games, or make things (like cookies) or just to watch clouds. Grandpa Sunshine, 9½" tall, has a curly white head of hair with moustache and beard and blue plastic eyes. He wears brown pants, a plaid shirt with a beige vest, and brown boots. Grandma Sunshine, 9" tall with white hair worn in a bun, wears a burgundy long-sleeved floral-print dress with lace cuffs and collar, blue apron with pockets, and black shoes. Both dolls have new head molds designed to make them appear older than Steve and Stephie. MARKINGS: Grandpa's back of head: c 1975 MATTEL, INC. TAIWAN; Back: c 1973/ MATTEL. INC./ TAIWAN. Grandma's back of head: c 1975 MATTEL, INC. TAIWAN; Back: c 1973/ MATTEL. INC./ TAIWAN. **$60.00.**

1976 THE HAPPY FAMILY GRANDPARENTS #9584 are African-American dolls using The Sunshine Family Grandparents' head molds. Grandpa Happy, with black-and-white hair, beard, and moustache and brown eyes, wears light blue jeans, a red plaid shirt, green vest, and brown boots. Grandma Happy, with curly white hair and brown eyes, wears a long orange gown with lace cuffs and collar, brown shoes, and a floral-print green apron with pockets. MARKINGS: same as The Sunshine Family Grandparents. **$65.00.**

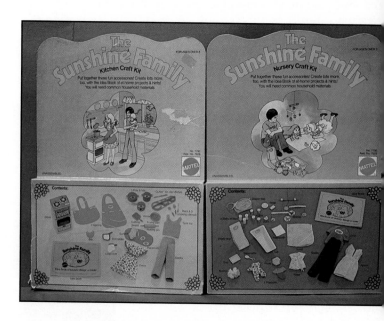

1976 KITCHEN CRAFT KIT #7792 repackages the 1974 set wit[h] a dress for Stephie, pants and tank top for Steve, stove, ho[t] mitt, pot holder, two aprons, casserole dish with lid, two pot[s] with lids, skillet, breadboard, fork, spoon, spatula, rolling pin[,] plate cutter, and utensil rack. **$25.00.**

1976 CAMPING CRAFT KIT #7790 is a reissue of the 1974 set with new packaging and slightly different contents. In this kit are denim shorts sets for Steve and Stephie, playsuit for Sweets, baby sleeping bag, lantern, camp stove, back pack flag, two pots, coffee pot with lid, three plates, and pan. **$25.00.**

1976 NURSERY CRAFT KIT #7793 is a reissue of the 1974 se[t] with pants and shirt for Steve, apron for Stephie, robe fo[r] Sweets, towel, two playsuits for Sweets, shorts for Sweet[s,] bathtub, infant seat, bunny, tray, rattle, washcloth, three bab[y] bottles, four jars, duck, soap, diaper bag, and mobile. **$25.00.**

1976 BACKYARD PICNIC PROJEC[T] **#9194** is a real wood craft kit contain[-] ing real wood pieces to assemble [a] bench for the patio. Also in this ki[t] are a dress for Stephie, pants fo[r] Steve, playsuit for Sweets, a grill, and eating utensils. **$35.00.**

1976 PLAYROOM PROJECT #9195 is [a] new real wood craft kit containing [a] die-cut wood horse, rocker, and to[y] chest, along with a dress for Stephie[,] playsuit for Sweets, plaid shirt fo[r] Steve, hammer, tool box, saw[,] wrench, pliers, screwdriver, and clamps. **$35.00.**

1976 BARBIE BABY-SITS #7882, the Sears exclusive sold in a brown catalog box from 1974 to 1975, was offered in a pink store box in 1976 with some notable changes. Sweets now wears a white floral-print robe with pink borders over a diaper; additional accessories include Barbie doll's pink apron, a phone list, bonnet for Sweets, bathtub, cradle, high chair, blanket, wash cloth, soap, duckie, teddy bear, baby dish, two baby bottles, a pink baby dress, and a bib. The most significant change is found on the note to Barbie on the back of the box, giving Barbie instructions on when to feed and bathe the baby—it is signed by a Mrs. Jones! Apparently, instead of Sweets, Mattel wanted the baby in this set to be called simply Baby, child of Mrs. Jones. MARKINGS: same as 1974 doll. **$35.00.**

1976 DRESS-UP KITS RICRAC #7269 contains a yellow dress for Stephie, white pants and shirt for Steve, green playsuit for Sweets, and ricrac for the clothes. **$16.00.**

1976 GARDENING CRAFT KIT #7791 is a reissue of the 1974 set with new packaging and altered contents. This set has coveralls for Steve, skirt and top for Stephie, shorts and top for Sweets, hats, lawn and leaf rakes, hoe, shovel, pruning shears, hedge shears, weeding fork, and trowel. **$25.00.**

1976 DRESS-UP KITS BRAIDED YARN #9192 contains a long blue dress for Stephie, green pants for Steve, white sweater and bonnet for Sweets, and yarn for making belts for the dolls. **$16.00.**

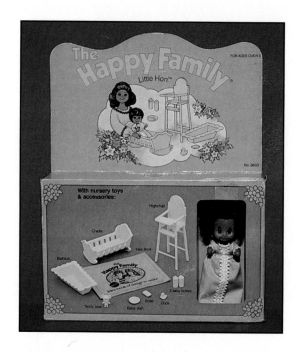

1976 BARBIE BABY-SITS #7882 from Sears has also been found with the baby dressed in a blue robe with white-petaled flowers. The box and other contents are identical. **$35.00.**

1977 LITTLE HON #9803 features the African-American Hon Happy wearing a blue dress with white lace decoration. Included with Little Hon are a high chair, cradle, bathtub, teddy bear, baby dish, soap, duck, and two baby bottles. This Little Hon set is very hard to find. MARKINGS: same as in The Happy Family set. **$65.00.**

1977 THE SUNSHINE FAMILY BABY'S ROOM #9804 packages Little Sweets with a brown, plastic corner room with starry window scene that snaps off for daytime. Included in Sweets' room are a bassinet/buggy, rocking chair, table, bathtub, scale, diaper pail, planters with ferns, two pictures for the wall, two baby bottles, two jars, soap, tray, rattle, and blanket. MARKINGS: Back of wall: C MATTEL, INC. 1976 U.S.A. **$75.00.**

1976 THE SUNSHINE FAMILY CRAFT STORE #9266 is an 18" 18" x 15" hardboard structure with open beam ceiling, swinging door, display cabinet with drawers, spinning wheel that really spins, pottery wheel that really works, chair, two wall shelves, counter, cash register, and stove. The idea book offers suggestions on making a broom from a straw and yarn, making a tub from a cup, and cutting a fabric welcome mat. **$70.00.**

77 THE SUNSHINE FAMILY FARM PRODUCE STAND 2072 is a rare Sears exclusive. **$65.00.**

1977 BARBIE BABY-SITTING ROOM #7804 is designed to complement the Barbie Baby-Sits doll sets. The Barbie Baby-Sitting Room is identical in structure to The Sunshine Family Baby's Room, except in the Barbie doll set, the floors and walls are pink, and the colors of other accessories vary as well. MARKINGS: same as The Sunshine Family Baby's Room. **$65.00.**

77 THE SUNSHINE FAMILY DOLL & CRAFT CASE 665 is a yellow vinyl carry case exclusive to ars. The Sears catalog number 49-31193 is inted on the front right corner of the case. The twork depicts Steve wearing his original 1974 tfit with light green pants and wine-colored rtle neck shirt, but Stephie is shown in her origi- 1976 red fashion. **$25.00.**

1977 THE SUNSHINE FAMILY FARM #9833 is the hardest to find item in the Sunshine Family line. The Sunshine Family Farm includes the barn and hayloft with opening doors, gate, fence, ladder, weather vane, pump that really pumps water into a water trough, milk can, milk stool, hoe, rake, shovel, bucket, axe, and rooster. Most amazing in this set is the cow that drinks from the trough and can then have its udders milked, and the hen that really lays six eggs! Suggestions in the idea book include making a bale of hay from a milk carton and yarn, making a silo from an oatmeal carton, and making a tree from a paper towel tube. **$140.00.**

1978 THE SUNSHINE FUN FAMILY #2321 announces, And now there are 4! Mom, Dad, big sister, and baby brother having fun together! The Sunshine Fun Family is a reworked Sunshine Family with more contemporary fashions and hairstyles. Mom Stephie has long, straight side-parted hair; and she wears blue eyeshadow — a sharp contrast to the earlier natural-look Stephie. Her dress has a beige floral bodice with long yellow skirt, and her shoes, not sandals, are yellow. Dad Steve now has a curly permed hairdo; he wears an off-white sweater with brown collar, brown pants, and yellow shoes. Daughter Sweets is now a 4¾" tall toddler with a newly designed head and body. Her long hair is tied on each side with orange ribbons. Sweets' top is yellow, and her shorts match Stephie's bodice. The new 3" baby boy is unnamed; he uses the old Sweets head and body molds. He has curly strawberry blonde hair and freckles, and his beige and brown playsuit complement Steve's outfit. The first Sunshine Fun Family sets on the market have a sticker on their lower left box front covering up the words, STORYBOOK INCLUDED. MARKINGS: Steve and Stephie: same as 1974; 4¾" Sweets' back of head: c 1977 MATTEL INC. TAIWAN; Sweets' back: c Mattel, Inc. 1977/ TAIWAN. Baby boy: Back of head: c 1973 MATTEL INC; Back: c 1973/ MATTEL, INC./ TAIWAN. **$65.00.**

1978 THE SUNSHINE FUN FAMILY #2321 sold a little later in the year have the STORYBOOK INCLUDED line visible on their box, and the storybook A Friend for Sweets is included. A Friend for Sweets recounts Sweets' loneliness at having only her Bear Sunshine as a companion; but she is delighted when a baby boy is born into the family on Christmas morning; his name is never given in the book. Stephie's bodice is a brighter yellow in this set, and the white paint now used on her eyes is more vibrant in this set. Steve's hair is fuller in this set, and his eyebrows and eyepaint are darker and thicker. The baby boy in this set has darker freckles. Markings: all same. **$65.00.**

1978 BEACH FASHIONS #2337 is one of four fashion sets created for The Sunshine Fun Family. Each carded fashion contains an outfit for each member of the familly. Beach Fashions contains a blue swimsuit, white coverup, and sandals for Mom; orange swimming trunks and yellow and orange jacket for Dad; white and red bathing suit and white terry cloth top for Sweets; and blue swimsuit for the new baby. The Happy Fun Family are shown modeling this fashion. **$30.00.**

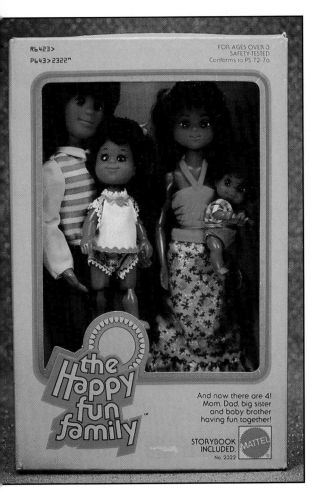

1978 THE HAPPY FUN FAMILY #2322 features the African-American Happy Family modified to late 1970s styles. In this set, Dad Hal wears a blue, white, and yellow striped shirt with blue pants. Mom Hattie wears an orange top and blue floral print skirt decorated with orange flowers. Hon, now 4¾" tall, wears a blue floral playsuit with white top. The new baby boy wears a playsuit matching Dad's shirt. This set is very hard to find. MARKINGS: same as The Sunshine Fun Family. **$85.00.**

1978 PARTY FASHIONS #2336 contains turquoise blue pants, jacket, shirt, and tie for Dad; powder blue dress for Mom; pink gown for Sweets; and white and turquoise playsuit for the baby. **$30.00.**

1978 WINTER FASHIONS #2339 contains a brown co[at] for Dad, a pink coat with white fur collar and blue pan[ts] for Mom, an orange snowsuit with fur collar for Sweet[s] and red wrap for the baby. **$30.00.**

THE SUNSHINE FUN FAMILY House with furniture, swing set & wading pool with squirting hose.

1978 THE SUNSHINE FUN FAMILY HOUSE is a two-story home with double beds in the parents' room, a single bed for Sweets and a cradle for the new baby in the room the children share, a sofa and trunk in the living room, a table with three chairs and a high chair in the kitchen, and a swing set and a wading pool with squirting hose outside. This is very rare. **$150.00.**

1978 PLAYTIME FASHIONS #2338 features white ten[n]is outfits for Dad and Mom, a red and white outf[it] for Sweets, and a romper for the baby. **$30.00.**

Star Spangled Dolls

As the United States of America approached its bicentennial in 1976, the entire country reflected on the past 200 years in measuring how far we as a nation had come, and how much farther we had to go. Mattel released a nostalgic series of Star Spangled dolls using The Sunshine Family's Steve's and Stephie's head and body molds in 1975. The dolls, dressed in attire appropriate to some past era in American history, were given actual names and stories on their boxes revealing their place in history. In the first two years of release, 1975 and 1976, four single female dolls and three male/female pairs of dolls were available in boxes with windows and beautifully illustrated liners. In 1977 only the four females were sold on blister cards. Rarest of all the Star Spangled Dolls are the Jazz Performers. If only all doll collections were this entertaining and educational.

MARKINGS: All girl dolls are 9" tall and have Stephie Sunshine's markings: c 1973 MATTEL INC on the back of the head and c 1973/ MATTEL. INC./ TAIWAN on their backs. All male dolls are 9½" tall with Steve Sunshine's markings of c 1973 MATTEL INC on the back of their heads and c 1973/ MATTEL. INC./ TAIWAN on their backs. NOTE: Advertisers offering The Sunshine Family mom with rare brown hair are mistakenly referring to one of the Star Spangled dolls. All Stephie dolls are blonde.

1975 COLONIAL GIRL #7941 is a blue-eyed blonde with ringlet curls in her hair. She wears a blue satin gown with yellow panel and sheer white sleeves, with yellow shoes. Her box story relates, "I'm Miss Alison Thompson. Every day my girlfriends and I go to school to learn needlecraft and sewing. Our whole city is alive with waiting and whispering. Will the British take the tax off tea? What will we do if they don't? Fight? It is so exciting! My father and his friend, Paul Revere, are patriots — I am too!" **$50.00.**

1975 INDIAN MAIDEN #7938 has dark brown hair and brown eyes. She wears a tan outfit with fringe on the bodice, sleeves, and hem. She wears moccasins, and she has a multicolored strand of beads around her neck and in both sections of her hair. Her box story reveals, "I'm Smiling Eyes from a Northern Plains tribe. My mother and sisters and I weave blankets in colors of the sun and sky. My brothers and father go each day to hunt deer for food and clothing. We welcome many travelers. Men named Lewis and Clark came and we gave them food and horses for their journey. We have been at peace with all peoples for many years. I hope it will always be so." **$60.00.**

1975 JAZZ PERFORMERS #7945 are the only African-American dolls this series. Louis wears white pants, a blue and white striped shirt w blue satin vest, hat, and shoes, and he carries a trumpet. Mellie wears long yellow lace dress with orange flowers at her waist and on her h Their box story reveals, "We're Mellie and Louis Harris from the port c where life is music and music is jazz. Louis plays the trumpet with Je Roll Morton, the famous piano player. I sing blues. We play in parks people dancing on the grass, at cotillions or in cabarets 'til the night filled with swirling colors and a sweet jazz wail. Our favorite place to pl is on street corners for the whole world to hear!" **$100.00.**

1975 LIBERTY PATRIOTS #7944 features Richard wearing a lavender colonial costume. He has brown eyes and curly, shoulder length hair. Regina wears a pale pink gown with floral panel and mobcap over her blonde head full of ringlet curls. Their box story states, "We're Regina and Richard Stanton. We live in the loveliest, largest and richest of all the colonial cities. Not only is it the home of the Liberty Bell, but it also has a library, a hospital, and even a college. Everyone here is very excited about independence. There is even talk that the declaration will be signed in our city. Tonight we go to a meeting to hear mo from our most honored Mr. Benjamin Franklin." **$70.00.**

1975 PIONEER DAUGHTER #7940 is a brown-haired, blue-eyed girl wearing a purple gown with floral, fringed shawl and pink bonnet. Her story reveals, "I'm Sara Jane Benson. My family, and 40 others in covered wagons, are heading west on the Northwest Trail. We've taken along all we own, from cows to plows. Sometimes I knit to pass time or I watch the beautiful countryside. I've seen herds of buffalo grazing — with wild flowers all around. Today we're going to Jim Bridger's fort. He's a famous frontier explorer and will help us reach the Pacific Ocean before winter comes." **$50.00.**

1975 SOUTHERN BELLE #7939 is a red-haired girl with blue eyes. She wears a three-tiered white gown with orange floral designs. A green belt matches the green band on her tan straw hat. Her story reveals, "I'm Rosa Lee Linden. I live with my family on a huge cotton plantation. Around here, cotton is king and daddy frets over dry spells and smiles when he can boast of his crop. We love company and guests are welcome all the time. Henry Clay, that fine old man who people are calling, 'the great compromiser,' even had supper with us all a week ago." **$50.00.**

1975 THANKSGIVING PILGRIMS #7943 features James with blonde hair and brown eyes dressed in a green Pilgrim uniform with white collar and cuffs. A tall black hat with buckle sits atop his head. The box photo shows him with dark brown hair. Louisa is a brunette with blue eyes. She wears a brown dress with white apron, cuffs, collar, and hat, and a brown cape. Their box story relates, "We are James and Louisa Winthrop from England. We have settled in Plymouth. Our first winter has been full of hardships and troubles — but this spring the Indian, Samoset, came. He is very wise and kind and has taught us how to catch fish, raise corn and stalk game. Our October harvest this year was small—but enough to make us rejoice that we have come this far. We had a feast of Thanksgiving to celebrate." **$70.00.**

1977 COLONIAL GIRL #7941 is now packaged on a blister card. Her story and outfit remain the same. **$40.00.**

1977 INDIAN MAIDEN #7938 is now packaged on a blister card. Her story and outfit remain the same. **$45.00.**

1977 SOUTHERN BELLE #7939 is now packaged on a blister card. Her hat is now white and lacy, instead of the tan straw hat found on the 1975 edition. Her story is unchanged. **$40.00.**

1977 PIONEER DAUGHTER #7940 is now packaged on a blister card. Her story and outfit remain the same. **$40.00.**

The Beans Family

This series is akin to The Sunshine Family with soft, bean-bag bodies and vinyl heads with rooted hair. Children could choose between four different Mama and Baby Beans sets — blonde, brunette, redhead, or African-American. Only one Daddy and Baby Beans set was made, a brunette father with blue eyes and a moustache. In 1977 three sets of large Baby Beans and Pets joined the line. All of the parents and the large babies have a Velcro tab on their hands for holding cloth objects. By 1979 four Shoe Baby Beans, tiny 2½" tall precious babies sold in miniature shoe boxes, were also available. Other Beans dolls were available in the 1970s, but those included here most reflect the family theme prevalent in The Sunshine Family and The Heart Family lines.

MARKINGS: All Mama dolls are marked on the back of the head c 1974 MATTEL INC. TAIWAN; Daddy and each Baby Bean (with pet) are marked on the back of the head c 1976 MATTEL INC.

1976 MAMA AND BABY BEANS #9197 includes a blonde 10" tall Mama with a foam/fiber filled body with vinyl head. This set has a blonde Mama with blue eyes wearing a brown floral-print gown with lace trim and apron over red-dotted leggings. Her 3¾" baby has a soft body and vinyl head with painted brown hair and blue eyes. The baby is wearing the same red-dotted yellow material as found on Mama's leggings. **$30.00.**

1976 MAMA AND BABY BEANS #9527 contains the African-American Mama with curly black hair and brown eyes. She wears a white floral print gown with blue stockings; her baby wears this same blue material in its outfit. **$35.00.**

1976 MAMA AND BABY BEANS #9198 features a brunette Mama with brown eyes holding a brown-haired baby with brown eyes. The outfits are identical for this set and the African-American set. **$30.00.**

1976 MAMA AND BABY BEANS #9199 includes a redheaded Mama with green eyes holding her redheaded, green-eyed baby. Mama wears a green floral-print dress with white apron and pink and yellow stockings; her baby wears a pink and yellow striped outfit. **$30.00.**

#9197 and **#9527** are also shown on page 103.

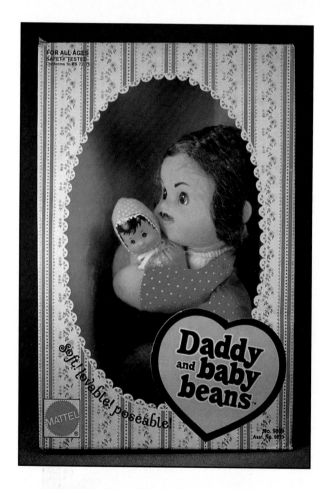

1977 DADDY AND BABY BEANS #9809 features blue-eyed, brown-haired Daddy with painted moustache wearing blue jeans, brown boots, and red top with white turtleneck. His baby has brown hair and blue eyes; it wears a yellow gown with white dots. **$30.00.**

1977 BABY BEANS AND PETS #9806 features a 10" tall brunette violet-eyed girl wearing a blue gingham gown with white apron clutching her pet chicken. **$30.00.**

1977 BABY BEANS AND PETS #9808 features a blonde-haired, blue-eyed boy, wearing overalls and a yellow and orange shirt, holding his white dog with brown ears. **$30.00.**

1979 SHOE BABY BEANS BALLERINA BEANS #2951 is part of the Shoe Baby Beans series, which is based on the Mother Goose rhyme about an old woman who lived in a shoe. The packaging on these dolls states, There was an old woman/ Who lived in a shoe,/ She had lots of SHOE BABY BEANS/ Who lived in shoes, too! Ballerina Beans is a 2½" tall soft-bodied ballerina with brown hair and brown eyes. She is packaged on a blister card inside her cardboard ballet shoe box. All four Shoe Baby Beans are marked on the back of their heads c 1978 MATTEL INC. TAIWAN. **$20.00.**

1979 SHOE BABY BEANS BEDTIME BABY BEANS
#2950 is a blonde, blue-eyed baby wearing a
blue sleeper. The tiny 2½" baby is packaged
inside a bunny slipper. **$20.00.**

1979 SHOE BABY BEANS PRETTY PARTY BEANS
#2953 is a red-haired girl with green eyes dressed
in a red outfit with lace-trimmed hood. This 2½"
baby is found inside a red cardboard saddle shoe.
$20.00.

1979 SHOE BABY BEANS SNEAKERS BEANS
#2952 is a brown-haired, brown-eyed boy with a
mischievous grin. He wears an orange hooded
playsuit, and resides inside a cardboard sneaker.
$20.00.

Honey Hill Bunch

   Much of doll playing is the child's wish to role play life as a glamorous grown-up (life in Barbie doll's world) or as a parent (caring for baby dolls). However, many children enjoy playing with a doll like themselves — a child. Mattel's Honey Hill Bunch contains a wide spectrum of children dolls certain to be a good match for any child in either looks or personality. The 1976 Honey Hill Bunch line includes a tomboy, a musician, a scholar, a momma's helper, a beauty, a toughie, and a little kid who follows the older children around; certainly most children can identify with one or more of these characters.

   All of these dolls have vinyl heads with rooted hair, and cloth bodies containing polyester fibers. One hand on each doll has a Velcro strip for use in holding their enclosed accessory. MARKINGS: All dolls have c 1975 MATTEL INC. with or without the word TAIWAN on the backs of their heads.

1976 BATTIE/SLUGGER #9095 is a redheaded tomboy with green eyes and freckles. She carries a baseball bat and boasts, "I can hit more 'homers' than anybody!" Interestingly, some box backs refer to Battie while others call her Slugger. **$25.00.**

1976 DARLIN' #9099 is a pretty blonde girl with blue eyes. She wears her hair in pigtails tied with pink ribbon, and she carries a pink purse. She boasts, "I'm so-o-o pretty! Don't you agree!" **$25.00.**

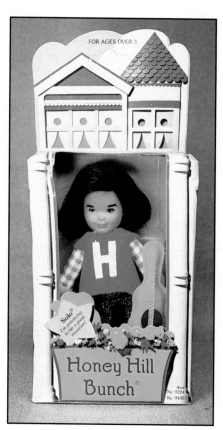

1976 I.Q. #9096 is an Asian student with black hair and brown eyes. I.Q. wears glasses and carries a cloth book, declaring, "I always get straight 'A's' in school!" **$25.00.**

1976 SOLO #9100 has darker skin, black hair, and brown eyes. Solo wears an H logo top (for Honey Hill Bunch) and carries a violin. Solo explains, "I'm practicing to be a great musician!" **$25.00.**

1976 LI'L KID #9097 is a swee blonde with blue eyes holding h pet Good Dog. A tag-along, Li'l Ki says, "Me 'n Good Dog wanta pla too!" **$25.00.**

1977 RICKETY RIG & 6 DOLLS #9977 is the ride-on vehicle the Honey Hill Bunch kids use. It was sold in two versions — without dolls **(#9781)**, **$40.00**; and with six dolls **(#9977)**, **$65.00.**

1976 SWEETLEE #9098 is a chubby-faced auburn-haired girl with blue eyes. Sweetlee carries a ginger-bread man cookie and claims, "I make the yummiest cookies in the world!" **$25.00.**

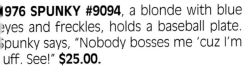

1976 SPUNKY #9094, a blonde with blue eyes and freckles, holds a baseball plate. Spunky says, "Nobody bosses me 'cuz I'm tuff. See!" **$25.00.**

1976 HONEY HILL BUNCH CLUB-HOUSE #9225 is "their special place to plot & plan & play!" Included with the clubhouse are a table, seesaw, barrel, tire swing, window shelf, wagon, tent, ladder, two plates and cups, two barrel chairs, and a tree. **$50.00.**

109

1976 HONEY HILL BUNCH CLUBHOUSE AND 4 DOLLS #9373 is a special exclusive edition of the regular clubhouse with four dolls included. These dolls are Darlin', Li'l Kid 'n Good Dog, Spunky, and Sweetlee. This set is very hard to find. **$85.00.**

1977 HAYSEED & CHUM #9714 contains Hayseed, a strawberry-blonde child with blue eyes and freckles, and his dog Chum, a St. Bernard. Chum has Velcro strips along each side of his body to hold his legs in position, and he has Velcro on his tongue for carrying his bone. MARKINGS: under Chum's chin: c 1976 MATTEL INC. TAIWAN. **$40.00.**

1977 CURLY Q #9713 is the only African-American member of the Honey Hill Bunch. She has curly auburn hair and brown eyes, and she carries a yellow cat. Curly Q asks, "How do you like my hair-do?" **$30.00.**

1978 IRISH EYES #2567 has brown hair and emerald green eyes. She carries two clovers. Her box says, "She's as Irish as can be!" Irish Eyes is hard to find. **$40.00.**

1978 MISS CHEEVUS #2568 has curly blonde hair and green eyes. Carrying a baseball diamond, "she's full of fun 'n jokes!" **$30.00.**

1978 SUNFLOWER #2566 is a brown-eyed blonde carrying a flower. Sunflower is hard to find. **$35.00.**

1978 BASKIN-ROBBINS ICE CREAM STORE #9979 is a vinyl carrycase that opens to reveal the interior of a Baskin-Robbins Ice Cream Store, complete with two counters, bench with table top, cash register, banana split, ice cream sundae, cone holder, and cups. A brown-haired boy employee with green eyes wears a brown hat, and a blonde-haired girl employee with blue eyes wears a pink hat and uniform; both hold ice cream cones. **$50.00. BUNNY BASKIN AND RICHIE ROBBINS #9978** were available as a pair in a baggie. **$55.00.**

111

Sweet 16

In 1976 Mattel released an 11½" young teen doll called Sweet 16. The doll uses a Barbie doll body, but her head and eyes are much larger than Barbie doll's. The Sweet 16 head originated on a Mattel doll made exclusively for the Japanese market called Living Eli in 1970.

Living Eli is Living Barbie doll's brunette friend. Twelve Sweet 16 fashions were sold on blister cards. These same fashions are used in the three Barbie's Super Fashion Fireworks sets sold exclusively at Kresge stores in 1977.

1976 SWEET 16 #9537 is a blonde doll with thin, pale blonde hair and large brown eyes. Sweet 16 uses a Barbie doll body with arms made from the original 1959 Barbie doll molds, but Sweet 16's body is hollow and very light, while the original Barbie doll's is solid and heavy. MARKINGS: Inside neck rim: c MATTEL INC. KOREA; Back: c MATTEL, INC./ 1958/ KOREA. **$40.00.**

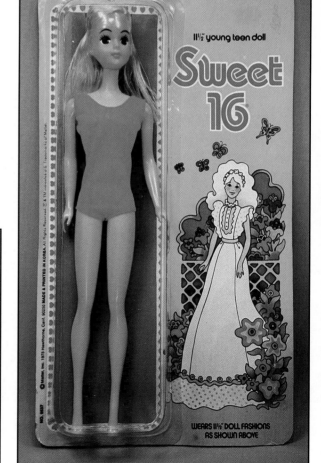

1976 SWEET 16 #9537 was also made with Francie doll's shorter arm molds, which have the palms posed toward the thighs. MARKINGS: same as above. **$35.00.**

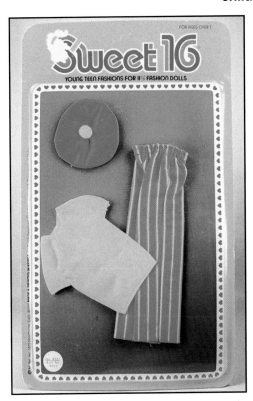

1976 SWEET 16 #9550 is an orange dress with yellow belt and yellow hat. All of these fashions are hard to find. **$20.00.**

1976 SWEET 16 #9551 is a pair of orange pants with yellow stripes, a yellow blouse, and an orange cap. **$20.00.**

1976 SWEET 16 #9552 is a red skirt with multicolored striped shirt and matching cap. **$20.00.**

1976 SWEET 16 #9553 is a yellow floral-print dress with matching scarf and white blouse. **$20.00.**

113

1976 SWEET 16 #9554 is a peach nightie with short robe. **$20.00.**

1976 SWEET 16 #9555 is a blue floral-design gown with pink waist bodice and white sleeves. **$20.00.**

1976 SWEET 16 #9556 is a pair of pink pants with a green belted shirt decorated with a pink floral design, matching scarf, and soda bottle. **$20.00.**

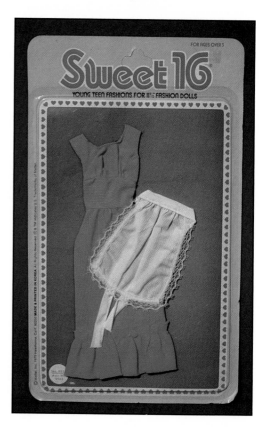

1976 SWEET 16 #9557 is a long pink dress with white apron. **$20.00.**

1976 SWEET 16 #9558 is a long red dress with white polka dots and floral designs, along with a white apron with matching red border. **$20.00.**

1976 SWEET 16 #9559 is a pair of white pants, a blue shirt with floral design, and a yellow top. **$20.00.**

1976 SWEET 16 #9559 is shown here with the same white pants and yellow top, but the shirt is a pink and white check design. **$20.00.**

1976 SWEET 16 #9560 is a long yellow skirt with red floral panel, yellow top, and net hat. **$20.00.**

115

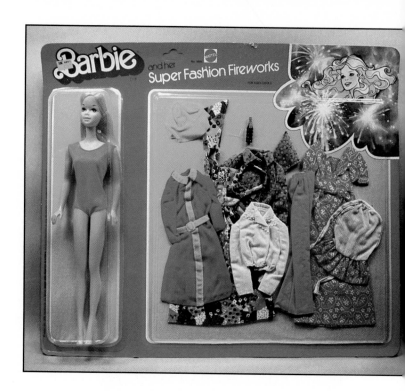

1976 SWEET 16 #9561 is a long orange dress with white floral design. **$20.00.**

1977 BARBIE AND HER SUPER FASHION FIREWORKS #9805 con tains Barbie doll with the same body (using original 1959 Barb arms and hands) and swimsuit as the 1976 Sweet 16 doll #953 The four extra fashions included in this set are Sweet 16 fashior #9550, #9553 (in a different color fabric dress/scarf), #9556, ar #9558 (with a different floral print). Barbie and Her Fashic Fireworks is a hard-to-find Kresge store exclusive. MARKING Inside neck rim: c 1965 MATTEL INC KOREA; Back: c MATTEL INC 1958/ KOREA. **$90.00.**

1977 BARBIE AND HER SUPER FASHION FIREWORKS #9805 has also been found packaged with four differ- ent Sweet 16 fashions. This set contains #9551, #9554, #9555, and #9557. The Barbie doll in this package has different arms with her palms facing behind her. MARKINGS: same. **$90.00.**

1977 BARBIE AND HER SUPER FASHION FIREWORK #9805 has been found in a third variation containing the remaining four styles of Sweet 16 fashions. Thi set contains #9552, #9559 (with blue shirt), #9560, an #9561. In this set, Barbie doll uses a third arm mol with hands posed to the sides. **$90.00.**

Young Sweethearts

Certainly the most romantically-themed series ever, Young Sweethearts introduces us to Michael and Melinda, described as "Made for each other. Hand in hand. Arm in arm. Playful. Lighthearted." Melinda's journal on the box back describes how she met Michael: "The first time I saw him, he was climbing in my old tree! 'What are you doing here?' we asked each other at the same time. We laughed and started talking. Then we shared lunch and wandered around the park all afternoon, past the pond and the wishing well. Now we come here all the time. It seems like we've been friends forever..." Michael is 12" tall with rooted hair and a new, completely poseable lifelike body. Melinda is 11½" tall with a new, completely poseable lifelike body. Michael's body was used by Mattel on later male dolls such as Shaun, Tom Comet, and even Ken. Melinda's body found later use on Spectra and Jazzie dolls. The Young Sweethearts line includes the Michael and Melinda set, available in two versions, four His 'N Hers Fashion Pairs, and a delightful Wishing Well Park playset.

1976 YOUNG SWEETHEARTS #9271 includes brown-eyed, brown haired Michael wearing off-white pants, a coral shirt with wine colored vest, and yellow shoes. Melinda, a blue-eyed blonde, wears a peach colored full-length dress with ivory top and sandals. The design on her bodice features two doves inside a heart, and she wears a crown of yellow flowers on her head. MARKINGS: Michael's back of head: c 1975 MATTEL INC TAIWAN; Back: c Mattel, Inc. 1975/ TAIWAN. Melinda's neck rim: c MATTEL, INC. 1975 TAIWAN; Back: c Mattel, Inc. 1975/ TAIWAN. **$50.00.**

1976 COUNTRY MATES! #9588 is the first of four His 'n Hers Fashion Pairs which feature an outfit each for Michael and Melinda. This set contains a floral sun dress with hat and purse for Melinda and tan corduroy pants and ivory shirt for Michael; the cuffs and collar of his shirt are in the same print fabric as Melinda's dress. No shoes are included with any of these fashions. All of these fashions are rare. **$40.00.**

1976 YOUNG SWEETHEARTS #9271 has also been found with one major difference — Melinda's dress in this set is bright yellow. This set with Melinda in a yellow dress is the harder of the two to find. MARKINGS: same. **$60.00.**

1976 PICNIC PINK!
#9586 contains pir
pants, pink shirt wit
two doves inside a hea
logo, and pink headbar
for Melinda, and
maroon pullover shi
and pink pants fc
Michael. **$40.00.**

1976 PARTY DAY BLUE! #9585 features
Melinda's long blue gown with lacy floral
bodice and blue heart-shaped diary,
along with Michael's white pants and blue
shirt. **$40.00.**

1976 YOUNG SWEETHEARTS WISHING WELL PARK #9538 contain
a wishing well with bucket, apple tree with removable apples
swing, pond with fountain, plastic flowers, plastic stone-look path
way, three swans, picnic cloth, fruit basket, two plates, two cups
dove, diary, and locket. The magic wishing well has two hidde
compartments; one is a hiding place for the locket, and the othe
gives secret answers to their questions. **$95.00.**

1976 SUNNY SUNDAY! #9588 features a two-piece
floral-design gown with lace collar and chain necklace with yellow felt heart pendant for Melinda and
brown pants, floral-sleeved top with red vest and
yellow bow tie for Michael. **$40.00.**

Pulsar

Pulsar, the ultimate man of adventure, offered children a unique alternative to Kenner Toy's popular Six Million Dollar Man series of dolls. 13½" tall Pulsar features a see-through chest cavity. When the button in his back is pushed, his heart beats, his lungs breathe, and his blood flows! As if those features aren't enough to interest even the most jaded child, Pulsar's face lifts up to reveal his brain, in which secret mission disks are inserted. The Pulsar line also includes Hypnos, Pulsar's arch enemy, and a Life Systems Center.

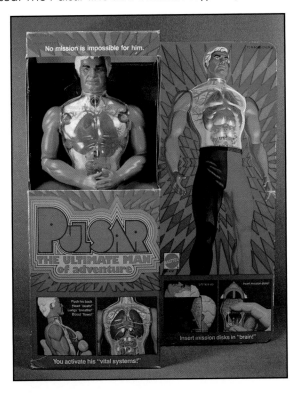

1977 PULSAR #9797 wears black and red pants with space boots. His matching jacket has a lightning bolt emblem on it. His transparent chest exposes workable vital organs. When his face is lifted up, his brain is revealed, in which two computer mission disks can be inserted. MARKINGS: Back: c MATTEL, INC./ 1976 U.S.A. **$70.00.**

1978 HYPNOS #2365 is described as the ultimate enemy. Also 13½" tall, Hypnos has hypnotic powers. When the buttons in his back and side are pressed, sparks appear and swirling cosmic colors hypnotize his victims. MARKINGS: c MATTEL INC 1978/HONG KONG. **$75.00.**

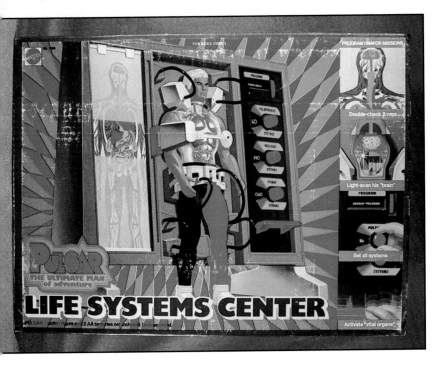

1977 PULSAR LIFE SYSTEMS CENTER #9899 measures 18" x 15" x 3½". The Life Systems Center is where Pulsar goes for diagnostic check-ups, including x-rays, light-scans of the brain, re-energizing, reprogramming, and activation of his vital organs. **$70.00.**

Rosebud

Beautifully elegant dolls. This is how Mattel described their Rosebud line of 1977 – 1978. While it may seem unusual to describe a child as elegant, that adjective soon proved to be appropriate. Four 4½" girls, three 4½" babies in gift sets, and three 7" dolls comprise the Rosebud line. The Rosebud line was planned to be expanded in 1980 with six new 4½" International Beauties, but the series was never released. The most enduring legacy of the 4½" Rosebud, A Baby Darling Rose, is her head and body mold, which was used heavily for all of the Heart Family toddlers and several Barbie doll sets. NOTE: Three different head molds are used on the 4½" Rosebud babies: A Baby Darling Rose and A Pink Heather Rose share the same head mold; A Scarlet Gem Rose, A Baby White Star Rose, A Lavender Lace Rose, and Baby Bettina all share a second head mold; A Baby Gold Star Rose uses a third head mold.

MARKINGS: All 4½" dolls have c MATTEL INC. 1976 TAIWAN on the backs of their heads, and c MATTEL, INC. 1976/ TAIWAN on their backs.

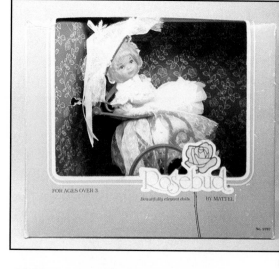

1977 A LAVENDER LACE ROSE #9787 is short-haired blonde baby with blue eyes wearing a sheer pink gown and bonnet. Included this set is a covered stroller. **$35.00.**

1977 A BABY DARLING ROSE #9783 is the first delicate little doll named after a real miniature rose. She is one of four 4½" Rosebud dolls with long hair wearing elegant dresses. A Baby Darling Rose is blonde with blue eyes. Her peach gown has a sheer white chiffon overlay and lace collar. **$20.00.**

120

1977 A BABY GOLD STAR ROSE #9784 is a brunette girl with brown eyes wearing a long yellow gown with a rose on her velvet bodice. **$20.00.**

1977 A SCARLET GEM ROSE #9785 a red-haired girl with green eyes wearing a pink gown with sheer white sleeves and lacy white over skirt. **$20.00.**

1977 A BABY WHITE STAR ROSE #9789 is a short-haired blonde baby with blue eyes wearing a fancy white gown with bonnet. The doll is packaged in a deluxe gift set featuring a rocking chair with cushion, nightstand with mirror, and a cradle. This is the hardest Rosebud item to find. **$55.00.**

1977 A PINK HEATHER ROSE #9786 is a short-haired baby with brown hair and brown eyes wearing a dotted pink gown and bonnet. A cradle is included in this set. **$35.00.**

1978 BABY BETTINA #2349 is a 4½" African-American girl with black hair and brown eyes, joining the Rosebud line this year wearing a blue gown with sheer white overskirt and lace bodice. Beginning in 1978 new Rosebud dolls are no longer named after real miniature roses. **$20.00.**

1978 MARISSA #2214 is one of three 7" tall Rosebud dolls. Marissa is a redhead with blue-green eyes. Her gown is white with yellow roses and a sheer yellow overskirt. MARKINGS: Back of head: c 1977 MATTEL INC. TAIWAN; Back: c Mattel, Inc. 1976/ TAIWAN. **$25.00.**

1978 SILVIE #2213, a brunette with brown eyes, wears a pink gown decorated with tiny rose designs covered by a sheer white overskirt. MARKINGS: same as Marissa. **$25.00.**

1978 STELLA #2466 is an African-American girl with dark brown hair and brown eyes. She wears a yellow gown with white borders and ribbons and a yellow bonnet. MARKINGS: same as Marissa. **$25.00.**

121

#1622 INTERNATIONAL BEAUTIES
#1620 Italy   #1618 France   #1617 U.S.A.

1619 Denmark   #1615 Japan   #1616 Spain

©Mattel Inc. 1980

**1980 ROSEBUD INTERNA-
TIONAL BEAUTIES featur
Italy #1620, France #1618
U.S.A. #1617, Denmar
#1619, Japan #1615, an
Spain #1616** in fashions rep
resentative of their respe
tive countries. The Matte
1980 retailer catalog show
these six 4½" dolls. The tex
describes them as elegan
dolls from around the worl
gracefully dressed in tradi
tional costume. Our swee
miss from Italy will feel righ
at home in the country or i
the city. There will be a
ooh-la-la for our prett

French doll. She's ready for a Sunday stroll. Our sweet little papoose from the U.S.A. is ready for a day at play! Ou
Denmark doll is all wide-eyed innocence and will surely fetch a few glances. Our Japanese doll is dressed for a quie
day in a teahouse or garden. And from Spain, our lovely doll is dressed in courting style. In 1980 Mattel launched th
wildly successful International Barbie line featuring Barbie dressed in traditional costumes of various countries, so it i
unfortunate that these Rosebud International Beauties never got to market.

Classic Beauty Collection

Poet John Keats wrote, "A thing of beauty is a joy forever." While e couldn't have been referring to Mattel's Classic Beauty Collection of 78, the four porcelain-look dolls in this set are certainly beautiful. eats' quote appears on the box front of each of these 16" dolls, and inside their booklet, Mattel adds, "Remember how dolls used to look? Now that same timeless quality and fine workmanship have been captured in this exclusive collection. Like famous artists' finest works, each doll is numbered, and only a limited quantity of each doll will be made. Each exquisite beauty is a jewel in herself. With delicate ladylike features, each face has a finely sculptured, almost enchanted look. Each lovely doll's eyes open and close, and each has a generous amount of long, thick, rooted hair that's sure to delight little girls everywhere. The flower print gown designs are hand chosen for each of these limited editions. Little girls — collectors too — can be sure that the doll they cherish today will remain a unique and beautiful treasure always."

1978 CYNTHIA #9986 is 16" tall and has light brunette hair with brown eyes and a brown dress. **$75.00.**

978 CECILIA #9987 is 16" tall. hese dolls were made in the J.S.A., and less than 5,000 of each were produced. **$75.00.**

1978 CATHERINE #9984. $75.00.

1978 CASSANDRA #9985. $75.00.

Gorgeous Creatures

Generations of children have grown up with stories, cartoons, and television shows featuring animals exhibiti human qualities such as talking, walking on two legs, and wearing human clothes. Classic examples include the W in Little Red Riding Hood, the Three Little Pigs, Bugs Bunny, and a multitude of Walt Disney characters, includi mice, ducks, and dogs, with all the abilities of humans. In the 1970s a popular children's show called ***The New Z Revue*** featured Henrietta Hippo, and everyone recognizes Miss Piggy. Mattel's line of four 7½" Gorgeous Creatur continues the tradition of human-like animals. A hippo, horse, cow, and pig are given fanciful names, pretty par hairdos, shapely bodies with moveable arms and legs, and a fashion ensemble that includes a glamorous gown, h stole, hanky, opera gloves, jewelry, shoes, and a picture of their boyfriend. A line of Gorgeous Creatures Fancy Fas ions was mentioned on some of the dolls' boxes, but no outfits were produced. In fact, the dolls were not even the 1980 Mattel retailer catalog, and only the hippo, horse, and cow were offered in the 1981 catalog.

MARKINGS: All four dolls are maked c MATTEL INC. 1979 PHILIPPINES on the backs of their heads; their backs rea c Mattel, Inc. 1979/ PHILIPPINES.

1980 COW BELLE #1741 wears a satiny blue gown with purp panels and sequins and a blue lamé bodice, blue lamé fingerle gloves, white boa, and feathered hat in her red hair. The com brush, mirror, and picture frame included with each of these dc is the same as used with Beauty Secrets Barbie of 1980. In fac the dolls' strap-on shoes, rings, and earrings are the same as use on Barbie dolls of this period. Cow Belle's boyfriend is a bull wh works at the stock market. Each of the dolls has a textured ted molded on their bodies. **$25.00.**

1980 MS. GIDDEE YUP #1743 wears a sparkly sil- ver gown with hot pink trim, fingerless pink gloves, a pink cape, and a pink flower with marabou feathers in her blonde hair. Her boyfriend plays polo. **$25.00.**

1980 PRINCESS PIG #1740 wears a pink satin gown with black lace bodice, black lace fingerless gloves, black boa, black net stockings, and a matching pink and black hat with pink feathers in her blonde hair. Her boyfriend is a professor of literature. **$25.00.**

1980 MS. HEAVENLY HIPPO #1742 wears a yellow satin pantsuit with silvery overskirt, sparkly yellow boa, and silver lamé bow with yellow feathers in her red hair. Her outfit is very similar to 1977's SuperStar Christie doll's original yellow fashion. Ms. Heavenly Hippo's boyfriend is a sailor. **$25.00.**

Guardian Goddesses

A popular television show of the late 1970s, *Wonder Woman*, featured a superheroine Amazon played by Lynda Carter. Mego's Wonder Woman toy line included two other Amazons with amazing strength and super powers. Mattel ventured into the superheroine doll genre cautiously with a test market series distributed to only several regions in 1980, including Ohio. The Guardian Goddesses, Sun Spell and Moon Mystic, are 11½" dolls using Barbie doll bodies with a newly-designed head mold. The story on their box reveals, "In another galaxy far away, there are beautiful goddesses who have unusual powers to guard people from danger in the universe. Two of these Guardian Goddesses, SUN SPELL and MOON MYSTIC, help people on Earth. To fight trouble or danger, they step into action. SUN SPELL is propelled to Earth spinning down a sun ray while MOON MYSTIC whirls on a moonbeam." Over their heroine action uniforms, the goddesses wear long gowns that quickly fall away when their legs are moved apart, causing their arms to spring outward. They have Ballerina Barbie doll's arm molds. Along with the two dolls, four themed outfits were sold. These items are very hard to find today. The head mold designed for Sun Spell and Moon Mystic was used on only one other doll ever — 1980's Italian Barbie.

1980 SUN SPELL #2757 has streaked fiery orange hair and green eyes. She wears a white plastic snap-on bodice with orange skirt and sparkly panties, panty hose, knee-high white plastic boots, and a gold lamé and white fabric cape with fiery design. Her cover-up outfit is a long satiny white gown with sheer overskirt attached to a white plastic bodice with gold lamé top. MARKINGS: Back of head: c 1978 MATTEL INC. TAIWAN; Back: c Mattel, Inc 1966/ TAIWAN. **$125.00.**

1980 MOON MYSTIC #2758 has dark, violet-streaked hair and blue eyes. She wears a blue plastic snap-on bodice with sparkly blue panties, blue pantyhose, knee-high blue plastic boots, and a silver lamé and blue fabric cape with crescent moons design. Her cover-up outfit is a long pink gown with sheer blue overskirt attached to a pink plastic chestplate with silver lamé top. MARKINGS: same. **$125.00.**

126

1980 ICE EMPRESS #2764 is the fashion worn by Moon Mystic as she takes on the power of ice to freeze an erupting volcano, saving a town. The outfit contains a se blue cape, blue pantyhose, blue lamé shorts and boot tops, plastic blue bodice, ice crown, and tall blue boots. **$50.00.**

1980 BLAZING FIRE #2763 is the identity Sun Spell adopts to dry up a raging flood with the powers of fire. The outfit features a fiery yellow, orange, and red cape, red panty hose, sparkly red lamé shorts, orange plastic bodice, matching helmet, and tall boots with red lamé tops. **$50.00.**

1980 LION QUEEN #2761 is Sun Spell's alias as she takes on the powers of a lion to stop stampeding elephants with a loud r-r-r-roar! The fashion contains a golden cape with lion head print, brown and white skirt, white bodice, golden boot tops, tall white boots, and lion headdress. **$50.00.**

1980 SOARING EAGLE #2762 is Moon Mystic's disguise as she takes on the powers of an eagle to flap her wings and blow away a tornado! This ensemble contains a blue, pink, and purple cape, purple lamé shorts and boot tops, plastic purple bodice, tall purple boots, and eagle headdress. **$50.00.**

127

Mattel predicted Starr, the terrific teen who's tops with everyone, would be the doll who'll take 1980 by storm! An 11½" high school student who has personality, looks, brains, athletic ability, she's the most popular girl in school. And everyone loves her! Starr and her exceptional, talented friends Kelley, Shaun, and Tracy all attend Springfield High School, where they are involved in many academic and extra-curricular activities, including playing in their own band. The girl dolls all have new bodies with movable shoulders and wrists, bendable elbows, knees, and feet (for flats or heels!), bending, twisting waist, and realistic hip action; textured, flesh-tone panties with floral designs with a star are etched on their bodies. Wires running through the dolls' arms and legs provide much of this poseability, and the jointed wrists add to the dolls' abilities. Shaun, Starr's boyfriend, uses the Young Sweethearts Michael body. All of the dolls come with many great plastic accessories and a 14-page Springfield High School Yearbook, which details the lives of these four students and serves as a catalog of available fashions. In 1980, four regular Starr and friends dolls were available, as well as one Starr department store special edition with free disco purse, and 10 fashions. In 1981, a new department store special with free record was added to the Starr line, along with five new fashions, a fashion case, and a Sportabout car. The packaging on all of these Starr items is noteworthy because the boxes are covered with a notebook-paper design.

MARKINGS: Starr, Kelley, and Tracy dolls' bodies are all marked on the back: c MATTEL INC 1979/ PHILIPPINES; Back of all girl's heads: c MATTEL INC 1979.

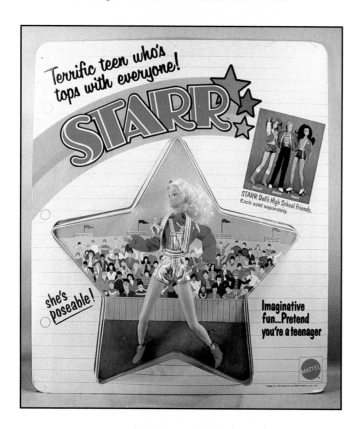

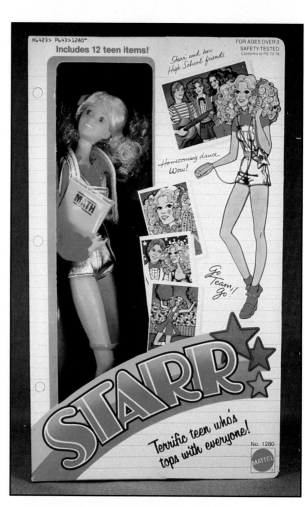

1980 STARR Retail Store Display #1871 introduces the world to Starr, "Terrific teen who's tops with everyone!" Starr is inside a five-sided clear plastic star, with an illustration of people in bleachers watching her — presumably as she leads cheers on the football field. The 19" x 22" display promises, "Imaginative fun...Pretend you're a teenager." Kelley, Shaun, and Tracy are shown in the photo above the star. Retail store displays are valuable and rare additions to collections. **$250.00.**

1980 STARR #1280 includes Starr with curly blonde ha and red hair bow wearing a silver lame disco shorts jum suit, red school jacket with the letter "S," silvery sta shaped purse, and red socks; also included are sandals ar high heel shoes, three books, tambourine, microphon telephone, soda, barrettes, and comb. Her box revea that she is "Most Popular, Homecoming Queen, chee leader captain, and member of the science club, gymna tics team, and journalism club." **$30.00.**

1980 KELLEY #1281 is Starr's redheaded, green-eyed best friend. Kelley is "most likely to succeed, valedictorian, editor of the yearbook, science club president, and member of the chess club." Mattel's retailer catalog calls Kelley the talking encyclopedia, while the Springfield High School Yearbook refers

to Kelley as the walking encyclopedia. Kelley wears green shorts, a white blouse, red school vest with an "S," and tan boots; she also has green shoes, three books, a banjo, telephone, clear glasses, a comb, and yogurt. **$35.00.**

1980 STARR #1280 was offerred as a department store special in 1980 with a free child-size disco purse; this purse is an enlarged version of the purse Starr doll carries. The stock number remained #1280. **$50.00.**

129

1980 KELLEY #1281 has been found with rare variation: some Kelley dolls have the St head mold! Kelley and Starr have differe head molds; Kelley's head mold has been us for both Mrs. Heart of The Heart Family a Jazzie, Barbie doll's teen cousin. Starr's he mold has never been used again. One m look closely to see the difference between t regular Kelley and the Kelley made with Sta head mold; Kelley has a more pronounc nose. **$60.00.**

1980 SHAUN #1283 is Starr's boyfriend and school heart-throb who's hand-some, smart, fun, and a great athlete. He seems to do everything well and easily. He is voted best all around and is class president, varsity football captain, and mem-ber of the drama and science clubs. He wears a striped shirt, jeans with suspenders, school jacket with an "S," and gymshoes; he also has a guitar, thre books, a telephone, football, radio, and hamburger. Shaun's boc

1980 SHAUN #1283 is shown here with a sec-ond style box. **$30.00.**

borrowed from Young Swee hearts Michael, allows him mo able wrists and torso, bendab elbows, knees, and feet, bendin twisting waist, and realistic h action. MARKINGS: Back of head. MATTEL INC. 1979; Back: c Matte Inc. 1975/ TAIWAN. **$30.00.**

980 TRACY #1282 is shown here with a second style box. **30.00.**

NOTE that the olors of the rain-ows behind the olls' names and he colors of the hree stars to the ight of their ames varies. The olors varied ecause a differ-nt color arrange-ent was used in 980 than in 1981.

1980 TRACY #1282 is Starr's zany friend who is lots of fun and very talented. Tracy stars in the school plays, draws well, and plays both the harmonica and bongo drums. She is the most humorous and most talented, is president of the drama club, and belongs to the dance and art clubs. Tracy has a wide smile and wears blue shorts with a yellow top, red school jacket with an "S," and red socks; she also has roller skates, blue shoes, three books, har-monica, bongo drums, a telephone, comb, and soda bottle. **$30.00.**

980 STARR BOOK BAG is a child-size red linen-rayon book bag nprinted with the official Starr emblem. It measures 12" x 12½" x 2½" nd has metal snap fasteners, two outside pockets, and adjustable houlder straps. This book bag was available for $2.99 until Jan. 31, 981. Some dolls' boxes have stickers on the box windows promoting his book bag. This premium is very rare since many doll collectors did ot open their dolls' boxes to find the order form or did not bother ending for a child's mail-in offer. **$40.00.**

1980 BEACH PARTY #1391 is one of four Fun Teen fashions available in 1980. Beach Party contains a blue and white swimsuit with coverup and towel for Starr. **$15.00.**

1980 CASUAL LIVING #1388 contains blue jeans and a pink top for Starr. **$15.00.**

1980 SCHOOL DAYS #1398 is a pa of tan pants and brown plaid shi for Shaun. This is a one-year fash ion. **$15.00.**

1981 STARR SPORTABOUT CAR #331 is 13" long and holds two dolls. The re car with yellow underside has a Star pennant and decals for customizin the car. MARKINGS: Underside: c 197 MATTEL, INC./ U.S.A. **$35.00.**

1980 CHEERLEADER CAPTAIN #1389 features a red bodysuit and red skirt with silver lamé panels, silver lamé vest, two red yarn pom pons, and white boots. This is one of six Deluxe Teen Fashions available in 1980. **$30.00.**

80 DISCO DANCING #1394 contains a pink ntsuit with pink overskirt, sparkly purple w tie, blue and purple metallic lamé purs- , and pink heels. This is a one-year fashion. 0.00.

1981 STARR AND FRIENDS FASHION CASE #3325 is an orange single-doll vinyl carrying case measuring 10½" x 12½". **$25.00.**

1980 50'S DANCE #1390 features a gray poodle skirt with pink sweater for Starr. This is a one-year fashion. **$20.00.**

1980 HOMECOMING QUEEN #1393 features a long blue gown with silver crown, HOMECOMING QUEEN sash, floral bouquet with red ribbon, and blue heels. Shown here is first-year packaging with a flat plastic bubble package. Two stars at the top of the package are blue, and the lower one is green. **$30.00.**

1981 HOMECOMING QUEEN #1393 is shown here as an example of how second-year packaging varied on the Deluxe Teen Fashions. The plastic bubble around the shoes and crown is raised higher than the rest of the window, and the stars at the top of the package are now blue, pink, and green, with the bottom stripe of the Starr rainbow orange on this card and pink on the 1980 card. **$30.00.**

1980 PROM NIGHT #1392 is Starr's red prom gown with white underskirt and white accents, matching shawl, white satin flower bouquet, and red heels. This is a one-year fashion. **$35.00.**

1980 PROM NIGHT #1395 is Shaun's tuxedo with black pants, white shirt, white jacket, red cummerbund and bow tie, and black shoes. **$30.00.**

1980 ROLLER DISCO QUEEN #1387 contains Starr's blue pants with gold belt and suspenders over a green striped shirt. An unattached purple collar with pink necktie and a pair of blue roller skates are included. This is a one-year fashion. **$30.00.**

1981 STARR #1280 was available as a department store special in 1981 with a free Starr 33⅓ record containing a song from Starr's band. The doll and contents are otherwise the same as the 1980 Starr. **$40.00.**

1981 AFTER SCHOOL DATE #3319 is one of two new additions to the Fun Teen Fashions series. After School Date contains Starr's red dress with yellow purse and math book. **$15.00.**

1981 KEEPIN' FIT #3320 is Shaun's red jogging pants with white Shaun logo tee-shirt. **$15.00.**

1981 FANCY FRILLS #3323 is one of three new Deluxe Teen fashions. Fancy Frills features Starr's pantyhose, slip, panties, and bra, along with a mirror, brush, and comb. **$35.00.**

1981 KEEPIN' FIT #3322 is Starr's jogging suit with red pants, red jacket, white Starr logo tee-shirt, sun visor, and white gym shoes. **$30.00.**

1981 SLUMBER NUMBER #3321 is the hardest to find Starr fashion. Slumber Number contains a blue robe, white teddy, Disco record, and blue sandals. **$40.00.**

Dazzle

After the Rock Flowers and Fashion Teeners lines of small fashion dolls were discontinued in the early 1970s, Mattel mainly concentrated on larger dolls for the rest of that decade. Then Kenner Toys redefined the small action figure market in 1977 with the introduction of 3¾" Star Wars figures that soon became the industry standard. Even Hasbro reduced their G. I. Joe dolls to 3¾" size and relaunched that series in 1982 with spectacular results. The time seemed right to release an all-new line of small-size fashion dolls. The Dazzle series was born in 1982 with a series of eight 4½" girls, all of whom resemble miniature Barbie dolls. Two distinctly different head molds are used for the Dazzle females — one uses a scaled-down version of the smiling, teeth-showing 1976-dated SuperStar Barbie head mold; the second head mold is a scaled-down version of the closed-mouth Walk Lively Steffie head mold. The female Dazzle dolls' arms resemble the Ballerina Barbie style arms. In addition, four extra boxed fashions, a Dazzle City playset, and a horse were available. In 1983 two new girls and two very rare boys were added to the line, along with two new fashions. A special promotion in 1983 packaged each girl in a free swimsuit on a special card alongside her original fashion. Two sets of catalog boxed dolls have also been found. A Dazzle Doozie car and Birthday Party and Wedding Fantasy four-doll packs were shown in the 1983 Mattel retailer catalog, but these items never reached the market.

MARKINGS: Back: c M.I. 1966 (this is a reduced-size Barbie torso).

1982 DAZZLE #5286 has the 1976 open-mouth, scaled-down SuperStar Barbie head mold. Dazzle has curly golden-blonde hair and wears a golden body-suit with sheer white overskirt. Dazzle's golden pantsuit uses the same material and style as 1981's Golden Dream Barbie. Each Dazzle series doll has painted, molded-on shoes with tiny holes in the center for use with the Dazzle posing stand. A comb is also included with each female. **$15.00.**

1982 CRYSTAL #5290 has long light brown hair. She has the 1971 scaled-down closed-mouth Walk Lively Steffie head mold. Crystal wears a long sparkly blue gown with white fuzzy boa. **$15.00.**

1982 DIAMOND #5289 has the open-mouth 1976 head with long braided blonde hair. Diamond wears a sparkly, long red belted gown with white coat. **$15.00.**

1982 GLIMMER #5292 has the open-mouth 1976 head with sandy blonde hair. Her sleeveless gown is purple with a white net overskirt. **$15.00.**

1982 GLISSEN #5295 has the closed-mouth 1971 head with blonde hair. Glissen wears a wedding gown with veil. **$18.00.**

1982 GLOSSY #5288 has the closed-mouth 1971 head with long blonde hair worn in two pigtails. Glossy wears a pair of jeans and a sparkly pink halter top. Her outfit is similar to 1982's Fashion Jeans Barbie. **$15.00.**

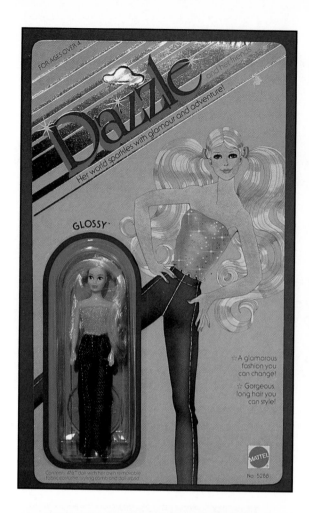

1982 RHINESTONE #5293 uses the 1976 open-mouth head mold. Her western outfit includes leathery pink pants, shimmery black top with silver belt and collar, and pink scarf. She has a strong facial resemblance to 1986's Greek Barbie. **$15.00.**

1982 SPANGLE #5291 uses the 1971 closed-mouth head mold. Spangle wears a gold metallic top with a sheer white skirt tied at the waist with a blue bow. **$15.00.**

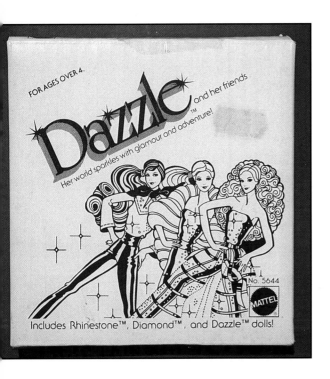

1982 DAZZLE AND HER FRIENDS #5644 packages Rhinestone, Diamond, and Dazzle in plastic bags inside a white catalog mailing box for J. C. Penney. The dolls are identical to those sold on cards. This set is hard to find in the original illustrated catalog box. **$45.00.**

1982 DAZZLE AND HER FRIENDS #5784 packages Glossy, Crystal, and Dazzle dolls in plastic bags inside a white catalog mailing box sold through J. C. Penney. This set is hard to find still in the illustrated catalog box. **$45.00.**

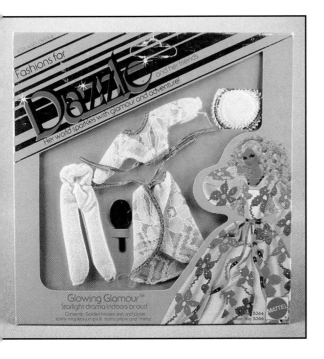

1982 GLOWING GLAMOUR #5364 is one of four separate fashions available for Dazzle in 1982. Glowing Glamour contains a white hostess skirt and jacket, satiny jumpsuit, satiny pillow, and hand mirror. **$12.00.**

1982 GOLDEN GEAR #5365 features a golden skirt with red fringe, golden pants, red plaid shirt, scarf, belt, spats, and horse blanket. **$12.00.**

141

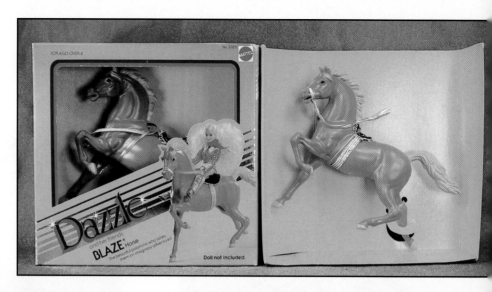

1982 BLAZE #5325 is Dazzle doll's beautiful palomino horse with silver saddle and bridle. MARKINGS: Inside left rear leg: PHILIPPINES. **$20.00.**

1982 SIZZLING SUN #5363 features a glittery blue swimsuit with matching skirt, golden sun hat, golden beach bag, long white robe, and yellow beach towel. **$12.00.**

1982 JAZZY JEANS #5362 contains a silve lamé jacke sparkly blue tank top, glittery red shorts, jeans, an silver lamé shoulder bag. **$12.00.**

1982 DAZZLE CITY #5373 features four movable rooms to arrange in many combinations. Dazzle Dance Hall contains a juke box, railing, microphone, and guitar. Dinner Club has a table and two chairs, and two plates and cups. Beauty Salon has a salon chair with hair dryer, counter, hand hair dryer, and comb. One Dazzle Drive Home contains a sofa, end table, lamp, and barbeque with cover and grill. **$30.00.**

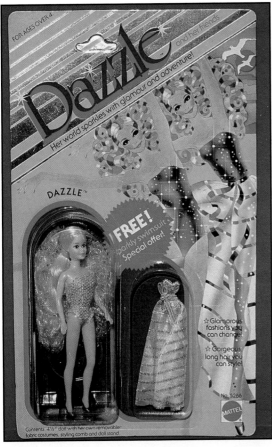

1983 DAZZLE #5286 is repackaged for 1983 with a free sparkly swimsuit special offer. Dazzle wears the free golden swimsuit, and her original outfit is packaged in a separate bubble on her card. Notice how the artwork on these second series dolls changes from the 1982 packaging. The dolls themselves are unchanged. **$20.00.**

1983 CRYSTAL #5290 is repackaged wearing a sparkly blue and black striped swimsuit with her original 1982 fashion at the side. **$20.00.**

1983 DIAMOND #5289 is repackaged wearing a silver glitter swimsuit with red horizontal stripes borrowed from new Dazzle line doll Shimmer; Diamond's original outfit is next to her. **$20.00.**

143

1983 GLIMMER #5292 is repackaged with a new sparkly white swimsuit, but her original purple gown is included in the package. **$20.00.**

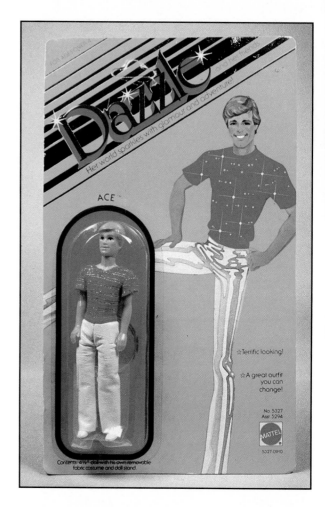

1983 ACE #5327 is the rare 4½" blonde male doll wearing white leather pants and a sparkly red shirt. He appears to be a scaled-down Ken doll. Ace is one of four Dazzle line dolls produced just before Mattel discontinued the line. Accordingly, all four dolls are hard to find, but the two male dolls, Ace and Glint, are nearly impossible to find. **$50.00.**

1983 GLINT #5326 is the rare brunette male Dazzle line doll wearing a tuxedo with sparkly white jacket. **$50.00.**

1983 SHIMMER #5891 has reddish-brown hair worn in pigtails. She has the 1971 closed-mouth Walk Lively Steffie head mold. Her outfit consists of a sparkly red and silver striped bodysuit with matching stockings and a white mini skirt. Because she is an end-of-production-run doll, she is hard to find. **$25.00.**

1983 SHIMMER #5891 was also released on a card with the free sparkly swimsuit offer. In this set, Shimmer wears a sparkly red swimsuit made from Diamond's dress material, and her striped fashion with skirt is packaged at the side. Shimmer's swimsuit is red because her original striped bodysuit is already too similar to a swimsuit. This set is rare. **$30.00.**

1983 STARLA #5890 is a blonde with unstreaked hair. She has the 1976 SuperStar Barbie head. Her dress is sparkly pink with silver highlights, and she wears a pink boa. **$25.00.**

Not pictured: **1983 GLISSEN #5295** is repackaged wearing a sparkly swimsuit with her wedding gown and veil at her side. **$20.00.**

1983 GLOSSY #5288 is repackaged wearing a sparkly swimsuit with her jeans and pink top also on the card. **$20.00.**

1983 RHINESTONE #5293 is repackaged with a swimsuit, her original western outfit is at the side. **$20.00.**

1983 SPANGLE #5291 is repackaged wearing the free swimsuit, and her original fashion is at her side. **$20.00.**

1983 BIRTHDAY PARTY DOLL PACK #4131 is shown in the 1983 Mattel retailer catalog as a four-doll gift set containing Dazzle, Glossy, Shimmer, and Ace; birthday cutouts were supposed to be on the package. In the catalog photo, Dazzle is wearing a sparkly red tube top and red pants, but the other three dolls are dressed in their original outfits. This set was never produced.

1983 WEDDING FANTASY DOLL PACK #4130 features the wedding of Glint and Glissen, with best friends Starla and Dazzle attending. Wedding cutouts were supposed to be on the packaging. The dolls shown in the photo for this set all wear their original outfits. This set was never produced.

145

Dazzle Doozie™
Off to new adventures in the most glamorous and expensive car of all! Dazzle Doozie™ is the super fantastic car you can make l-o-n-g-e-r. So Dazzle doll can take lots of friends with her on each exciting trip. Car expands to hold 10 dolls! There's plenty of space for luggage, too. Luxury play features include luggage rack and strap, 2 suitcases, TV set, rumble seat, car blanket, "wire" wheels and driving lights. 4-color chip package. **For ages over 4. # 4042 Std. Pak 6**

1983 DAZZLE DOOZIE #4042 is the most glamorous and expensive car of all! This expandable pink car can hold up to ten dolls and features a TV set, rumble seat, luggage rack, car blanket, wire wheels, and driving lights. The car was advertised on the backs of the 1983 Dazzle line dolls, but it was only pictured in the 1983 Mattel retailer catalog. It was never mass produced.

146

1983 STARLA #5890 also has been found on the free sparkly swimsuit card. Her pink swimsuit is made of the same material as her dress. This set is rare. **$30.00.**

1983 DRESSY DREAMS #4251 is one of two new fashions added for 1983. This fashion contains a long pink negligee, dressing gown, teddy, and half slip. This fashion is hard to find. **$22.00.**

1983 PRETTY PARTY #4252 contains a long blue dress, white net overskirt, white hat, and a pink cardboard present. This outfit is hard to find. **$22.00.**

The Heart Family

"Fun is being part, of the family that's all Heart," according to an advertising jingle used by Mattel. What fun indeed! The Heart Family line of dolls, produced from 1985 to 1990, grew to epic proportions by its conclusion. Introduced as Barbie doll's friends, The Heart Family, packaged in blue boxes in contrast to Barbie doll's hot pink boxes, never quite became part of the Barbie doll line in most collectors' eyes. Even The Heart Family dolls' packaging only mentions the Barbie doll's friends phrase in 1985. After 1985, the dolls were left to flourish without the Barbie name propping them up. Originally The Heart Family consisted of Mrs. Heart, a pretty young mother, Mr. Heart, her husband, and their twin babies, a boy and a girl. A new baby joined the family in 1986, along with an English Sheepdog, Trueheart. In 1987 The Heart Family Grandparents arrived. The family really expanded in 1988 with the addition of six Baby Cousins. In 1989 six additional Neighborhood Kids moved in, and in 1990 Disneyland Kids on Parade befriended the family. Through these years, 20 different Heart Family fashions were sold separately, along with numerous playsets including a rare Loving Home, a Playground, two different cars, a camper, a bicycle, two nurseries, and a Dumbo Ride. Adding to the enormity of this collection is the fact that most adult Heart Family dolls are available in Caucasian or African-American editions, sold individually as a parent with child or in four-doll deluxe sets. The Heart Family was especially popular in Europe, where many European-only items were available; after The Heart Family was discontinued in the United States, Mattel Europe continued releasing Heart Family babies, called Barbie's Li'l Friends, from 1992 to 1994.

MARKINGS: All Caucasian Mrs. Heart dolls (except the Kiss & Cuddle version) use the Kelley (Starr's friend) head mold, marked: c MATTEL INC 1979 on the back of the head. All African-American Mrs. Heart dolls use the Walk Lively Steffie head mold, marked: c 1971 Mattel Inc. on the inside neck rim. ALL Mrs. Heart dolls have the SuperStar Barbie body with permanently bent arms marked: c MATTEL, INC. 1966/ TAIWAN (or PHILIPPINES or CHINA) on their backs. They all have a gold band painted on their left hand ring finger.

All Caucasian Mr. Heart dolls use SuperStar Ken's head mold, marked: c Mattel, Inc. 1977 on the inside rim. All African-American Mr. Heart dolls (except the Disneyland Dad) use the African-American Sunsational Malibu Ken head, marked: c 1983 MATTEL INC on the back. ALL Mr. Heart dolls use the SuperStar Ken body with permanently bent arms, marked: c Mattel, Inc. 1968/ TAIWAN (or CHINA) on the back. First-year Dads do not have a wedding band painted on their left hands; all Dads sold beginning in 1986 do have this band.

ALL babies are marked c MATTEL INC. 1976 with or without country of origin on the back of their heads; their bodies are marked c Mattel, Inc. 1976 on their backs, with or without country of origin. These babies' heads and bodies originated on the 1976 Rosebud, A Baby Darling Rose doll.

It is amazing how facial paint and hair can change the appearance of dolls. Shown here are the dolls who contributed heads and/or bodies to make The Heart Family: 1978 SuperStar Ken, 1980 Kelley, and two 1976 Rosebud babies — A Pink Heather Rose and A Baby Darling Rose.

1985 MOM & BABY #9078 features mother and daughter packag together with matching outfits — soft pink dresses with tiny white flo ers and white bib collars, edged with lace, and tights. The baby is scer ed with baby powder. Mattel's 1985 retailer catalog describes Mom Baby as having a fresh, contemorary look. Both have delicate swe faces and big, blue eyes. Interestingly, all versions of the Mom fro 1985, including those in the Deluxe Sets, have gold wedding ban painted on their left ring fingers, while none of the Dads this year ha wedding bands. **$25.00.**

1985 MOM, DAD, AN BABIES DELUXE SET #94 contains Mom, Dad, and t twins in one set. Also include in this set are a baby carrier tote bag, and diapers. Th Mattel catalog describes Th Heart Family world as a ve special place, filled with lo and joy and fun adventure Days include trips to the pa the zoo and lots of oth wonderful places. Nights a filled with story telling, qui talks and heaps of hugs ar kisses. Life together is wo derful and so much fu **$55.00.**

1985 DAD AND BABY #9079 packages father and son in matching outfits. Dad wears a light blue shirt and white pants with suspenders and pink tie. The baby boy wears a blue and white playsuit with suspenders, a pink bow tie, and a blue hat. The baby is scented with baby powder. **$25.00.**

1985 MOM & BABY #9718 is the African-American version using the Walk Lively Steffie head mold for the Mom, but the same head mold for the baby girl. The African-American versions of The Heart Family dolls are somewhat harder to find than their white counterparts, but they aren't as widely collected. **$25.00.**

1985 DAD & BABY #9719 is the African-American version using an ethnic head mold for the Dad, but the same head mold for the baby boy. **$25.00.**

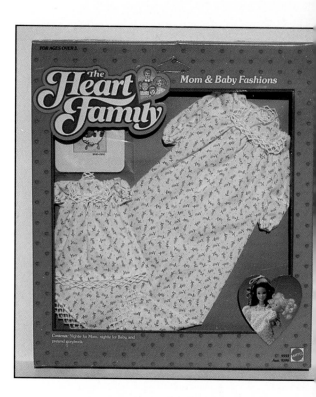

1985 MOM, DAD & BABIES DELUXE SET #2052 contains the African-American dolls in the same outfits and with the same accessories as their Caucasian counterparts in the #9439 set. **$55.00.**

1985 MOM & BABY FASHIONS #9593 is the first five Heart Family fashions available in 1985. Ea fashion includes an outfit for the adult as well a matching outfit for the baby. This outfit featur white floral-print nightgowns for Mom and daug ter, and a Mother Goose storybook. **$20.00.**

1985 MOM & BABY FASHIONS #9594 contains a pleated white skirt, striped nautical shirt, and white pumps for Mom and a blue and white dress with tights and ribbon for daughter. **$20.00.**

1985 MOM & BABY FASHIONS #9595 features yellow jumpsuit with white blouse and yelle shoes for Mom and a matching one-piece jum suit for daughter. **$20.00.**

1985 MOM & BABY FASHIONS #9596 contains a dainty white pinafore dress with shoes for Mom and a matching pinafore dress and tights for daughter. **$20.00.**

1985 DAD & BABY FASHIONS #9597 contains Dad's pin-stripe blue suit with navy socks and shoes and a blue velvet romper suit for son. This is the hardest to find Heart Family fashion. **$30.00.**

1985 BABIES' PLAYSET #7891 includes a rocking horse, walker, pink dress with tights, blue overalls with white shirt, a blue sleeper, a pink sleeper, brush, rattle, bottle, toy bunny, two diapers, and a blanket. **$25.00.**

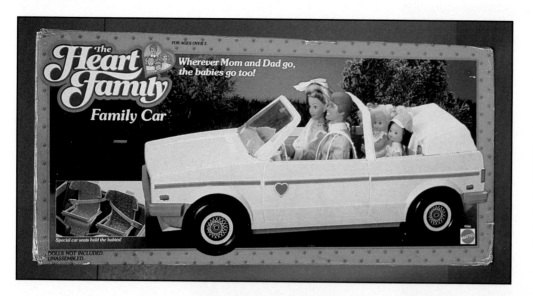

1985 FAMILY CAR #9566 is a baby blue Volkswagen Cabriolet with medium blue interior. One pink and one blue carseat for the babies are included. The license plate has a heart shape followed by the word FAMILY. The trunk opens for storage. MARKINGS: Bottom of car: Mattel, Inc./ 1981. **$45.00.**

1985 LOVING HOME #9691 is the rarest of the Heart Family toys. Two stories high and measuring 28" x 29", the Loving Home features a living room, kitchen, and babies' room setting. The home comes furnished with a kitchen table with two chairs, dinnerware, a rocking horse, and walker. **$135.00.**

1985 NURSERY #7937 features a baby bath that transforms into a bed along with a highchair, bed ruffle, quilt, pillow, sheet, two bibs, mattress, diaper pail with lid, soap, rattle, tray, dish, ball, bottle, jar, duck, rag doll, spoon, bear, washcloth, and towel. **$35.00.**

152

1986 NEW ARRIVAL MOM & BABY #2412 caught the attention of the media. The innovative set features Mom in a pink velour maternity smock that, when worn, makes her appear to have a large, expectant figure. When the smock is removed, a slim pink dress with lacy skirt remains — along with a precious new baby! The baby has a sweet face and uses the Sunshine Family baby Sweets body. This set also come with a blanket, bunny toy, rattle, birth certificate, photo album, bottle, towel, sleeper, and three diapers. MARKINGS: Back of baby's head: c M.I. 1985; Baby's back: c 1973/ MATTEL, INC./ TAIWAN. **$40.00.**

1986 NEW ARRIVAL SET (Black) #2499 contains African-american versions of the Caucasian New Arrival Set. These dolls were only available in this set. Dad now has a gold wedding band on his left hand. The baby uses the same head and body molds as the white New Arrival baby. **$55.00.**

1986 NEW ARRIVAL SET #2415 contains both Mom with new baby and Dad, who was not sold in this outfit separately. Dad wears white pants with a pink shirt, purple vest, and purple tie; he now has a gold band on the ring finger of his left hand. This set includes several accessories not given with the New Arrival Mom & Baby set: a hospital suitcase, camera, and flower bouquet. **$55.00.**

153

1986 SURPRISE PARTY DAD & BABY GIRL #2382
features Dad wearing a lavender suit with striped
pink shirt and yellow tie, holding his daughter wearing a yellow party dress. The pink package contains
a toy bear for the girl. **$35.00.**

1986 SURPRISE PARTY MOM & BABY BOY #2381 features Mom
in a pretty party dress now packaged with her son, wearing a
blue playsuit. Since female dolls sell best, perhaps the parents
switched babies to make the Dad sets better sellers. Inside the
yellow package is a yellow truck for the boy. **$35.00.**

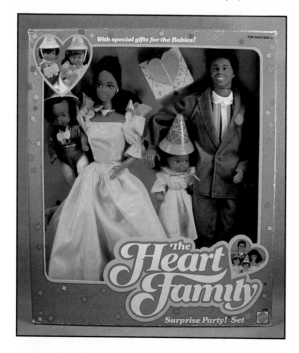

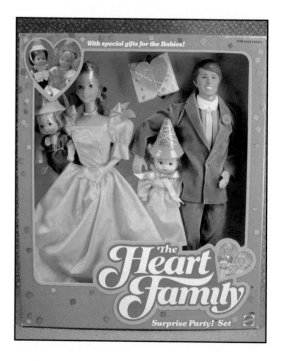

1986 SURPRISE PARTY! SET (Black) #2512
features an African-American Mom, Dad,
and their twins in one set. **$50.00.**

1986 SURPRISE PARTY! SET #2383 combines the Mom and Dad sets with their
twins. **$50.00.**

1986 BEACH OUTFIT #2623 is one of eight new fashions introduced in 1986. Six of the outfits are called Family Fashions and feature coordinating outfits for Mom, Dad, and the babies. The other two new fashions are Mom & Baby Fashions. Only the **Nightgown #9593** and **Jumpsuit #9595** from 1985 were carried over for sale in 1986. Beach Outfit features a white swimsuit with multicolored dots, yellow terry robe, mirrored red sunglasses, and a beach bag for Mom, and a matching bathing suit and red sunglasses for daughter. **$20.00.**

1986 TRUE HEART #2371 is the Heart Family's big, furry female English sheepdog. The poseable, combable dog comes with two feeding dishes, a brush, medallion, ribbon, leash, and collar. **$35.00.**

1986 HIKING OUTFIT #2621 contains Mom's white jumpsuit with red and blue stripes, red belt, knee-high red socks, and gym shoes, along with a denim baby carrier, white blouse, and striped jumpsuit for daughter. **$20.00.**

1986 BEACH OUTFIT #2624 features Dad's red swimtrunks, striped tee-shirt, mirrored blue sunglasses, towel, and beach bag, along with matching swimwear and sunglasses for son. **$20.00.**

155

1986 HIKING OUTFIT #2622 contains Dad's short denim jumpsuit and gym shoes, along with a striped baby carrier, denim overalls and white shirt for son. **$20.00.**

1986 JOGGING OUTFIT #2619 features a pink jogging suit with blue sleeves, headband, and gym shoes for Mom, and a matching sweatsuit and visor for daughter. **$20.00.**

1986 JOGGING OUTFIT #2620 features Dad's blue sweatshirt with pink sleeves, blue sweatpants, headband, and jogging shoes, along with son's one-piece sweatsuit and visor. **$20.00.**

1986 TUXEDO DRESS #2625 contains Mom's pink and white tuxedo dress with white pumps, and a tuxedo dress and tights for daughter. **$22.00.**

1986 BICYCLE BUILT-FOR-4 #2685 is the family's tandem bike equipped with seats for Mom and Dad, as well as two passenger seats for the babies. A picnic basket is included. **$30.00.**

1986 VALENTINE DRESS #2627 features Mom's white heart-print Valentine's dress with pink pumps, along with a matching dress and tights for daughter. **$22.00.**

1986 PLAYGROUND #2789 has two swings, a glider, a slide, a sand-box, four ladders, a trap door, a baby bench, two cups and saucers, a pail and shovel, and a ball. **$65.00.**

1987 KISS & CUDDLE MOM & BABY BOY #3140 features Mom dressed in her most beautiful outfit — a red velvet dress with lace collar and hem. She has specially designed arms to simulate hugging, and a new head mold with closed mouth. When her lip-stick is applied, she will leave kiss prints on the babies. Her son wears a red suit. MARKINGS: Mom's back of head: c MATTEL INC. 1986; Mom's back: c MATTEL, INC. 1966/ TAIWAN. **$40.00.**

1987 KISS & CUDDLE DAD & BABY GIRL #3141 features Dad in a red jacket with navy blue pants, white shirt, and red tie. His arms are specially designed to hug his children. His daughter wears a red velvet dress with lace collar and tights. Lipstick is included for her to use so that she too can kiss and leave her kiss print. **$35.00.**

1987 KISS & CUDDLE SET #1966 packages the Mom & Baby Boy and Dad & Baby Girl together in one box. **$65.00.**

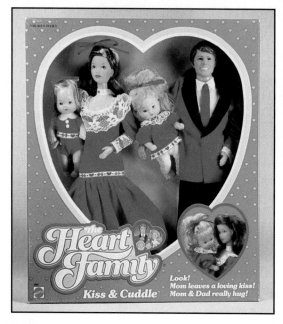

1987 KISS & CUDDLE MOM & BABY BOY (Black) #3768 features the African-American Mom with the regular Walk Lively Steffie head mold — her lips were already closed, so Mattel did not redesign her head for use with lipstick as they had to do with the Caucasian Kiss & Cuddle Mom. Neither the Caucasian nor the African-American baby girls needed head redesigns, either, since their mouths were already closed. **$40.00.**

1987 KISS & CUDDLE DAD & BABY GIRL (Black) #3769. **$35.00.**

1987 GRANDMA HEART SET #4448

Grandma has come to visit, and she's brought a gift for her granddaughter! Grandma Heart uses a new head mold with wrinkles sculpted into her face. She has brown and white hair worn in a bun, and her dress is lavender with lace heart trim. She carries a cloth rag doll and has a package containing pajamas. MARKINGS: Back of head: c MATTEL, INC. 1986; Back: c MATTEL, INC. 1966./ TAIWAN. Rag doll's label: c Mattel, Inc. 1986. Grandma Heart and Grandpa Heart are the hardest to find Heart Family members. **$55.00.**

1987 KISS & CUDDLE SET (Black) #3174. $65.00.

1987 GRANDPA HEART SET #4449

Grandpa has come to visit, and he brought a gift for his grandson. Grandpa Heart has a newly-designed head with wrinkles molded into his forehead and face. His hair is black and white, and he wears a white cardigan sweater over gray pants, and a lavender striped shirt with tie. He carries a stick horse for his grandson, and the gift in his box contains overalls. MARKINGS: Back of head: c MATTEL, INC. 1986; Back: c Mattel, Inc. 1968/ TAIWAN. Both Grandma Heart and Grandpa Heart have golden wedding bands painted on their left ring fingers. **$60.00.**

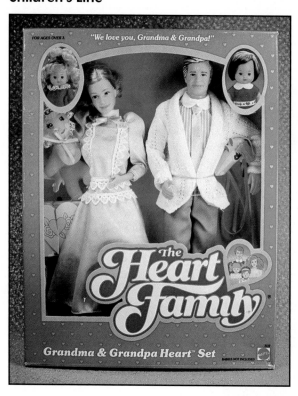

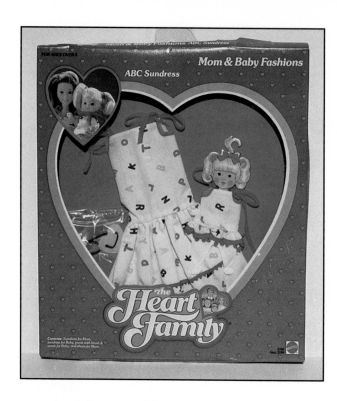

1987 GRANDMA & GRANDPA HEART SET #3132 pairs the Grandma Heart Set with the Grandpa Heart Set. **$85.00.**

1987 ABC SUNDRESS #3196 is one of four new Mom & Bab Fashions for 1987. The only fashions carried over from 198 are the jogging fashions **#2619** and **#2620**. ABC Sundress fea tures an alphabet-print white sundress and red pumps fo Mom and a matching sundress, stockings, and purse wit brush and comb for daughter. Notice how the baby fashion in this series use a paper doll to model the outfit. **$18.00.**

1987 BUTTERFLIES IN LACE DRESS #3195 contains a blue satiny dress and white pumps for Mom and a matching dress with lace tights for daughter. **$18.00.**

1987 CANDY CANE DRESS #3194 is a holiday-theme red dress with candy-cane design and red pumps fo Mom, with a matching dress and lace tights fo daughter. **$18.00.**

987 CAMPING FUN! #3146 is the first of three Heart Fami-
Playsets featuring outfit pieces for the family as well as
emed accessories. Camping Fun contains a play campfire,
vo camping stools, a frying pan, two pots, a lantern, two
elmets, along with a jacket, pants, and boots for Mom; a
cket, jumpsuit, and shoes for Dad; a jumpsuit, shorts, and
oose hood for son; and a jumpsuit, shorts, and bunny
od for daughter. These sets had very limited distribution.
45.00.

1987 RAINCOAT #3197 contains a shiny yellow
raincoat, polka-dot muffler, and red boots for
Mom, and a raincoat, rain hat, muffler, and yellow
rain boots for daughter. **$18.00.**

3147 *Snow Fun!*™ Set

987 SNOW FUN #3147 contains ski pants, socks, boots
ith skis, sweater, scarf, hat, and glasses for Mom; boots
ith skis, socks, ski pants, sweater, scarf, and hat for Dad;
wo baby carriers for the babies to allow them to ride
long while their parents ski, and snowsuits, scarves, sun-
lasses, and ear muffs for each baby. **$45.00.**

1987 WATER FUN #3148 contains an inflatable
heart-shaped pool, innertube, two deck chairs,
beach ball, four towels, swimsuit with sunglasses for
Mom; swimsuit for Dad; swimsuit and sunglasses for
daughter; and swimsuit and sunglasses for son.
$45.00.

161

1987 FAMILY CAR #9566 is now pink with a blue interior. The license plate on this Volkswagen Cabriolet still has a heart followed by the word, FAMILY. **$50.00.**

1988 BATHTIME FUN DAD & BABY GIRL #4617 features Mr. Heart wearing a blue and white striped jumpsuit with yellow apron decorated with pink and blue hearts; his daughter is wrapped in a pink towel. **$25.00.**

1988 BATHTIME FUN MOM & BABY BOY #4615 features Mrs. Heart wearing a pink and white striped jumpsuit and yellow apron with pink and blue hearts; her son is wrapped in a blue towel. It's bath time! As the box front says, With The Heart Family, bathtime is always funtime! **$25.00.**

1987 DOUBLE STROLLE[R] #2293 features a doub[le] white stroller with canop[y] that transforms into a ca[r]riage at naptime, a bab[y] blanket, and pillow. **$20.00.**

1988 BATHTIME FUN MOM & BABY BOY (Black) #4751. $25.00.

988 BATHTIME FUN DELUXE SET #4618 is a hard find set pairing Mr. and Mrs. Heart with their abies in one package. **$65.00.**

988 BATHTIME FUN DAD & BABY RL (Black) #4752. $25.00.

1988 BABY WETS #7173 feature the Heart Family twin babies. They really drink from their bottles and then wet their diapers. Two cloth diapers, four disposable diapers, two bottles, and a brush are included. The babies in this set use a new head mold used only here. A black set of Baby Wets babies is shown on the back of the African-American Bathtime Fun dolls, but these were never on the market. The backs of Baby Wets heads are marked c MATTEL, INC. 1987. Their bodies are still marked c MATTEL, INC. 1976. **$25.00.**

1988 HONEY & HIGHCHAIR #5396 is the first of six baby cousins to visit the Heart Family. Each cousin comes with a special accessory. Honey's special accessory is her highchair. All of the cousins use the same head and body molds as the original Heart Family babies. **$22.00.**

1988 JANET & POTTY CHAIR #5397. $22.00.

1988 KENNY & TRICYCLE #5394 features Kenny wearing an "H" for "Heart" on both his jacket and his cap. His tricycle pulls a wagon. **$22.00.**

1988 KEVIN & HIGHCHAIR #5395 contains The Heart Family's first African-American cousin, Kevin. **$22.00.**

1988 NELLIE & ROCKING HORSE #5399 is shown here to identify two box styles in use during the two years these Baby Cousins remained in production. Above Nellie's window, one box says "NELLIE & ROCKING HORSE," the second box style says "NELLIE & ROCKING HORSE INSIDE." Such a minor difference makes no difference to most collectors, but the two boxes are shown here to point out that there are slight differences among boxes. **$22.00.**

1988 MELODY & WALKER #5398 is an African-American cousin. **$22.00.**

1988 BATHROBE AND SLIPPER SET #7142 is the first of only three Baby Fashions available in 1988. All of the adult fashions were discontinued. These fashions are sold on blister cards, while the earlier fashions were boxed with windows. This set includes yellow robes for both the boy and girl. The boy's robe has a blue collar, belt, and slippers, while the girl's robe has a pink collar, belt, and slippers. **$16.00.**

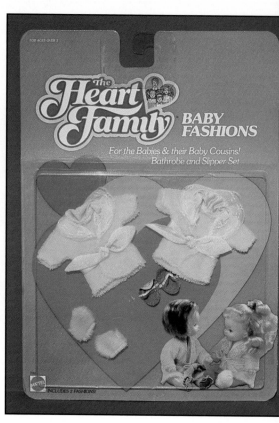

1988 SAILOR SUITS #7162 features a sailor dress with blue tights and cap for the girl and a blue sailor suit and hat for the boy. **$16.00.**

1988 BATHROBE AND SLIPPER SET #7142 shown here mispackaged with two girl's robe on the same blister card, even though the blu slippers are correct. Mistakes such as this ac value to the item. **$20.00.**

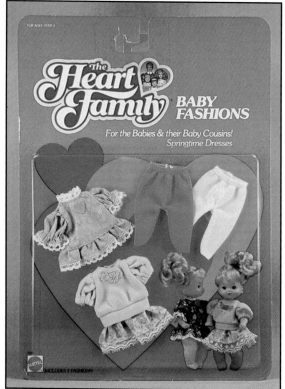

1988 SPRINGTIME DRESSES #7168 has two girl's fashions — a blue dress with white leggings and a lavender dress with pink tights. **$16.00.**

1988 THE HEART FAMILY BATHTUB #5157 is a blue bathtub wit working faucet and shower nozzle. Towels, washcloths, soap, bub ble bath, tray, and back scrubber are included. **$25.00.**

1988 THE HEART FAMILY CAMPER #3316 is a pink pop-up camper that folds flat for towing. When raised, a large blue tent pops up. A storage drawer is in the base of the camper. A table with four collapsible chairs, table service, and a cooler are included. This is hard to find. **$70.00.**

1988 ROCK 'N PLAY MUSICAL NURSERY #4674 features a musical crib that, when wound up, plays a lullaby as a lever rocks either the rocking chair or the horse; the wind-up action also causes a train on the railing to move back and forth, and pictures rotate in the headboard. **$45.00.**

1988 PLAY CENTER #4755 is a changing table that opens to a play area, complete with chalkboard, easel, wagons, blocks, a changing pad, and a drum set. **$20.00.**

1989 SCHOOLTIME FUN TEACHER MOM & BOY #3281 features Mrs. Heart in a pink dress with blue heart-shaped glasses with her son, wearing a school uniform. A lunchbox, thermos, ruler, pencil, scissors, brush, and shoes are included. The Fun Book included with these dolls contains a dot to dot picture, a rhyming game, a maze, photos of the 1989 Heart Family line, and coupons. The photo of the Schooltime Fun Teacher Mom in this booklet shows her with pink glasses. **$28.00.**

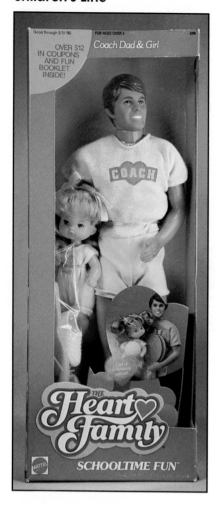

1989 SCHOOLTIME FUN COACH DAD & GIRL #3288 features Mr. Heart wearing a blue tee-shirt with "COACH" logo, yellow shorts, and tennis shoes, along with his daughter wearing a pink gym suit and shoes. Two tennis rackets, a soccer ball, and brush are included. **$28.00.**

1989 SCHOOLTIME FUN TEACHER MOM & BOY (Black) #2821 features Mrs. Heart wearing a pink dress with yellow glasses — the white Mrs. Heart has blue glasses, and the box photos for this African-American version show her with blue glasses. Other contents are the same. **$28.00.**

1989 SCHOOLTIME FUN COACH DAD & GIRL (Black) #281 **$28.00.**

1989 SUNSHINE FUN PALS SAND SET #2644 features The Heart Family twins wearing beach sunsuits. Also included are two visors, a sandcastle, sand pail, shovel, beachball, brush, and a fish-shaped sand-sifter. **$28.00.**

1989 SUNSHINE FUN PALS WATER SET #2645 features The Heart Family twins wearing striped bathing suits. The girl in this set has dark brown hair and brown eyes — a big change from the 1985 girl with light blonde hair and blue eyes! Also included in the set are two pairs of sunglasses, a water float, towel, brush, and a dolphin ring toss game with three rings. **$32.00.**

1989 DARIA & DESK #2678 is the first of six Neighborhood Kids who play with The Heart Family twins after school. Their slogan is "We're Neighborhood Kids every one! One for all and all for fun!" Each of the Neighborhood Kids features a personalized accessory that really works. A pink bunny pops out of Daria's desk when she closes its top. **$18.00.**

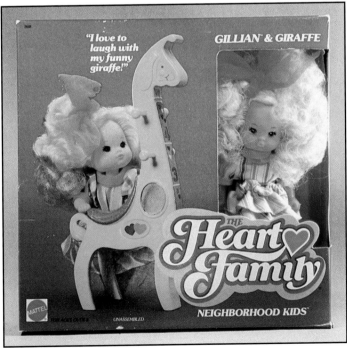

1989 DARRIN & DESK #2681 also has a desk from which a bunny pops, but his bunny is blue. **$18.00.**

1989 GILLIAN & GIRAFFE #2648 features a smiling ride-on giraffe with growth chart and mirror. **$18.00.**

1989 PLEASANCE & PONY #2682 features the first Hispanic friend of The Heart Family. Even her box is printed in both English and Spanish. Her box says, "My pony & I rock 'n play!", but in The Heart Family Fun Book, Pleasance's rhyme is printed in full: "My pony & I love to play, as we rock-along all day!" **$22.00.**

1989 TAWNY & TRIKE #2687 features the only African American Neighborhood Kid. Tawny's trike pulls wagon. **$18.00.**

1989 WINDY & WAGON #2647 features red-haired Windy and her wagon with moving ducks. **$18.00.**

1989 SCHOOLTIME FUN SCHOOLHOUSE #3434 features a working clock with ringing bell, revolving table, merry-go-round, two bunny chairs, cat 'n mouse clock, magic lesson board, teeter totter, spinning globe, drawing board/easel, computer, and two hang-up lesson boards. **$45.00.**

89 SUNSHINE FUN PLAYSET #2760 features
pool/sandbox, water-squirting elephant
de, swing, pail, shovel, seashell, whale, boat,
d flying disc. **$22.00.**

**1990 THE HEART FAMILY VIS-
ITS DISNEYLAND PARK MOM
& GIRL #7555** contains Mom
wearing a pink dress with Disneyland shirt featuring Minnie
Mouse, along with her daughter wearing a romper with
Dumbo on it, a skirt, and a Mickey Mouse hat. A Disneyland visor,
balloon, Minnie Mouse charm, poster, and shoes are included. The
Heart Family visited Disneyland Park in 1990 to celebrate its 35th
anniversary. **$45.00.**

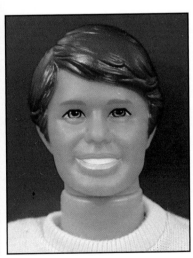

1990 THE HEART FAMILY VISITS DISNEYLAND PARK DAD & BOY #7556 contains Dad wearing striped pants and a
lue shirt with Disneyland above an illustration of Mickey Mouse; his son wears a romper with Donald Duck featured
n the shirt and a Mickey Mouse hat. Also included are a Disneyland visor, balloon, brush, child-size Mickey Mouse
harm, shoes, and poster. **$45.00.**

1990 THE HEART FAMILY VISITS DISNEYLAND PARK MOM & GIRL—DAD & BOY GIFT SET
#7250 pairs the Mom & Girl set with the Dad & Boy set in one package. This is very hard to find. **$95.00.**

1990 THE HEART FAMILY VISITS DISNEYLAND PARK MOM & GIRL (Black) #7557. $45.00.

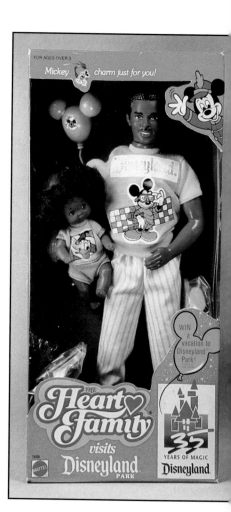

1990 THE HEART FAMILY VISITS DISNEYLAND PARK DAD & BOY (Black) #7606 features the first change to the African-American Mr. Heart's head. His modified afro hairstyle had become outdated, so in this set he adopts the head mold of 1988's Island Fun Steven (a Barbie doll friend). This is also the first Mr. Heart with a moustache. This is a hard to find doll. **$48.00.**

90 KIDS ON PARADE DONALD DUCK BOAT & GIRL
082 features a redheaded girl wearing a Mickey Mouse
t, Donald Duck shirt, and blue pants packaged with a
use ears balloon and a Donald Duck boat. The Donald
ick boat attaches to other vehicles in the Kids on
rade series, or it can be used with the Dumbo Ride.
5.00.

1990 KIDS ON PARADE MICKEY MOUSE TRAIN & BOY
#1078 features a blonde boy wearing a Mickey Mouse
hat, white Mickey Mouse tee-shirt, and blue shorts,
along with a Mouse ears balloon and a Mickey Mouse
train. **$35.00.**

**1990 KIDS ON PARADE MINNIE MOUSE
CAR & GIRL #1079** features a blonde girl
with crimped hair wearing a Mickey Mouse
hat and lavender Minnie Mouse outfit,
along with a Mouse ears balloon and a pink
Minnie Mouse car. **$35.00.**

**1990 KIDS ON PARADE MINNIE
MOUSE CAR & GIRL (Black) #1124** is
the African-American version with
her hair in a different style — it is
worn in two pigtails. **$35.00.**

173

1990 KIDS ON PARADE PLUTO PLANE & GIRL #111 features a Hispanic girl wearing a Pluto shirt wit shorts and a Mickey Mouse hat, along with a mous ears balloon and a yellow Pluto plane. **$35.00.**

1990 DUMBO RIDE #1076 is a wind-up ride that goes up and down while The Heart Family babies ride in the two Dumbo vehicles, which have wheels and are detachable for use in a parade. Up to four Kids on Parade or Dumbo vehicles fit on the Dumbo Ride at once. A bench and vendor stand with hot dogs, hamburger, and toys for sale are included. **$45.00.**

The Heart Family Foreign Exclusives

1985 THE HEART FAMILY LOVING HOME #9691 sold in Europe features a two-story house with elevator, a rooftop terrace, different illustrated room scenes, and different furniture than the Loving Home sold in the U.S. Most notably absent from the U.S. set is the elevator. The U.S. home contains a casual dining table and chairs, while the European set is formal. **$175.00.**

Not shown: **1986 MR. BOBBIE #2371** is The Heart Family's dog, True Heart, using a different name as part of the Barbie doll line in Europe. Most shocking is the fact that Mattel's catalogs in the U.S. refer to True Heart as a she, but in Europe Mr. Bobbie is male — and the dogs are identical, down to the blue heart-shaped "1" medallion they wear on their collar. In the United Kingdom, True Heart is packaged as Bonnie or Toufou. **$40.00.**

1986 BUNK BED PLAYSET #3866 features a pink bed for the girl and a blue bed for the boy, along with sleepers for each. **$25.00.**

1986 BOX #3867 is a foreign-market exclusive playpen with sliding beads. **$20.00.**

986 DRESSER/ARMOIRE is a blue moire with spaces for the babies' othes, as well as a changing table d storage area for diapers, diaper ail, and toys. **$30.00.**

1986 STOVE/OVEN features a range with opening door in a wall unit containing two drawers, a stove top with burners, a microwave oven, and a cupboard. **$30.00.**

1986 TABLE & CHAIRS features a white dining table with blue and pink border, two adult chairs, and two booster chairs that attach to the sides of the table for the babies. Tableware is included. **$30.00.**

1986 TOY CHEST/BENCH is a blue toy box with opening lid that doubles as a bench when the cushion and pillow are added. **$20.00.**

1986 TRICYCLE #3868 features a pink tricycle with wagon not sold separately in the U.S. **$20.00.**

1988 BABY WETS DELUXE SET #4663 features the blonde Baby Wets babies, sold in the U.S. wearing diapers, dressed in a blue playsuit and a lacy dress, along with Mom wearing a pink dress with lacy overskirt and Dad wearing a turquoise jacket with white pants, pink shirt, and blue scarf. **$95.00.**

1989 GIRL AND TRIKE is a Caucasian version of the U.S. African-American Tawny and Trike sold on the international market. In the 1980s, Europe sold very few black Barbie-family dolls, but the altered Tawny as a white girl is a Heart Family collector must-have. The outfit, tricycle, wagon, and even hair ribbon are identical; only the doll's race has been changed. **$50.00.**

1989 SCHOOLTIME FUN TEACHE DAD & GIRL #3288 was available Europe as a music/art teacher, wearir long blue pants with white stripes, long-sleeved yellow shirt with blue ar white bow tie, and a pink apron! Ho different from our U.S. Coach Da who wears yellow shorts and a blu tee-shirt! The girl in the European s wears a long pink dress with an apro that matches Dad's. In the U.S. the g wears a one-piece pink gym su **$65.00.**

989 GIRL & DESK #2678 from Canada is lled Daria & Desk in the U.S. Some foreign arkets eliminated the names from the U.S. eighborhood Kids, referring to each of the x children in the series as Boy or Girl. **$35.00.**

1990 KINDERGARTEN FRIENDS #4804 is one of six Kindergarten Friends sold exclusively on the international market. The girl shown here has red hair, freckles, and blue eyes. She wears a white raincoat with rain hat. **$35.00.**

989 PLAYGROUND FRIENDS Six Playground Friends exclusive Europe were available, consisting of four girls and two boys. blonde girl in a pink romper, a blonde girl in a violet dress with ce vest, a brunette girl in a white dress, a boy in a star-design p and hat, a red-haired girl in a star-design skirt and cap, and a oy in a yellow playsuit are featured. **$40.00 each.**

1990 KINDERGARTEN FRIENDS consist of four girls and two boys sold in Europe. This back of box photo shows all six, including the red-haired girl in a rain coat. **$35.00 each.**

177

Not shown: **1988 JANET & POTTY CHAIR #5397** shown in the Summer 1989 *Barbie Journal* wit blonde hair! In the U.S. Janet has brown hair. **$40.00**

1989 SCHOOLTIME FUN TEACHER MOM & BOY #328 is featured on the package of the foreign-boxe School & Playground and in German booklets with a outfit slightly different than used in the U.S. Her outf in some foreign markets has a white blouse with separate pink jacket, and she wears yellow glasse when her jacket and skirt are removed, she has on shorts and top exercise outfit. The U.S. doll wears one-piece pink dress. The boy included varies as we — in Germany he wears a more traditional uniform blue pants and suspenders with white stripes an matching cap, and a yellow shirt; the U.S. boy has solid blue outfit, including his shirt, and no ca **$50.00**

1990 MUSICAL CAROUSEL is in the style of the U.S. Dumbo Ride, but in this carousel, two rabbits and two ducks provide the rides. **$60.00**.

1992 BARBIE LI'L FRIENDS #2205 is a blonde girl with brown eyes wearing a black and white jacket and black skirt. **$35.00**.

1992 BARBIE LI'L FRIENDS #2206 is a blonde girl with green eyes wearing a white dress with green and pink decoration. **$35.00**.

1992 BARBIE LI'L FRIENDS #2202 is the first doll in the Li'l Friend series of dolls that continued The Heart Family line on the interna tional market. This first series contains five doll sold individually plu three gift sets containing dolls with an accessory. This is a redhead ed girl with brown eyes wearing a purple outfit. **$35.00**.

1992 BARBIE LI'L FRIENDS #2203 is a brown-haired, blue-eyed g wearing a white sweatshirt and pink leggings. **$35.00**.

1992 BARBIE LI'L FRIENDS #2204 is a blonde girl with blue eye wearing a green shirt and geometric print dress. **$35.00**.

178

**1992 BARBIE LI'L FRIEND & ROCKING HORSE
2150** contains a brown-haired blue-eyed girl
earing a blue shirt and white skirt, along with her
ocking horse. This is rare. **$50.00.**

1992 BARBIE LI'L FRIEND & WAGON #2152 contains a
blonde, brown-eyed girl wearing a blue dress, along with
her wagon. This is rare. **$50.00.**

992 BARBIE LI'L FRIEND & WALKER #2153 contins a blonde-
aired, blue-eyed girl wearing a pink top with multicolored
ants, along with a walker. This is rare. **$50.00.**

993 BARBIE LI'L FRIENDS #3536 features a blonde-haired,
olet-eyed girl wearing an orange jumpsuit with purple dots
nd stripes, under a pink skirt. **$25.00.**

**993 BARBIE LI'L FRIENDS
3537** is a brown-haired, violet-
yed girl wearing a multicolored
riped top with pink and purple
ants. **$25.00.**

**993 BARBIE LI'L FRIENDS
3538** is a blonde girl with blue
yes wearing a blue top and pas-
l floral-print pants. **$25.00.**

**993 BARBIE LI'L FRIENDS
3539** is an auburn-haired girl
ith green eyes and freckles
ho is dressed in an orange
ress with yellow ribbons.
25.00.**

1993 MOM & BABY #9078 The 1985 Heart Family Mom and Dad, each with baby, were reissued in India in 1993 with several differences. India packaging refers to The Heart Family as Barbie's friends and Barbie's neighbors. Mom h light blonde hair in India, while the original U.S. doll has sandy blonde hair wi brown streaks. This India Mom has a pink dress 1¼" shorter than the U.S. doll The India doll's complexion is lighter, and her eyes are a lighter blue. The ba girl has a longer lace collar than the U.S. girl, and the India girl's stockings hav no feet to them. A photo of the dolls on the India **Bunk Bed Playset** shows M Heart with blonde painted hair using 1984's Crystal Ken head mold, and Mr Heart with blonde hair using the 1972 Walk Lively Steffie head mold, but the may be pre-production samples. **$35.00.**

1993 PLAYGROUND FRIENDS KENNY #5394 is one of five Playground Friends sold exclusively on the India market. Kenny has curly brown hair, a red shirt, and red plaid pants. **$20.00.**

1993 PLAYGROUND FRIENDS NIKITA #3207
has brown hair. She wears a white satiny
dress with blue accents. **$20.00.**

**1993 PLAYGROUND FRIENDS
SUNNY #3209** is a brown-haired
boy with brown eyes wearing
denim overalls. **$20.00.**

**1993 PLAYGROUND FRIENDS SUSAN
#5397** is a blonde girl wearing a red
dress with white blouse. **$20.00.**

**1993 PLAYGROUND FRIENDS WINDY
#3206** is a blonde girl wearing a lacy
white dress. **$20.00.**

1994 BARBIE LI'L FRIEN[**#11853** is a honey blonde hair[girl with olive green eyes a[freckles wearing a strawber[print jumpsuit with red hat. S[has a straw purse with napk[**$20.00.**

1994 BARBIE LI'L FRIEN[**#11854** is a blonde, blue-ey[girl wearing a swimsuit and s[hat. She has a pail and shov[**$20.00.**

1994 BARBIE LI'L FRIEN[**#11855** is a brown-haired g[with green eyes wearing a y[low rain coat and rain hat and black and white pants. She has a lunchbox and thermos. **$20.00.**

1994 BARBIE LI'L FRIENDS #11856 is the only boy in the series. He has blue eyes and dark brown hair. He wears[rainbow striped shirt with orange shorts, and he kicks his soccer ball. **$20.00.**

1988 HEART FAMI[**NAUTICAL OUTF[** **#5265** contains outf[for Mom and daught[**$45.00.**

1988 HEART FAMILY COUNTRY LACE DRESS #5256 is the first of the European exclusive Family Fashions that uses the Baby Fashion, sold carded in the U.S., with matching fashions for Mom and Dad that were not available in the U.S. These are blue floral print dresses with white lace trim. **$45.00.**

1988 HEART FAMI[**NAUTICAL OUTF[** **#5267** contains outf[for Dad and so[**$45.00.**

182

1988 HEART FAMILY ROBES #5266 contains robes and slippers for Mom and daughter. **$45.00.**

1988 HEART FAMILY ROBES #5274 contains robes and slippers for Dad and son. **$45.00.**

1988 HEART FAMILY SPRING-TIME FLOWER DRESS #5260 has a pastel dress and top for Mom and daughter. **$45.00.**

The Heart Family Legacy

After being discontinued in 1990, a revised Heart Family-like line was planned, consisting of Midge, Barbie doll's best friend since 1963, and her new husband Alan (spelled Allan in 1964), who married in 1991. 1992 Barbie fashion booklets contained a photograph of new family Midge, Alan, and their twin infants! Mattel may have felt that well-known Midge was a strong enough attraction to carry a new family line of dolls similar to The Heart Family, whose blue boxes and unclear ties to Barbie may have contributed to the line's demise. The Midge, Alan,

and babies set never reached the market to the dismay of many collectors, and Alan was dropped from the Barbie family line while Midge appeared in new toy lines through 1998 with no further mention of her being married.

The Heart Family continues to leave its mark on the world of Barbie dolls. A number of Barbie family dolls have been packaged with either the Rosebud/Heart Family babies or the tiny New Arrival infant, who never again appeared with any of The Heart Family dolls or playsets after its lone appearance in 1986. Listed here are the dolls with The Heart Family babies, along with selected photos showing original or special uses of the baby.

Midge® and Alan™ have adorable twin babies that magically hold their bottle and toys. #5717, #5718

183

1993 LOVE TO READ BARBIE DELUXE GIFT SET #10507 is a Toys 'R' Us exclusive. **$50.00.**

1997 AMERICAN INDIAN #17313. **$22.00.**

Not shown:
1991 BABYSITTER SKIPPER #9433. $25.00.
1991 BABYSITTER SKIPPER (BLACK) #1599. $25.00.
1991 BABYSITTER COURTNEY #9434. $25.00.
1993 MERMAID SKIPPER AND THE SEA TWINS #10506. $22.00.
1994 BABYSITTER SKIPPER #12071. $16.00.
1994 BABYSITTER SKIPPER (Black) #12072. $16.00.
1994 DR. BARBIE #11160. $50.00.
1994 DR. BARBIE (Black) #11814. $50.00.
1995 DR. BARBIE (Black) #14315. (Toys 'R' Us exclusive.) **$22.00.**
1995 TEACHER BARBIE #13914. $30.00.
1995 TEACHER BARBIE (Black) #13195. $30.00.
1995 TEACHER BARBIE (Hispanic) #16210. $32.00.
1996 AMERICAN INDIAN #14715. $28.00.
1996 DR. BARBIE #15803. (Toys 'R' Us exclusive.) **$22.00.**
1996 DR. BARBIE (Black) #15804. (Toys 'R' Us exclusive.) **$22.00.**

1995 DR. BARBIE #14309 is a Toys 'R' Us exclusive. **$22.00.**

Princess of Power

THE STORY OF SHE-RA ILLUS-TRATED COMIC BOOK.

A new Mattel boy's action figure fantasy adventure series, Masters of the Universe, featured He-Man, a muscle-bound champion and prince of the planet Eternia. Launched in 1982, the series became very popular and was incorporated into an animated television series. Hoping to capture the girl's market, Mattel created He-Man's long-lost sister Princess Adora, Princess of Power, who was raised on the planet Etheria — a world filled with beauty, magic, and fantasy. Living in Crystal Castle, Princess Adora transforms into She-Ra, the most exciting and powerful woman in the universe, when danger threatens — usually instigated by the jealous enemy Catra. The Princess of Power series introduced eight 5½" human characters in 1985, an owl, three horses, an enchanted swan, a castle, and three horse and figure sets. In 1986 She-Ra and Catra got new costumes, six new humans joined the line, a three doll gift set, and eight Fantastic Fashions debuted; also new were three horses with crystal bodies, a cat, three new doll and crystal horse sets, a Butterflyer carry case, a Sea Harp carriage, and Crystal Falls playset. In 1987 She-Ra and Catra received new powers, three new characters joined the line, another eight fashions debuted, and two horses were redesigned — but other planned introductions shown in the catalog (three Star Sisters and their bird) were never released. Each character comes with an illustrated comic book.

MARKINGS: All 1985 females (except Double Trouble) are marked c M.I. 1984 on the back of their heads; all females' bodies of 1985 are marked either c M.I. 1984/ TAIWAN or c MATTEL, INC. 1984/ TAIWAN.

1985 SHE-RA #9182 is the the most powerful woman in the universe. Her crown turns around to become a helmet, and she has an action waist. All of the female dolls in this line come with a comb. She-Ra also has a cape, skirt, sword, and shield. Her enclosed comic book, "The Story of She-Ra," reveals her origin and reunion with her brother, He-Man. A promotional **SHE-RA #9182** has a free necklace for the child. **$40.00.**

PRINCESS OF POWER ILLUSTRATED COMIC BOOKS

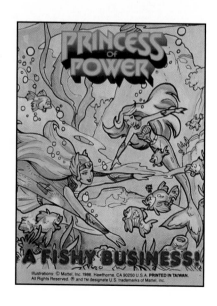

1985 ANGELLA #9186 is the winged guide whose wings spread when her halo is pressed to simulate flight. Her comic book is called, "Journey to Mizar." **$20.00.**

1985 BOW #9183 is She-Ra's special friend. His heart, visible through his chest plate, beats for She-Ra when the button on his back is pressed. He has a removable headband, quiver of six arrows, and a red cape. His comic book is called, "The Hidden Symbols Mystery". **$20.00.**

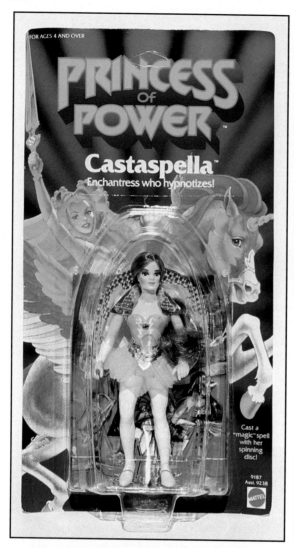

1985 CASTASPELLA #9187 is the enchantress who hypnotizes with her spinning hypnotic disc, worn on her back. Her comic book is "Disappearing Treasures." **$20.00.**

1985 CATRA #9184 is the raven-haired jealous beauty who becomes a cat when her mask is put on. She has a scratching action waist. Her comic book is "Journey to Mizar" (some comic books were repeated with certain characters). **$20.00.**

1985 DOUBLE TROUBLE #9185 is a helmeted glamorous double agent whose face changes from smiling to frowning when the wheel in her back is turned (thus turning her face 180 degrees inside the helmet). Double Trouble's counterpart from Masters of the Universe is Man-E-Faces, who has three different faces inside his helmet. Her comic book is "Adventure of the Blue Diamond." MARKINGS: none on head. **$20.00.**

1985 FROSTA #9189 is Ice Empress of Etheria whose snowflake wand spins and whistles. She freezes whatever she pleases, and she has an action waist. The Ice Empress name was first used with the 1980 Guardian Goddesses series. Her comic book is "Adventure of the Blue Diamond." **$20.00.**

189

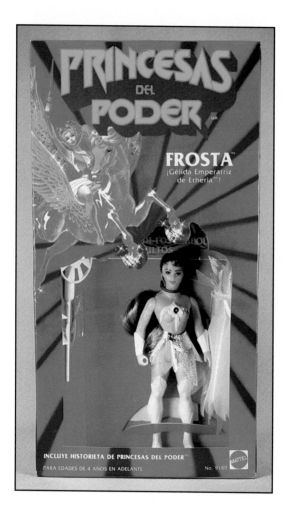

1985 ARROW #9721 is Bow's true-blue horse with multi-colored wings. The horses in the Princess of Power line all have combable manes and tails. **$25.00. (A BOW AND ARROW** set **#9817** pairs Bow and Arrow in one box **$50.00.**)

1985 FROSTA #9189 is shown here as sold in Mexico, where the Princess of Power dolls were sold in window boxes instead of on blister cards. The artwork in her comic book is identical to the U.S. doll's, but words are in Spanish. Collectors of foreign-market items are often surprised to learn how U.S. dolls are altered or re-named for sale in other countries. For instance, in France, Sweetbee is called Buttina, Peekablue is called Irisa, Mermista is called Sirena, and Flutterina is called Aeria. **$25.00.**

1985 GLIMMER #9188 is the guide who lights the way with her headdress and staff that glow in the dark. Her comic book is called "Disappearing Treasures." **$20.00.**

190

1985 KOWL #9190 is the "know-it-owl" whose secret panel on his stomach lifts to reveal color-coded answers to questions asked of it: red means no, yellow means maybe, and green means yes. The comic book included is called "The Hidden Symbols Mystery." MARKINGS: none. **$20.00.**

985 STORM #9722 is Catra's shimmery silver horse ith multicolor wings. **$25.00.**

1985 CATRA AND STORM #9818 pairs Catra and Storm in one set. **$50.00.**

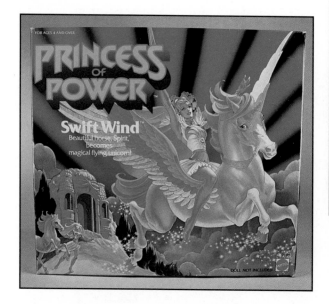

1985 ENCHANTA #9681 is the 8¾" high and 11½" long flying pink swan with jeweled collar, pink saddle, and soft pink mar that carries She-Ra and her friends to new adventures. **$35.00**

1985 SWIFT WIND #9191 is She-Ra's horse/unicorn. As Spirit, she is Princess Adora's pearly-pink horse; when the unicorn mask and multicolor wings are attached, Spirit becomes Swift Wind, She-Ra's flying unicorn! **$25.00.** (**A SHE-RA AND SWIFT WIND set #9400** pairs She-Ra and Swift Wind in one box. **$50.00.**)

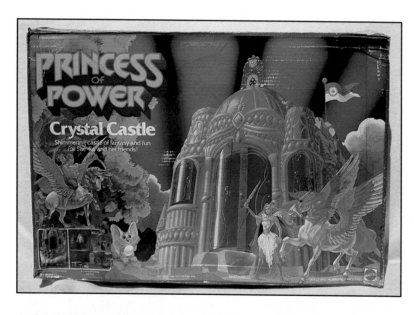

1985 CRYSTAL CASTLE #9193 is the spectacular home of Princess Adora/She-Ra with opening crystal windows and doors, a crystal throne elevator that carries She-Ra to the top, and a secret passage. The four-room castle is 18½" high and 13½" long. Furnishings include a crystal bed with canopy, treasure chest with disappearing jewels, table with map of Etheria, flag, chandelier, clothes stand, two chairs, bedspread, fireplace, mirrored vanity, pillow, and plush rug. **$120.00.**

1986 STARBURST SHE-RA #2450 features She Ra in a new costume that allows her to b Princess Adora with a lovely pink cape when h arms are down; when her arms are raised, h golden lamé starburst cape is revealed. She al has a headdress, skirt, sword, shield, and com Her comic book is "Across the Crystal Light Bar er." She introduces a new head mold designe for greater head movement, marked: c M. 1985; her back is marked c MATTEL, INC. 198 **$25.00.**

1986 ENTRAPTA #2636 is Catra's helper who uses her long pink and purple hair to trap She-Ra and her friends after first tricking them into coming near with her golden beauty. Entrapta has a golden headband and collar, skirt, and shield. Her comic book is "A Born Champion." MARKINGS: same as dolls of 1985. **$22.00.**

1986 FLUTTERINA #2453 is the beautiful lookout with fluttering butterfly wings who secretly follows Catra to learn of her plans. When the child holds her string and pulls from both ends, Flutterina glides up and down the string as her wings flutter. Her comic book is "A Most Unpleasant Present." Some of the new 1986 dolls have the word, "NEW!" in the top left corner of their card, while others do not. MARKINGS: Back of head: c M.I. 1985; Back: c MATTEL, INC. 1985. **$20.00.**

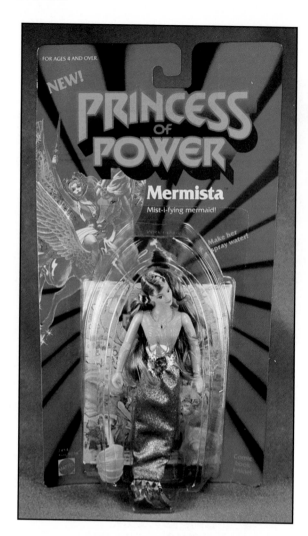

1986 MERMISTA #2454 is the blue-haired mist-i-fying mermaid who sprays a water mist. **$22.00.**

1986 PEEKABLUE #2452 is the green-haired watchful feathered friend of She-Ra. Each feather has an eye, to allow her to see in all directions. Her enclosed comic book is "A Fishy Business." MARKINGS: same as Flutterina. **$22.00.**

1986 PERFUMA #2455 is the scent-sational flower maiden who opens her petals into a beautiful blossom which releases a perfume that puts those smelling it to sleep. Her comic book is "A Most Unpleasant Present." **$20.00.**

1986 SCRATCHIN' SOUND CATRA #2451 makes a scratching sound when the lever on her back moves her arm in a "scratching" action. Her comic book is "A Born Champion." **$24.00.**

1986 SWEETBEE #2635 is She-Ra's honey of a guide with antennae and turn-around wings that glow in the dark. Her comic book is "A Born Champion." **$22.00.**

1986 CLAWDEEN #9627 is Catra's glamorous pink cat with saddle, harness, hair ribbon, brush, and comb. Clawdeen taught Catra how to become a cat and now carries her to new adventures. **$30.00.**

1986 CRYSTAL MOONBEAM #2434 is the brother of the Cry Sun Dancer horse. Crystal Moonbeam has a crystal violet bo with blue wings, tail, and mane. Crystal Moonbeam protec Crystal Castle at night. **$35.00.** (A **PEEKABLUE AND CRYST MOONBEAM set #2900** pairs the doll and horse in one bo **$65.00.**)

1986 DEFENDERS OF GOOD #1052 is a department store special containing Perfuma, She-Ra, and SweetBee in one package. This is hard to find. **$95.00.**

986 CRYSTAL SUN DANCER #2435 is the crystal
nk horse with yellow mane and tail that guards
rystal Castle by day. **$35.00.** (A **SWEETBEE AND
RYSTAL SUNDANCER set #2899** pairs the doll and
orse in one box. **$65.00.**)

1986 CRYSTAL SWIFT WIND #2433 is She-Ra's crystal pink unicorn with yellow wings and combable pink mane and tail.
When the unicorn mask is removed, Spirit, the crystal horse is
revealed. Swift Wind became crystal when, journeying to Crystal World, the legend that anyone who touched the ground
would turn to crystal proved to be correct! **$35.00.**

986 DEEP BLUE SECRET #2836 is one of eight
ard to find Fantastic Fashions created for
he-Ra and her friends (a second set of eight
ashions were produced in 1987). Deep Blue
ecret is an ocean blue outfit with a secret
nap of the sea hidden behind the blue fish
hield. A Fantastic Fashions booklet, included
vith several of the dolls, illustrates and
escribes the eight 1986 fashions. **$18.00.**

1986 STARBURST SHE-RA & CRYSTAL SWIFT WIND #2898 pairs
the doll and unicorn in one gift set package. This is a hard set to
find. **$85.00.**

The **Fantastic Fashions booklet,** included with several of the dolls, illustrates and describes the eight 1986 fashions.

1986 FIT TO BE TIED #2825 is a blue ballgown worn by Princess Adora when dancing with Bow. The long blue scarf is actually a life-saving rope. **$18.00.**

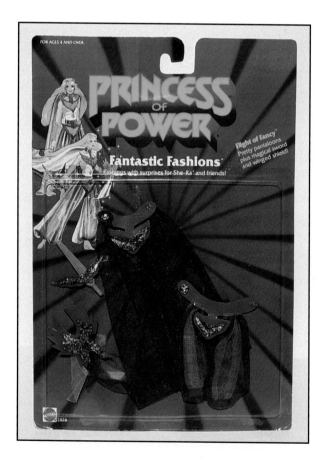

1986 FLIGHT OF FANCY #2828 is She-Ra's flying costume when riding with Crystal Swift Wind. A magical winged sword and shield fly to her side when trouble arises. **$18.00.**

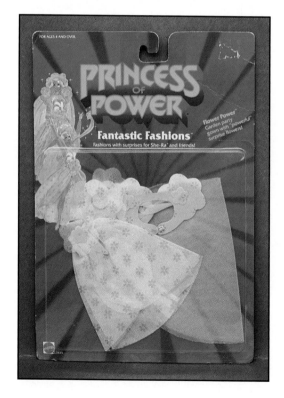

1986 FLOWER POWER #2835 is a lime green garden fashion with shoulder posies that pull out to push trouble away. **$18.00.**

**1986 HOLD ON TO YOUR HAT
#2826** is a party dress with a parasol that is really a sword cover and a hat that doubles as a shield. **$18.00.**

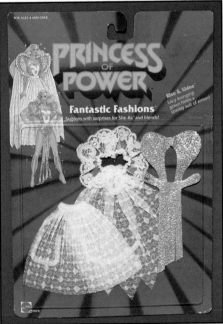

86 READY IN RED #2827 is a sparkly d winter outfit with fur trim. Turned side out, the skirt can be used as a it of armor, and the cape doubles as et to trap Entrapta. **$18.00.**

1986 RISE & SHINE #2824 is a lacy lounging gown covering a sparkly suit of armor. **$18.00.**

1986 VEILS OF MYSTERY #2824 is a dress with layers of hot pink veils that cover a secret sword. **$18.00.**

1986 BUTTERFLYER #2903 is a wing butterfly collector's case that carr She-Ra and her friends anywhere Etheria as quickly as the wind. The B terflyer has a molded human face w hair and arms. **$35.00.**

1986 CRYSTAL FALLS #2456 is a three-level waterfall flowing from an orchid; it features a lounge shell, reflecting mirror, shell pool, hand pump, clothes hook, and towel bar. **$65.00.**

1986 SEA HARP #2902 is a musical sea horse that once lived below Crystal Falls. Sea Harp summons help by playing a musical message and carries She-Ra and her friends to adventures. **$30.00.**

1987 BUBBLE POWER SHE-RA #3023 has a Bubble-Blower with bubble liquid which blows bubbles. A comic book "Don't Rain on My Parade" is included. **$100.00.**

1987 LOO-KEE #1969 is the elf who really moves when wound up, as his eyes look around. His comic book is "Where Hope Has Gone." **$100.00.**

1987 SHOWER POWER CATRA #3021 is an extremely rare figure on an oversized card featuring Catra's Shower Squirter. The comic book "Don't Rain On My Parade" is included. **$100.00.**

1987 NETOSSA #1835 is the only black character in this series. She uses her cape as a capturing net. Her comic book is "Where Hope Has Gone!" **$32.00.**

1987 SPINNERELLA #3053 whirls and swirls on her stand. She is hard to find. Her comic book is "Where Hope Has Gone." **$175.00.**

1987 ROYAL SWIFTWIND #3050 is She-Ra's unicorn with a white body and pink mane and tail. His saddle is golden, as are the edges of his wings. This is the hardest to find animal of the series. **$60.00.**

1987 SILVER STORM #3150 has an iridescent body with black mane and tail. Silvery saddle armor and cat mask are included. **$55.00.**

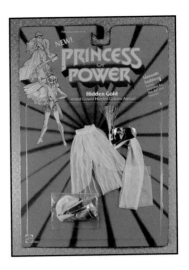

1987 SECRET MESSENGER #2830. $25.00.

1987 FROSTY FUR #2831. $25.00.

1987 HIDDEN GOLD #2832. $25.00.

1987 BLUE LIGHTNING #2833. $25.00.

1987 REFLECTIONS IN RED #2834. $25.00.

1987 COLORFUL SECRET #2837. $25.00.

1987 HEART OF GOLD #2838. $25.00.

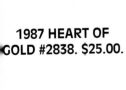

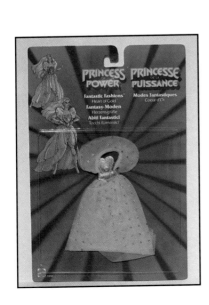

1987 WINDY JUMPER #2839. $25.00.

Never Released Princess of Power Toys

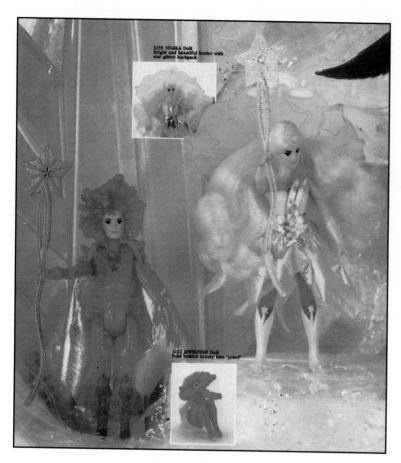

1987 JEWELSTAR #3212 is one of three Star Sisters shown in the 1987 Mattel retailer catalog. The Star Sisters were advertised as COMING SOON! on the backs of 1987 cards, but the Princess of Power line was discontinued before these dolls and their Glory Bird were released. The catalog states that "Long ago, an evil sorceress imprisoned the Star Sisters inside a gleaming star and sent it shooting towards Etheria. It came to rest in a cave beneath Crystal Castle where it was discovered by She-Ra. Starla, Tallstar, Jewelstar, and Glory Bird pledged their loyalty and magical powers to her!" Jewelstar has a sparkly pink body which can be folded into a jewel.

1987 STARLA #3155 is the yellow-haired bright and beautiful leader with star glitter backpack.

1987 TALLSTAR #3156 is the pink-haired lookout whose extending body allows her to grow.

1987 GLORY BIRD #3137 is the Star Sisters' flying friend with perch. His wings flap.

C.U.T.I.E.

C.U.T.I.E. is an abbreviation for Coolest Ultra Tiny Individuals on Earth. Measuring only between 1¼" and 2¼" tall, the C.U.T.I.E. dolls are called the wildest, wackiest, most colorful group of miniature dolls ever, according to Mattel's 1987 retailer catalog. The back of the dolls' boxes tell the story behind C.U.T.I.E.: Before there were C.U.T.I.E. dolls, there were just plain dolls. Girls tried to get them interested in what they liked. But nothing happened. Then one day, along came a wild, wacky group of dolls called C.U.T.I.E. And life was never the same. C.U.T.I.E. dolls loved doing what little girls did, going where little girls went. And girls wanted to take them along — everywhere! Why, they were the coo-coo-coolest dolls around! Five different 10 packs of these tiny dolls were available, as well as random assortments of four packs sold on blister cards. In addition, a C.U.T.I.E. child-size fashion purse was available, as well as a free mail-away poster.

1987 BITSY BABIES #3459 includes 10 teeny tots: Cry Baby, Tickle Toes, Sweetums, Dimples, Baby Skates, Burples, Apple Dumplin', Coochie Coochie, Coddles, and Coochie Coo. **$8.00.**

1987 GYM DOLLIES #3460 includes 10 workout girls: Harriet Hardbody, Mara Thon, Miss Fit, Goldie Gloves, Workout Wilma, Anna Aerobic, Sweaty Betty, Twinkle Toes, Bitty Builder, and Shapely Shirley. **$8.00.**

Children's Line

1987 LOVEY DOVEYS #3462 includes 10 dream girls: Tu[...] March, Singa Longa, Leah Tard, Cherry Blossom, Rita Read[...] Mrs. Sippie, Momma Mia, Mary Mee, Holly Woodstar, a[...] Terri Cloth. **$8.00.**

1987 ROCKITY ROLLERS #3465 includes a 10 member rock 'n roll band: Mello-Dee, P. Anna, Jazzie, My-Donna, Wanna-Bee, Strumma, Rockababe, Punkie, Teeny Tooner, and Bopper. **$8.00.**

1987 TINY TRENDIES #3463 includes the year's top fashic[...] models: Debbie Deb, Reel E. Cool, Too Hip, Trendy Wend[...] Gotta Bop, Fasheena, Rani Rad, Modesty, Amy Awesome, ar[...] B. Cool. **$8.00.**

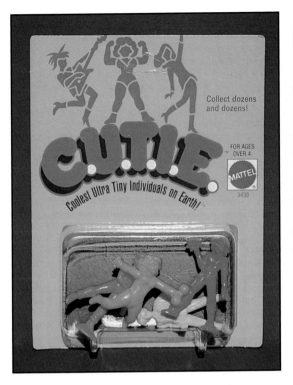

1987 C.U.T.I.E. FIGURE PAKS #3438 contain a random assortment of C.U.T.I.E. figures, packaged four per blister card. The same stock number, #3438, is used on every pak. **$3.00 each.**

1987 FREE C.U.T.I.E. COLLECTOR POSTER was available by mail with two UPC proofs of purchase from C.U.T.I.E. Figure Paks or one UPC proof of purchase from a 10-pack set. The poster shows the city in which the C.U.T.I.E.s live, and all of them are pictured in two rows along the bottom of the poster. The poster offer expired December 31, 1988. **$10.00.**

1987 C.U.T.I.E. HOT FASHION PURSE #3649 is a large, child-size purse with six pockets. Three C.U.T.I.E. figures are included. **$12.00.**

Hot Looks

Mattel had limited success with large-size fashion dolls in the 1970s — most notable are the 19" Cynthia and Quick Curl Casey dolls and the 18" SuperSize Barbie. By 1987, a well-thought out line of five poseable, soft-bodied 18" fashion dolls called Hot Looks appeared. These Hot Looks dolls are international teenage fashion models who work for the Hot Looks Modeling Agency. Each of the dolls has a detailed biography printed on her box to make the child well acquainted with each model. The 12 extra boxed fashions available for the dolls are grouped into three groups — Warm Colors, Hot Colors, and Cool Colors — and children were educated as to which fashion group would best suit the hair, face, and skin tone of their dolls. An extra Super Accessory Kit containing shoes, belts, and jewelry was also available. In 1988 four new models were supposed to join the line, but they were never produced. Eight new fashions reached the market in new boxes, joining eight fashions carried over from 1987, all now easily identifiable by the letters A through P on their box fronts. Three additional Go In Style fashion kits were also available. MARKINGS: All Hot Looks dolls are marked on the back of their heads: c MATTEL, INC. 1986.

1987 CHELSEA #3704 is "the adventurous one." She has strawberry blonde hair and green eyes. She wears a blue and white striped shirt, orange vest, blue stretch pants, a blue headband, socks, high-top shoes, and earrings. Each of the Hot Looks models comes with a comb and a Hot Looks Portfolio, which is a catalog of available Hot Looks fashions. Chelsea's box contains this biography:

NATIONALITY: British
CHELSEA SAYS: "I live for adventure"
FAVORITE COLORS: SUPER WARM colors — "They're daring, like me!"
HOBBY: To go on safari in the jungle
WHAT'S BEST ABOUT BEING A MODEL? Travel!
FAVORITE SONG: Surfin' Safari
$35.00.

1987 ELKIE #3702 is "the athletic one!" She has dark blonde hair and lavender-blue eyes. She wears a pastel jacket, yellow tee-shirt, pink stretch pants, iridescent white belt, floral cap, socks, earrings, and high-top shoes.
NATIONALITY: Swedish
ELKIE SAYS: "Exercise is my life!"
FAVORITE COLORS: SUPER COOL colors — "They're so cool!"
HOBBY: Snow skiing and aerobics
WHAT'S BEST ABOUT BEING A MODEL? The action and excitement!
AMBITION: To ski in the Olympics
$35.00.

1987 MIMI #3703 is "the romantic one!" She has curly light blonde hair and blue eyes. She wears a lavender satin jacket, pink sweater, lacy white skirt, blue lace tights, pastel lace hair ribbon, purple shoes, and earrings.
NATIONALITY: French
MIMI SAYS: "I have a passion for fashion!"
FAVORITE COLORS: SUPER COOL colors — "How romantic!"
HOBBY: Reading romance novels
WHAT'S BEST ABOUT BEING A MODEL? The clothes!
HER DREAM: To fall in love with Prince Charming
$35.00.

1987 STACEY #3701 is "the party girl!" She has brown hair and brown eyes. She wears a red jumpsuit, white print blouse, belt, yellow hair bow, striped socks, yellow sandals, earrings, bracelet, and comb.
NATIONALITY: U.S.A.
STACEY SAYS: "I just wanna have fun!"
FAVORITE COLORS: SUPER HOT colors — "They're attention getters!"
HOBBY: Going to parties
WHAT'S BEST ABOUT BEING A MODEL? "Meeting interesting people"
AMBITION: "To be a music video vee-jay."
$35.00.

1987 ZIZI #3899 is "the creative one She wears zebra-stripe pink pants wi matching jacket, white tee-shirt, ye low belt, pink beret, yellow sock black sandals, earrings, and bracelet.
NATIONALITY: Kenyan
ZIZI SAYS: "I love center stage!"
FAVORITE COLORS: Super Hot colors "They give me energy!"
HOBBY: Dancing with friends
FAVORITE AMERICAN FOOD: Ice cream
AMBITION: "To dance with Micha Jackson in a music video."
$35.00.

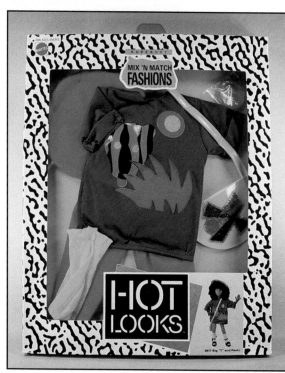

1987 BIG "T" AND PANTS #3817. $15.00.

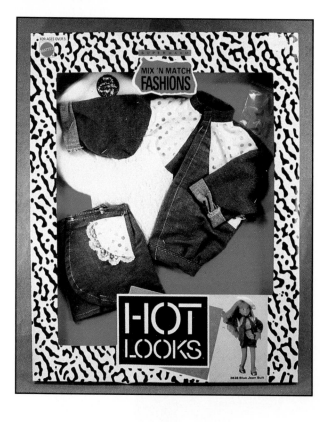

1987 BLUE JEAN SUIT #3838. $15.00. (This fashion is renamed E — Blue Jean Suit in 1988.)

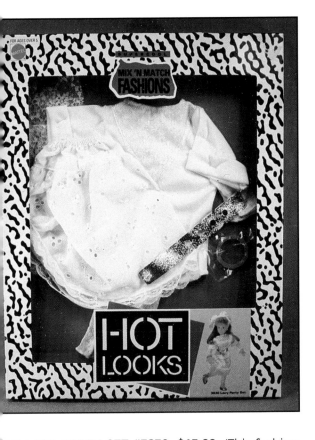

1987 LACY PARTY SET #3830. $15.00. (This fashion renamed L — Bright White Party Dress in 1988.)

1987 LEATHERY SKIRT SET #3820. $15.00.

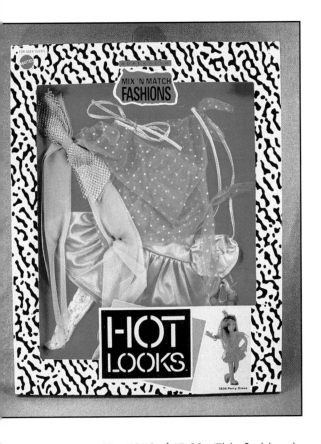

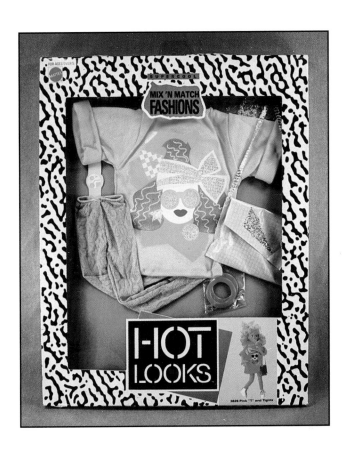

1987 PARTY DRESS #3836. $15.00. (This fashion is renamed A — Peach Party Dress in 1988.)

1987 PINK "T" AND TIGHTS. $15.00. (This fashion is renamed K — Pink "T" and Tights in 1988.)

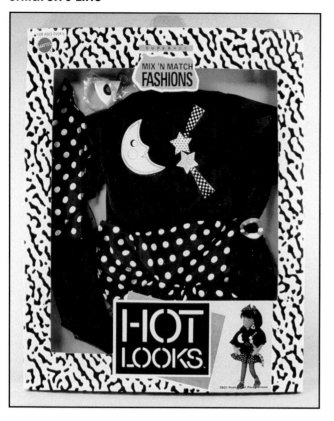

1987 POLKA DOT PARTY DRESS. $15.00. (This fashion is renamed F — Designer Dot Dress in 1988.)

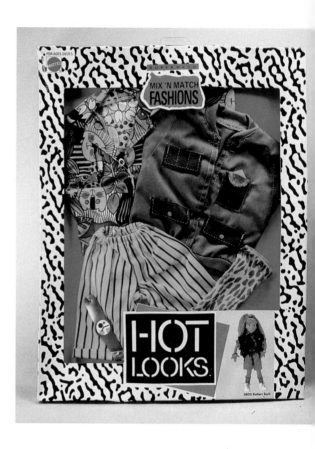

1987 SAFARI SUIT #3833. $15.00.

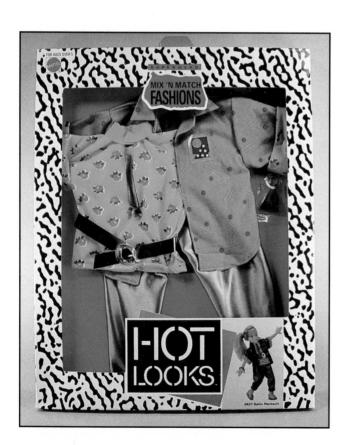

1987 SATIN PANTSUIT #3837. $15.00.

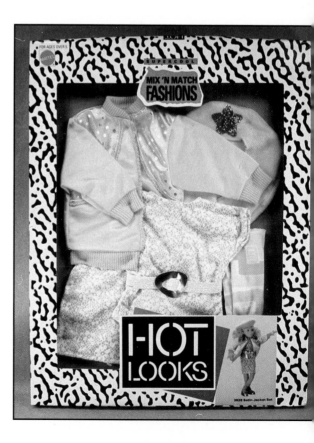

1987 SATIN JACKET SET #3828. $15.00. (This fashion is renamed O — Satin Jacket Set in 1988.)

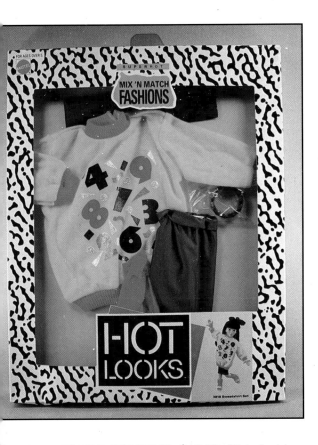

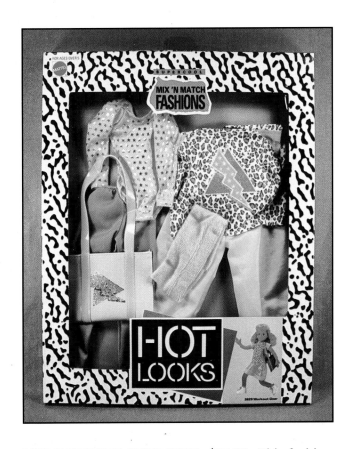

987 SWEATSHIRT SET #3818. $15.00. (This fashion renamed D — Sweatshirt Number in 1988.)

1987 WORKOUT GEAR #3829. $15.00. (This fashion is renamed H — Workout Gear in 1988.)

1987 HOT FASHIONS EVENING OUT #4021 contains everything to be a Hot Looks fashion model. $15.00.

987 HOT FASHION BEAUTY SET #4020 contains a child-size brush, comb, and hand mirror. $15.00.

1987 SUPER ACCESSORY TOTE #3874 includes two pa[ir] of shoes, two belts, two bracelets, two pairs of earring[s,] two scarves, watch, and purse. **$18.00.**

1987 HOT LOOKS JEWELRY SET #4025 contains over 60 pieces. **$15.00.**

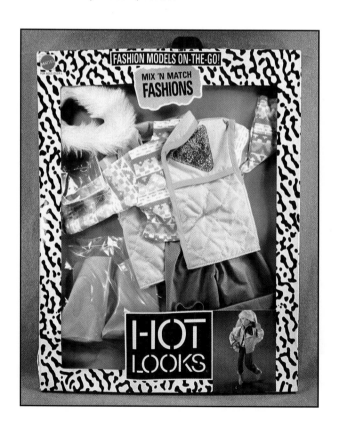

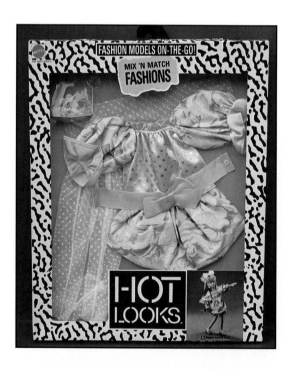

1988 B — ELEGANT EVENING OUTFIT #5754 is one of eig[ht] new Hot Looks fashions released in 1988. The new fashio[n] all have a letter designation, "A" through "P," preceding th[e] outfit name. Eight fashions from 1987 were carried over [to] 1988 — these carry-overs are renamed in the checklist o[n] the back of the outfit boxes, but the eight carry-overs we[re] not released in the new style boxes. The 1988 fashions a[re] harder to find. **$20.00.**

1988 C — SNOW FUN SET #5753. $20.00.

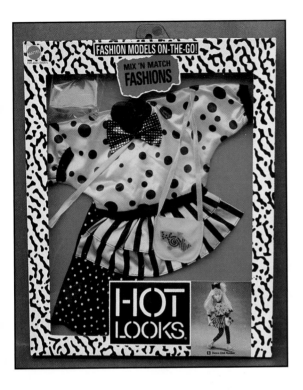

1988 G — DANCE CLUB NUMBER #5737. $20.00.

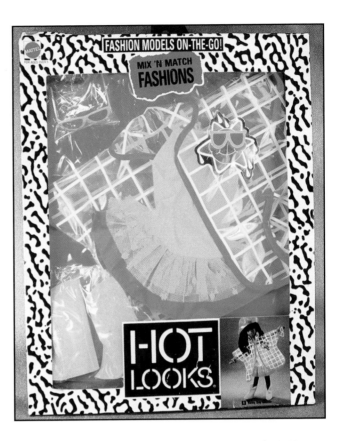

1988 I — RAINY DAY SLICKER #5751. $20.00.

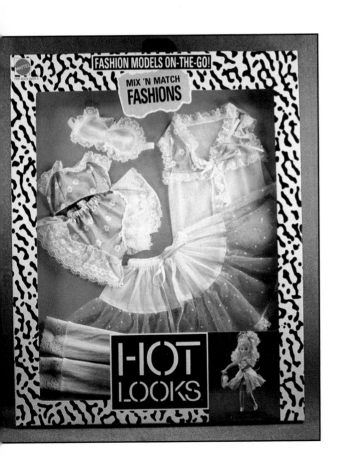

1988 J — PRETTY PETTICOAT SET #5752. $20.00.

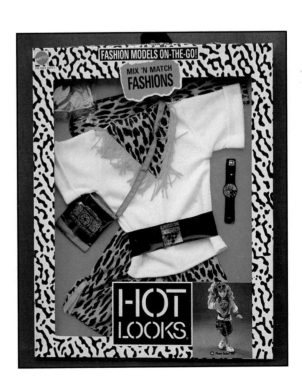

1988 M — PHOTO SAFARI SET #5761. $20.00.

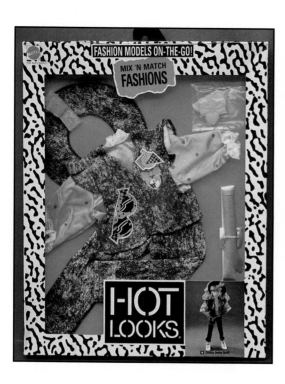

1988 N — COUNTRY DENIM SET #5763. $20.00.

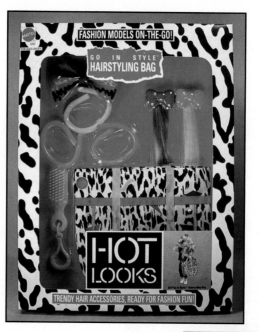

1988 GO IN STYLE HAIR STYLING BAG #57
includes a bow, two ha
piece barrettes, keycha
brush, and three ha
curlers. **$14.00.**

**1988 GO IN STYLE
ACTION PACK #5710**
includes tennis shoes,
visor, socks, headband,
and sunglasses. **$14.00.**

1988 P — CYCLING CHIC #5741. $20.00.

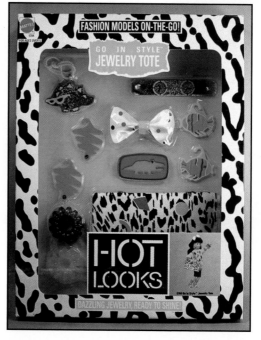

**1988 GO IN STYL
JEWELRY TOT
#5704** includes
dinosaur necklace
watch, two spira
bracelets, alligato
pin, two pairs of ea
rings, and pin-o
bow. **$14.00.**

Never Released Hot Looks Dolls

5817 SHAWNA™ Doll   5522 SACHI™ Doll

1988 SACHI #5522 is one of four Hot Looks dolls shown in the Mattel Toys 1988 catalog that never reached the market. Sachi is described in the catalog as a sweet rock 'n roller from Japan! Her flared skirt, baseball jacket and bobby sox are a fashion blast from the past! An Asian doll like Sachi would have been a wonderful addition to the Hot Looks Model Agency.

1988 SHAWNA #5517 is a lovely redhead with green eyes. The catalog describes her as, "the lovely lassie from Scotland who loves to wear just a wee bit o' lace. Shawna reflects the romance of the popular country look!"

1988 STARR #5510 revives the Starr name first used in the 1980 11½" Springfield High School fashion doll. This version of Starr is from Hollywood. The catalog states, "She's famous for fun! Starr has that sunny California look, complete with blonde hair and cool shades!"

1988 STEFF #5516 is called "the Australian wonder from down under!" She wears walking shorts with suspenders — perfect for exploring the outback.

5510 STARR™ Doll   5516 STEFF™ Doll

Lady Lovelylocks

Lady Lovelylocks is a beautiful princess who lives in the Kingdom of Lovelylocks with friends Maiden Fairhair, Maiden Curlycrown, and Prince Strongheart. The magical Pixietails, forest pets with long silky tails, have befriended Lady Lovelylocks and her friends, and are often seen in their hair. The Pixietails magically assist Lady Lovelylocks against the jealous Duchess Ravenwaves and her gnomes. The Lady Lovelylocks toy line of 1987 includes five 8½" dolls, a horse, a dog, three baby dragons, four fashions, the Pixietail Treehouse, and Castle Lovelylocks. In 1988 the Lady Lovelylocks line revolves around Enchanted Island; five new dolls, three Hide 'N Peeks, three Lilytops, a gift set, a bedroom, four new fashions, and the Sea Magic Salon are available. Only three dolls are made in 1989, the final year of production, along with six Curlykittens, two new fashions, and a mail-away Barbie doll.

Two different head molds are used with these dolls — the Lady Lovelylocks head mold, which has a small nose, small chin, and small lips, and the Duchess Ravenwaves head mold, which has a greater dip between the eyes where the nose begins, wider lips, and firmer chin.

1987 LADY LOVELYLOCKS #3057 is the beautiful princess with magical purple, orange, and yellow streaks in her blonde hair. She comes with three Pixietails to wear in her or the child's hair. Her dress is iridescent pink with satin pink bodice and sheer white sleeves. MARKINGS: Back of head: c 1986 TCFC; Back: c 1986/ THOSE/ CHARACTERS/ FROM/ CLEVELAND/ INC/ TAIWAN. **$25.00.**

1987 MAIDEN FAIRHAIR #3058 is called the gentle maiden with long flowing hair. She wears a blue gown with sheer white sleeves, and three Pixietails come with her. MARKINGS: same as Lady Lovelylocks. **$25.00.**

987 MAIDEN CURLYCROWN #3056 is the cheerful, redheaded maiden. She wears a yellow gown with white underskirt and sheer white sleeves. She has three Pixietails. MARKINGS: same as Lady Lovelylocks. **$25.00.**

1987 DUCHESS RAVENWAVES #3606 is the gorgeous jealous beauty with raven-black hair and violet eyes. Her gown is a stunning purple satin with layers of sparkly, sheer blue, pink, and purple panels. She has two mischievous Comb Gnomes to assist her. Her head mold is different from Lady Lovelylocks. Duchess Ravenwaves and Prince Strongheart were late additions to the 1987 line — the first Lady Lovelylocks booklet does not even mention them. MARKINGS: Back of head: c 1986 TCFC MIC; Back: c 1986/ THOSE/ CHARACTERS/ FROM/ CLEVELAND/ INC. **$30.00.**

1987 PRINCE STRONGHEART #3610 is the handsome brown-eyed young prince. He wears blue satin pants with gold and silver dots, a white shirt, a golden belt, and a flowing blue cape with a secret pocket in which to hide a Pixietail. He has a secret map of the kindom which is hidden in his pouch. His arms are more muscular than the girls' arms, but he does use the same chest cavity as they do, and the same head mold as Lady Lovelylocks. MARKINGS: head: same as Lady Lovelylocks; Back: c 1986/ THOSE/ CHARACTERS/ FROM/ CLEVELAND/ INC. **$25.00.**

219

3748 BOUNCYCURL Baby Dragon

1987 BOUNCYCURL BABY DRAGON #3748 is one of three baby dragons that help groom the Pixietails. Bouncycurl is blue with yellow hair. A Pixietail, comb, brush, and mirror are included with each dragon. **$14.00.**

1987 SILKYPUP DOG #3107 is Lady Lovelylocks' pink dog wit shimmery pink hair. Silkypup comes with three Pixietails, leash, and a comb. **$17.00.**

1987 SILKYMANE HORSE #3108 is the lavender female horse of Lady Lovelylocks. Silkymane comes with five Pixietails, a saddle, reins, and a comb. **$20.00.**

1987 MERRYCURL BABY DRAGON #3755 i an adorable purple dragon with pink hair **$14.00.**

3761 SWEETCURL Baby Dragon

1987 PARTY DRESS #3122 is the first of four 1986 Lady Lovely-locks Fashions, each of which comes with a Pixietail. A Lady Lovely-locks paper doll is used to model each outfit. Lady Lovelylocks Fashions are hard to find. **$16.00.**

1987 SWEETCURL BABY DRAGON 3761 is a sweet pink dragon with purple hair. **$14.00.**

1987 RIDING OUTFIT #3130. $16.00.

1987 PICNIC DRESS #3123. $16.00.

1987 SLUMBER SET #3124. $16.00.

1987 CASTLE LOVELYLOCKS #3816 opens with a child's speci[al] key to a courtyard containing a swing, slide, gazebo, perche[s] for the Pixietails, and a basket-elevator for the Pixietails to ri[de] to the guard tower. Eight Pixietails are included. **$55.00.**

1987 PIXIETAIL TREE HOUSE #3110 is a tree-house that opens down the middle to reveal the Pixietail's home, complete with a seat, vanity, and mirror for Lady Lovelylocks and a tiny table and chairs for the Pixietails. **$25.00.**

1988 ENCHANTED ISLAND LADY LOVELYLOCKS #4639 intr[o]duces the year-long Enchanted Island theme, based upon th[e] discovery of that island by Lady Lovelylocks. There she meet[s] Maiden GoldenWaves and Maiden MistyCurls, as well as thre[e] Hide 'N Peeks and three Lilytops. Enchanted Island Lady Love[ly]lylocks has a tan complexion; her short dress becomes [a] swimsuit when the iridescent skirt is removed. Three Pixietail[s] are included. **$20.00.**

1988 ENCHANTED ISLAND MAIDEN FAIRHAIR #4641 has a removable irides-cent pink skirt over her lovely pink swimsuit. She comes with two Pixietails. **$20.00.**

1988 ENCHANTED ISLAND MAIDEN CURLYCROWN #4640 has ankle-length orange hair. She wears a pleated lavender skirt over her one-piece swimsuit. She comes with two Pixietails. **$20.00.**

1988 ENCHANTED ISLAND MAIDEN MISTYCURLS #7090 is a beautiful black girl with pink streaks in her black hair who has the ability to transform into a mermaid. Her fish tail can be pulled shorter for a party dress look. She comes with two Sea Magic Pixietails. Maiden MistyCurls uses the Lady Lovelylocks head mold. **$24.00.**

1988 ENCHANTED ISLAND MAIDEN GOLDENWAVES #4642 is a beauti-ful girl with tan skin and pale yellow hair who has the ability to trans-form into a mermaid. Maiden GoldenWaves wears an iridescent fish tail that can be pulled shorter and folded into a pretty skirt. She has two Sea Magic Pixietails, which look like tiny seahorses. She uses Duchess Ravenwave's head mold. **$24.00.**

5390 PEARLYPEEK™ doll

1988 PEARLYPEEK #5390 is the shy Hide 'N Peek Enchant[ed] Island forest friend with pink hair with purple streaks. A gold[en] PixiePetal crown, comb, and one Sea Magic Pixietail is inclu[d]ed. MARKINGS: Back of head: c 1987 T. C. F. C. **$16.00.**

1988 LADY LOVELYLOCKS & SUNNYPEEK #7319 pairs the 1987 first edition Lady Lovelylocks with light skin tone with her new Enchanted Island friend Sunnypeek, the shy Hide 'N Peek who hides behind her own lilac and pink hair. Three Pixietails are included in this set. **$40.00.**

1988 PERKYPEE[K] #5389 is the s[hy] Hide 'N Peek fore[st] friend with blue a[nd] green hair. A pi[nk] PixiePetal crow[n,] comb, and one S[ea] Magic Pixietail included. **$16.00.**

1988 SUNNYPEEK #5387 is the shy Hide N Peek forest frien[d] with lilac hair containing pink streaks. A blue PixiePetal crow[n,] comb, and one Sea Magic Pixietail is included. **$16.00.**

1988 LILYSPRINKLE #4644 is a yellow water baby with curly yellow hair, purple lilypad hat, and one Sea Magic Pixietail. The faces on these water babies are adorable. **$15.00.**

1988 LILYBUBBLE #4645 is a light purple water baby with curly purple hair. The water babies have lilypad hats for use in ferrying Sea Magic Pixietails across the water. Lilybubble has a pink lilypad hat and one Sea Magic Pixietail. MARKINGS: Bottom: c 1987 T. C. F. C. CHINA. **$15.00.**

1988 LILYSPLASH #4643 is a light blue water baby with curly blue hair, yellow lilypad hat, and one Sea Magic Pixietail. **$15.00.**

1988 MASQUERADE GOWN #5152 is one of four Enchanted Island fashions. Each of these fashions comes with a Sea Magic Pixietail and PixiePetal. **$12.00.**

225

1988 PLUSH WRAP #5148. $12.00.

1988 SATINY ROBE #5154. $12.00.

1988 FAIRY TALE BEDROOM #3839 contains a bed with seash[...] headboard, two nightstands with lamps, dresser with shell mirr[...] table, and beauty accessories. **$22.00.**

1988 TEA TIME DRESS #5147. $12.00.

1988 SEA MAGIC SALON #5424 is a sea shell-shaped beauty salon for Lady Lovelylocks featuring a retractable mirror, reclining swan chair, comb, rollers, blow dryer, apron, sea shell compact case, shampoo bottle, perfume bottle, and four Sea Magic Pixietails. **$22.00.**

1989 BALLERINA MAIDEN FAIRHAIR #1740 is dressed in a pretty blue ballet costume with ballet slippers, headband, and one Pixietail. **$20.00.**

1989 SPARKLE PRETTY LADY LOVELYLOCKS #1493 introduces Shimmershine hair on Lady Lovelylocks. She is dressed in a pink ball gown and wears a sparkly crown in her blonde, Shimmershine-streaked hair. The crown can be worn in a child's hair as well. Butterfly Pixietails with Shimmershine hair are included. **$25.00.**

1989 BALLERINA LADY LOVELYLOCKS #1740 features Lady Lovelylocks wearing a lavender ballet costume, ballet slippers, headband, and one Pixietail. She is dressed for the Royal Ballet. **$20.00.**

227

Children's Line

1989 CURLYKITTENS PURPLE #2355 is one of six CurlyKittens with silky hair and tails. Each CurlyKitten is scented w[ith] fresh flowers. A butterfly Pixietail and ribbons are included with each. With the cancellation of the Lady Lovelylo[cks] line in 1989, Mattel gave these kittens a line of their own called Little Pretty in 1990, which consisted of over 24 k[it] tens and puppies using these CurlyKittens molds. The Little Pretty basic pet assortment included kittens and pupp[ies] using names from earlier doll lines. Some Little Pretty animal nam[es] include Mimi, Zizi, Flutterina, Rosebud, Ginger, Catra, Peekablue, Bo[?] Little Sweets, and Perfuma. It is fascinating to note how Mattel reus[es] names so as not to lose the trademark rights to them. The CurlyKitte[ns] are also available in orange (#2342), yellow (#2352), blue (#2340), p[ink] (#2321), and white (#231[?]). **$12.00 each.**

1989 BIRTHDAY PART[Y] DRESS #1742 is one [of] two new fashions f[or] 1989. A Pixietail is inclu[d]ed with each. End of pr[o]duction run items such [as] these two items, pr[o]duced just before a line [is] discontinued, are usua[lly] the hardest items [to] locate for collector[s]. **$22.00.**

1989 STARLIGHT BLUE BARBIE #3553 was offered as a mail-in offer in 1989 for Pixietail points and cash. Starlight Blue Barbie wears a one-piece blue party dress with lacy overskirt. The doll came in a brown catalog box with a packet of blue shoes. The same doll in a pink box, called Fashion Play Barbie, was sold in Europe. **$40.00.**

228

1989 GARDEN PARTY GOWN #174[2] **$22.00.**

Spectra

Lacy...Spacy...Out-of-this-world! — is the slogan used to describe the futuristic Spectra line. The first toy shown in the Mattel 1987 retailer catalog, Spectra clearly looked like she would be a hit — yet the Spectra line was discontinued within a year, not even making a return appearance in the 1988 catalog. Spectra and her four friends are fashion dolls from outer space, with shiny, metallic-looking poseable bodies, shimmery hair, sparkly make-up, and fanciful fashions. Along with Spark, her metallic-domed, robotic dog, Spectra and her friends travel the galaxy on their adventures. The entire Spectra line consists of 11½" Spectra, her three girl-friends, 12" boyfriend, dog, a gift set containing Spectra and Spark, a Buffatron bed, two Space Magics accessory sets, and 12 boxed fashions. A mail-away Shimmeron travel kit was available, and a Selectron toy shown in the 1987 catalog never reached the market. Why didn't the line enjoy greater success? Perhaps Spectra was just ahead of her time. In 1987, the doll's retail price was about $16.00 each, pricing them above most of the Barbie dolls out at that time, a factor which probably contributed to the line's quick demise. The vast appeal of Spectra today is known by both savvy fashion doll collectors and space toy collectors alike.

1987 SPECTRA #3344 is the outer space star and leader of the Shimmerons — teenage friends from the planet Shimmeron who have journeyed to Earth to find out why the Earth is "number one for teenage fun"; in the process, they are discovering skate-boards, hot dogs, rock music, and shopping malls. Spectra has long pink hair with shimmery iridescent strands, a sparkly, lacy white dress with matching hair bow, pink shoes, comb, and Shimmeron collector card, which reveals her favorite food is man-in-the-moon burgers, and her favorite pastime is stirring up excitement on Earth! The doll shown here does not have earrings, and her box has a top lid window. Spectra has a new head mold, marked c MATTEL, INC. 1986 on the back of her head. All of the female dolls in this line use the Young Sweetheart's Melinda's body, although their wrists and ankles do not bend because of the metallic paint finish. The girls' backs are marked c MATTEL, INC. 1975; nly Spectra's back also marks the country, MALAYSIA. **$25.00.**

229

1987 ASTRAGOLD #3356 has yello[w] hair with golden strands and a gol[d] tone body. She wears a sparkly aq[ua] blue party dress with net stockin[gs] and yellow shoes. Her Shimmeron co[l]lector card reveals that her favori[te] food is space chips 'n dip, and h[er] favorite pastime is making new Ear[th] friends! She has a new head mold d[if]ferent from Spectra's, marked c MA[T]TEL INC 1986 on the back. **$25.00.**

1987 SPECTRA #3344 is shown here with pink, five-point star earrings in a box that has no window on the top lid, and her lower left box front says, "Spectra Booklet inside!" Each doll in the Spectra line has been found with two styles of boxes — one has a clear plastic window in the top box lid, the second box style has no window in the box top. Spectra is the only doll to have earrings; the other dolls remained the same inside both styles of boxes. **$32.00.**

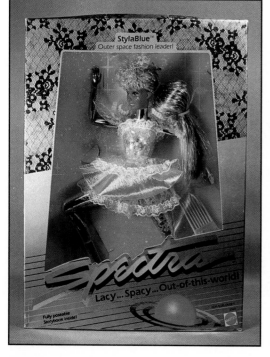

1987 STYLABLUE #3363 has blu[e] hair with shimmery strands and [a] blue metallic-look body. She wears [a] short tiered pink dress with lac[e] pink stockings, matching hair bo[w] and blue shoes. Her Shimmeron co[l]lector card reveals that her favorit[e] food is Shimmeron pie a la mod[e] and her favorite pastime is checkin[g] out the latest fashion trends o[n] Earth! She uses Spectra's hea[d] mold. StylaBlue is harder to fin[d] **$30.00.**

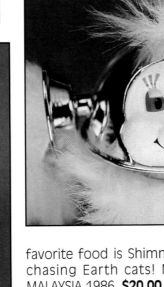

1987 TOM COMET #3374 is the cute number one sports fan and fix-it man in the galaxy. He has rooted blue hair with silver strands and a shiny blue body. He wears a metallic-look net shirt, iridescent pants, and blue shoes. His Shimmeron collector card reveals that his favorite food is Shimmeron space dogs, and his favorite pastime is meeting Earth girls! Tom Comet has a new head, marked c MATTEL, INC. 1986 on the back, and his body is the Young Sweethearts Michael's body with unbending wrists and ankles, marked c Mattel, Inc. 1975/ TAIWAN. **$35.00.**

1987 SPARK #3628 is Spectra's whimsical outer space dog. When wound up and patted on the head, Spark rolls along the floor with open eyes, which close when he stops to rest. Spark's Shimmeron collector card reveals his favorite food is Shimmeron space bits, and his favorite pastime is chasing Earth cats! MARKINGS: Back of head: c MATTEL, INC./ MALAYSIA 1986. **$20.00.**

987 ULTRAVIOLET #3353 has olet hair with shimmery rands and a shiny purple ody. She wears a yellow mpsuit with lacy overskirt, atching hair bow, and violet oes. Her Shimmeron collec- r card reveals her favorite ood is galactic granola bars, d her favorite pastime is gging through the galaxies! e uses the same head mold AstraGold. **$25.00.**

231

1987 SPECTRA & SPARK DELUXE SET #3627 pairs Spectra without earrings with Spark in one gift set box. A special Spectra & Spark Shimmeron collector card is included. **$50.00.**

1987 AT-HOME WEAR #3724 is one of 12 Space Lace Fashions from the planet Shimmeron. None of the fashions include shoes, but a Shimmeron collector card depicting the outfit is included with each. Eleven fashions are for the girls, and only one outfit is available for Tom Comet. At-Home Wear is a shimmer blue top and bloomers. **$15.00.**

1987 BALL GOWN #3616 contains a net golden-dot skirt with molded plastic snap-on bodice. **$15.00.**

1987 CASUAL PANTSUIT #3617 features blue net pants, pink net jacket and socks, and pink molded plastic snap-on bodice. **$15.00.**

987 DRESS-UP OUTFIT #3727 contains a frilly pink kirt, pink fur boa, and molded plastic snap-on odice. **$15.00.**

1987 EVENING GOWN #3729 contains a pink skirt and pink molded plastic snap-on bodice. **$15.00.**

987 EXERCISE OUTFIT #3723 contains a bright yellow bodysuit with a golden chain net shirt, leg warmers, and headband. **$15.00.**

1987 PARTY DRESS #3614 is a lace skirt with pink snap-on bodice. **$15.00.**

233

Children's Line

1987 SLEEP SET #3620 contains an iridescent lace teddy with lacy pink robe. **$15.00.**

1987 SHOPPING OUTFIT #3728 is a lacy lavende jumpsuit with iridescent top, along with an irides cent purse. **$15.00.**

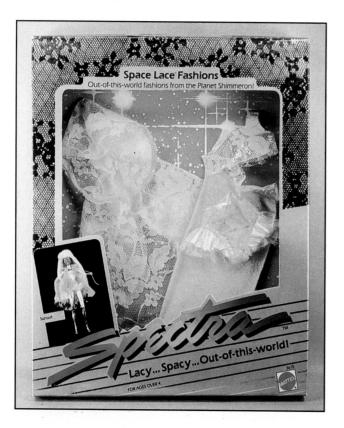

1987 SUNSUIT #3615 is a yellow sunsuit with hooded jacket and yellow towel. **$15.00.**

234

1987 TRAVEL WEAR #3619 contains an iridescen blue coat, skirt, and handbag with purple plastie snap-on bodice. **$15.00.**

1987 BUFFATRON #3626 is called Buffamatic in the catalog. The Buffatron features a pink fur bed with canopy that buffs and shines Spectra's shiny body, as she uses the built-in powder puff, mirror, and perfume sprayer. A hand mirror, cosmic comb, and Shimmeron collector card are included. **$30.00.**

987 TUXEDO #3730 is the hardest to find outfit this series. It contains an iridescent blue jacket ith white sleeves and an iridescent jumpsuit with nk bow tie. **$20.00.**

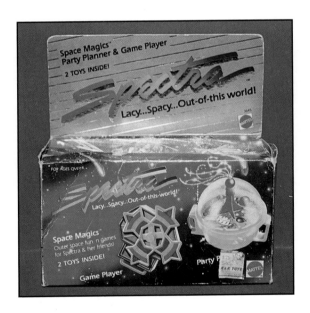

987 SPACE MAGICS BODY BUFFER & FASHION ELECTOR #3644 contains a hand-held body buffer hat really buffs when wound up, along with a wind-p fashion selector with arrow that spins atop illus-rations of Spectra's fashions, before coming to stop n a randomly-chosen outfit. The Space Magics sets re hard to find. **$20.00.**

1987 SPACE MAGICS PARTY PLANNER & GAME PLAYER #3645 features a wind-up party planner that randomly chooses activities for the party based upon where the red ball stops under the dome, along with a game player that plays several games. **$20.00.**

3861 SELECTRON Fashion Playset

1987 SELECTRON #3861 is shown in th
1987 Mattel retailer catalog, but it neve
reached the market. The Selectron
Spectra's closet where she sits in he
swiveling space chair watching fashic
colors appear on her computer scree
while her fashion tree rotates. When th
color she desires is on the screen, th
computer is stopped, and the matchin
fashion is at hand on the fashion tree.

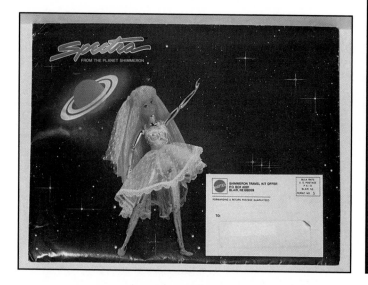

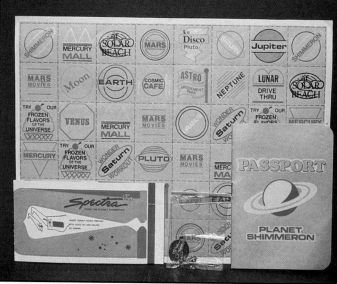

1987 SHIMMERON TRAVEL KIT was advertised on all dolls' packaging. For one
dollar, the child received a fabulous Shimmeron Travel Kit containing a map of
exciting places between Shimmeron and Earth, Shimmeron passport with a
sheet of stickers to show places visited, Spectra necklace, shimmering pink
star, child-size Spectra glasses with red lenses, and a letter from Spectra. This
travel kit is extremely rare in unused condition with mailing envelope. **$35.00.**

Jazzie

Hoping to fill the void left when Barbie doll's 'Mod'ern cousin Francie was discontinued in the mid-1970s, Mattel launched her modern-day equivalent in 1989 in the form of Jazzie. Many similarities exist between Francie and Jazzie: both are Barbie doll's cousin, both have slimmer bustlines and flat feet, both have their own lines of distinct friends and fashions, and both were incorporated into mainstream Barbie doll beach lines preceding their cancellations. Many collectors consider 1980 Starr as the model upon which Jazzie was designed; in fact, Starr's lack of ties to Barbie doll may have limited her appeal. Jazzie's premiere high school line greatly parallels Starr's line — both contain high school students sold in white boxes featuring the lead doll, her boyfriend, and two girlfriends. Mattel launched Jazzie on a grand scale — five different Jazzie dolls were offered in 1989 besides her three high school friends. But by the second year of release, Mattel began strengthening Jazzie's ties to her cousin Barbie, discontinuing her friends, adding Wears Barbie Fashions on the doll's packaging and changing from the Jazzie trademark white boxes to the more familiar Barbie doll hot pink packaging. From 1991 through 1993 Jazzie's only appearances were as part of the Barbie doll beach lines.

All female dolls in the Jazzie line use the Young Sweethearts Melinda's upper torso combined with Starr's lower body, including textured panties (minus the tiny star in the design) and legs with non-poseable flat feet. MARKINGS: Their back markings are c MATTEL, INC. 1975/ MALAYSIA. All versions of Jazzie use the 1980 Kelley head mold, marked c MATTEL INC. 1979.

1989 HIGH SCHOOL JAZZIE #3635 is the cool teen cousin of Barbie, called the coolest teenager yet in the Mattel catalog. High School Jazzie has thigh-length blonde hair and blue eyes. Each doll in this High School line features coordinating outfit pieces that can be worn in different ways for five fresh looks. Jazzie wears white bike shorts, a hot pink skirt with black and white waistband, white tee-shirt, denim-look jacket, and blue gym shoes. All of the girl dolls come with hair picks. **$30.00.**

1989 HIGH SCHOOL CHELS
#3698 is Jazzie's friend w
red hair and green eye
Chelsie wears blue cycli
shorts, blue skirt and jack
white crop top, one piece
coiled jewelry, and pink g
shoes. Chelsie uses Trac
(Starr's friend) head mo
marked c MATTEL INC. 19
$35.00.

1989 HIGH SCHOOL DUDE #3637 is Jazzie's boyfriend with dark brown hair frosted with blonde streaks and blue eyes. Dude wears denim shorts, a white and pink tee-shirt, denim jacket, and white gym shoes. Dude uses the Rocker Derek head mold and Ken doll body. He is hard to find. MARKINGS: Back of head: c MATTEL INC. 1985; Back: c Mattel, Inc. 1968/ MALAYSIA. **$35.00.**

1989 HIGH SCHOOL STACIE #3636 is Jazzie's African-American friend wearing pink cycling shorts, pink satin jacket with "HS" (for High School), white sweatshirt, blue crop top, black belt, two pieces of coiled jewelry/hair decorations, a hair pick, and white gym shoes. Stacie uses Walk Lively Steffie's head mold, marked on the inside neck rim: c MATTEL INC 1971 MALAYSIA. High School Stacie is the hardest to find doll in the Jazzie line. **$40.00.**

1989 TEEN LOOKS CHEERLEADER JAZZIE #3631 has blue eyes and crimped blonde hair. She wears a blue crop top with HS on it, lime green cycling shorts, pink skirt, yellow piece of coil jewelry, green and pink pompon, and pink gym shoes. **$25.00.**

1989 TEEN DANCE JAZZIE #3634 features blonde, curly-haired Jazzie in an outfit that transforms from hot dance dress to classy prom dress or trendy minidress. Eight different looks are possible by mixing and matching her black minidress, pink, blue, and yellow skirt ruffles, large pink bow, ruffle corsage, black pantyhose, pink shoes, and three pieces of coil jewelry. **$35.00.**

239

Children's Line

NOTE: the boxes on first-year Jazzie dolls are found with several variations. The inside box liner is usually a pink collage of photos of real high school students and items in their lives, but solid dark pink liners are also found with these dolls. The phrase Wears Barbie fashions appears in the upper left corner of some girls' boxes, and some Dude boxes have the phrase Wears Ken fashions. Jazzie doll *can not* wear all of Barbie doll's fashions — Jazzie's hips are wider, making some of Barbie doll's pants, shorts, and panties too tight for her. These box variations do not affect the values.

1989 TEEN LOOKS WORKOUT JAZZIE #3633 features Jazzie with violet eyes and blonde hair wearing a blue bodysuit, orange crop top, yellow exercise briefs, pink tennis shoes, and two pieces of coil jewelry. **$25.00.**

1989 TEEN LOOKS SWIM SUIT JAZZIE #3632 is the only brown-eyed Jazzie ever produced! She wears a two-piece pink and green swimsuit, two detachable pink sleeves, an orange sarong skirt, and two pieces of coil jewelry. **$28.00.**

1989 TEEN SCENE FASHIONS #3773 is one of 12 fashions made for Jazzie. Six deluxe fashions with shoes belong to the Teen Scene Fashions series, and six fashions without shoes comprise the Totally Cool Fashions series. In the Mattel catalog, Jazzie dolls using Starr bodies with bendable wrists and larger chests are shown modeling these 12 fashions. #3773 features a green top, black skirt with pink suspenders, black belt, and pink shoes (these are the Spectra shoes). **$15.00.**

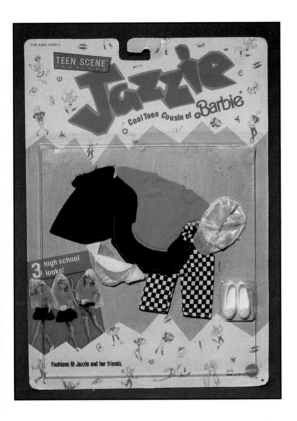

1989 TEEN SCENE FASHIONS #3774 contains a pink top, black skirt, black and white checked pants, iridescent white cap and belt, and white Spectra shoes. **$15.00.**

1989 TEEN SCENE FASHIONS #3775 features a white top with black dots on the sleeves and apron, black and white striped shorts, pink skirt, white cap, white belt, and white Spectra shoes. **$15.00.**

1989 TEEN SCENE FASHIONS #3776 is a black and white striped top with pink bow, pink skirt with black waist, black belt, pink shorts, and white Spectra shoes. **$15.00.**

1989 TEEN SCENE FASHIONS #3778 contains pink shorts (although the catalog photo shows blue), pink jacket with blue sleeves, white tee-shirt, black belt, and pink Spectra shoes. **$15.00.**

1989 TEEN SCENE FASHIONS #3777 features blu shorts, denim-look skirt with green suspenders, blu green, and denim shirt, white iridescent belt, ar blue Spectra shoes. **$15.00.**

1989 TOTALLY COOL FASHIONS #3781 contains a blue skirt, green waist band/halter top, and shirt. **$12.00.**

1989 TOTALLY COOL FASHIONS #3780 is the first of s Totally Cool Fashions which each contain three fashic pieces. None of these have shoes. #3780 has whit shorts with black dots, a blue waist band/halter top, an a red and white striped shirt. **$12.00.**

1989 TOTALLY COOL FASHIONS #3783 contains a black skirt, pink top, and zebra-print yellow and black pink top. **$12.00.**

1989 TOTALLY COOL FASHIONS #3784 features black and white striped shorts with black suspenders, yellow top, and a pink shirt. **$12.00.**

1989 TOTALLY COOL FASHIONS #3785 contains a denim-look skirt, yellow belt/top, and cartoon print shirt. **$12.00.**

1989 TOTALLY COOL FASHIONS #3786 features confetti-sprinkled white cycling pants, matching top, and green belt/top. **$12.00.**

1989 JAZZIE BURGER KING #4209 is called the "cool hango for Barbie, Jazzie, and their friends!" The Jazzie Burger King a redecorated version of 1983 Barbie Loves McDonald's. Th restaurant has a menu board, counter with built-in trash b hamburger cooking center, table with bench seats, fenc soda fountain, two cash registers, four trays, spatula, fo cups, four bags of french fries, four hamburger patties wi buns, and four Burger King sandwich boxes. This is very ha to find. **$85.00.**

1989 JAZZIE VOLKSWAGE CABRIOLET #3804 is Jazzie white car with pink and blu stripes and white interio This is the same make of c as used with The Heart Fam ly. The license plate read Jazzie, and bumper sticke include, "I LOVE SHOPPIN and "I LOVE COOL DUDES **$45.00.**

1990 RECORD SHOP #4030 is one of three stores comprising the Barbie Galleria shown in the Mattel 1990 catalog. Jazzie's name appears on the signs and floors of all three stores, which also include the Fashion Wraps Boutique #4024 and Sports Shop #4028. She is illustrated modeling one of the fashions in the Fashion Wraps Boutique. Teen Scene Jazzie is featured on an album cover in the Record Shop. Most interesting about the catalog photo of the galleria is the photo of an unreleased Jazzie wearing a fashion that would be sold on a Toys 'R' Us exclusive doll called Cool Looks Barbie.

1990 SUN LOVIN' JAZZIE #4088 is sold in a hot pink box. She wears a two-piece yellow and purple bikini under her pink tank top and white shorts. Her hair reveals purple streaks, and her shirt decal changes color, when they are placed in sunlight. A visor, pink tennis shoes, flying disc, hairbrush, and child-size color-changing press on fingernails are included. **$25.00.**

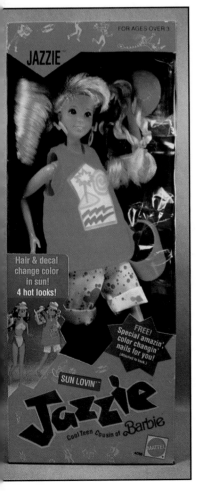

1990 COOL LOOKS BARBIE #5947 is shown here wearing the same fashion shown on Jazzie in the Barbie Galleria. Even the earrings are the same as Jazzie's. The outfit looks like something a teenager would wear, so perhaps original plans were for Cool Looks Jazzie. **$25.00.**

1991 HAWAIIAN FUN JAZZIE #9294 absorbed into the annual Barbie d swimsuit line with this doll. Hawaii Fun Jazzie wears a two-piece swimsu and she comes with a blue hula ski bracelet with watermelon scent, ar sunglasses. Notice the unusual "Z" ey paint design. **$20.00.**

1991 TEEN SCENE JAZZIE #5507 wears a coral mini dress, black pants with gold braid trim, black jacket with golden design, gold-speckled black tulle skirt, black top, black bowler hat, black Spectra shoes, three bracelets, and earrings. Teen Scene Jazzie is meant to reflect the life of a mega star. **$30.00.**

1991 TEEN SCENE JAZZIE #5507 shown here in a variant box. This sty box is very hard to find. **$40.00.**

1992 SUN SENSATION JAZZIE #5473 wears a gorgeous blue lamé swimsuit with steering wheel necklace and golden star-shaped earrings. She has silky sun-streaked blonde hair with golden bands in her hair, and she comes with a hairbrush. Jazzie is not pictured in the group photo of the Sun Sensation dolls shown on the back of the dolls' boxes (including her own), so her inclusion in this series may be a last-minute addition. **$25.00.**

1993 GLITTER BEACH JAZZIE #4935 wears a two-piece glittery swimsuit with headband, a blue and pink jewel necklace, and silvery earrings. A hairbrush is included. This is the last Jazzie doll produced. **$15.00.**

1991 I'M INTO...BARBIE #0548-3 is a store display sign that is attached to the shelves below the dolls. This sign is significant because it shows Teen Looks Workout Jazzie (second from left) among the Barbie family dolls — Christie, Kira, Skipper, Ken, and Barbie. **$25.00.**

247

Fashion Friends

K-Mart Stores sold three exclusive Mattel fashion dolls in 1991 called Fashion Friends. The dolls have no names, except for the designations Party Dress, Pretty Teen, and Swimsuit. The Party Dress and Swimsuit dolls greatly resemble Barbie dolls; in fact, they use Barbie doll bodies with a newly designed head mold. Pretty Teen resembles a Skipper doll; and she uses Skipper doll's body. While not officially members of Barbie doll's family, the ties to Barbie are increased since the adult dolls' boxes say, "Wears all Barbie Fashions," and the young teen girl's box says, "Wears all Skipper Fashions." Twelve additional carded fashions were available.

1991 FASHION FRIENDS PARTY DRES
#7026 contains an 11½" blonde do
with blue eyes wearing a one-piece pir
dress with sparkly top. A brush and pir
pumps are included. MARKINGS: Back o
head: c MATTEL INC 1990; Back: c MAT
TEL, INC. 1966/ CHINA. **$20.00.**

1991 FASHION FRIENDS PRETTY TEEN
#7010 is a 10" young teen girl with
blonde hair and big blue eyes. She
wears a tee-shirt, blue skirt/yellow bike
pants, and white gym shoes. A yellow
brush is included. MARKINGS: Back of
head: c MATTEL INC 1990; Back: c MAT-
TEL INC 1987/ CHINA. **$20.00.**

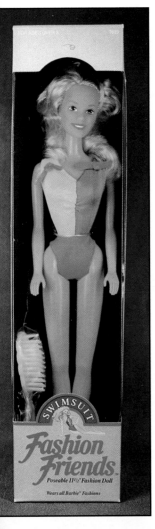

1991 FASHION FRIENDS SWIMSUIT #7019 features an 11½" blonde doll with blue eyes. She wears a yellow, blue, and pink swimsuit, and she comes with a yellow brush. She uses the same head as Fashion Friends Party Dress. MARKINGS: same as Fashion Friends Party Dress. **$20.00.**

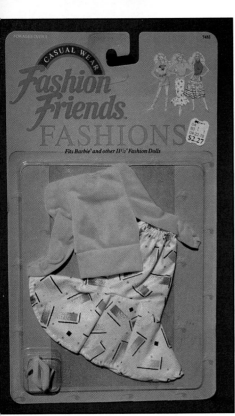

1991 CASUAL WEAR #7480 is the first of seven Casual Wear fashions with shoes. This fashion has a blue skirt, white blouse, and blue pumps. These fashions originally cost only $2.27. **$10.00.**

1991 CASUAL WEAR #7482 contains a pink shirt, white shorts with red floral print, red belt, and red shoes. **$10.00.**

1991 CASUAL WEAR #7483 has a lavender skirt, pink jacket, floral print blouse, and shoes. **$10.00.**

1991 CASUAL WEAR #7481 is a yellow blouse with white skirt and yellow pumps. **$10.00.**

249

1991 CASUAL WEAR #7484 has white pants, a pastel blouse, and white pumps. **$10.00.**

1991 CASUAL WEAR #7485 contains a lavender top, skirt, and pink shoes. **$10.00.**

1991 CASUAL WEAR #7486 has a yellow sweatshirt, blue skirt, yellow leggings, and yellow gym shoes. **$10.00.**

1991 DRESS COLLECTION #7488 is the first of five Dress Collection fashions with shoes. These fashions are a little better quality, and a real bargain in 1991 at only $2.97. **#7488** contains an aqua skirt with white palm-tree print, matching top and cap, and yellow pumps. **$14.00.**

1991 DRESS COLLECTION #7490 is a white jacket with pink floral design, matching skirt, top, and pink pumps. **$14.00.**

1991 DRESS COLLECTION #7489 has a multicolored halter top, matching skirt with red flounce, carry bag, and pumps. **$14.00.**

1991 DRESS COLLECTION #7492 has a blue skirt, red shirt, white cap, white scarf, and white pumps. **$14.00.**

1991 DRESS COLLECTION #7491 features a long red shirt, red and white striped bathing suit, white pants, and red tennis shoes. **$14.00.**

251

Shani

"Shani means marvelous in the Swahili language...and marvelous she is!" the back of Shani's box says; "With her friends Asha and Nichelle, Shani brings to life the special style and beauty of the African American woman. Each one is beautiful in her own way, with her own lovely skin shade and unique facial features. Each has a different hair color and texture, perfect for braiding, twisting, and creating fabulous hair styles! Their clothes, too, reflect the vivid colors and ethnic accents that showcase their exotic looks and fashion flair!" In initial planning stages, Shani was called Mahogany, Asha was called Cinnamon, and Nichelle was called Cocoa. Early press photos of Mahogany, Cinnamon, and Cocoa show dolls with jointed wrists and divided fingers.

By the time the dolls were released, the names changed and the arms were simplified, yet they are still among the most preferred arm molds used on a Barbie-size doll. In 1991 the three dolls and four fashions were available. In 1992 Shani's boyfriend Jamal joined the line; other new items were the girls sold in beach fashions, three additional fashions, a Sears exclusive set, and Shani's Corvette. In 1993 the girls got new body molds; four beach dolls and four Soul Train dolls were available. Shani was last produced in 1994, as she briefly joined the Barbie doll line.

1991 SHANI #1750 wears a purpl and pink gown that transforms int a bathing suit with cover-up. Sh has a new style of golden earring that quickly became a favorite c collectors. She has newly designe arms, known as Shani arms, tha gracefully poise down and to th side. Mattel lists Shani and he friends in their official list of Barb doll's friends. MARKINGS: Back c head: c 1990 MATTEL INC.; Back: MATTEL INC. 1966/ MALAYSIA **$35.00.**

1991 ASHA #1752 is a favorite with collectors. Her fabulous coral and golden lamé gown becomes a mini dress and jacket. MARKINGS: Back of head: c 1990 MATTEL INC.; Back: same as Shani. **$55.00.**

1991 NICHELLE #1751 wears a beautiful dark pink gown with yellow bodice that transforms into a ballerina costume. MARKINGS: Back of head: c 1990 MATTEL INC.; Back: same as Shani. **$35.00.**

991 SHANI FASHIONS #1872 is the first of four ashions from 1991. Each outfit contains two different looks. **#1872** is a leathery white skirt with natching jacket, gold lamé top, and white pumps. he panels on the jacket's lapels use the same fabic as Asha's bodice. **$16.00.**

1991 SHANI FASHIONS #1884 contains a yellow suit dress, long pleated skirt, brown suede suitcase, and yellow pumps. **$16.00.**

1991 SHANI FASHIONS #1896 features a green jacket with golden braid fringe, yellow minidress made from Nichelle's bodice material, and blue pumps. **$16.00.**

1991 SHANI FASHIONS #1969 contains a pink bodysuit, full multicolored skirt, and pink pumps. **$16.00.**

1992 BEACH DAZZLE SHANI #5774 wears a two-piece swimsuit made from the material in Asha's 1991 gown's bodice. Shani traded Asha swimsuit material since the 1991 Shani already wears a swimsuit under her gown. A hair tie and hair pick are included. **$20.00.**

1992 BEACH DAZZLE ASHA #5777 wears a two-piece swimsuit made from the material in Shani's 1991 gown's bodice. A hair tie and hair pick are included. **$25.00.**

1992 BEACH DAZZLE NICHELLE

#5775 wears a two-piece swimsuit made from her 1991 gown's bodice material. A hair tie and hair pick are included. **$20.00.**

1992 JAMAL #7795 wears a yellow party tux, which becomes a casual suit when the white shirt, gold lamé bow tie with collar, and gold lamé cummerbund are replaced with a colorful shirt. He also has a solid tan tie (instead of paisley as shown on the box back) and a long gold lamé tie, both attached to collars. He has a painted moustache and debuts a new head mold. MARK-INGS: Back of head: c 1991 MATTEL INC.; Back: c Mattel Inc. 1968/ MALAYSIA. **$35.00.**

SHANI #0835 wears a 3-in-one gown that transforms from formal evening gown to luncheon fashion to party minidress. This doll was shown in the Mattel 1992 Girls Toys catalog but was never released.

1992 SIZZLING STYLE FASHIONS #5968 ontains a black gown with gold lamé coat ith tassles and black shoes. **$18.00.**

1992 SIZZLING STYLE FASHIONS #5967 features a golden coat with belt along with a shiny scarf and black pumps. The Sizzling Style Fashions are much harder to find than the 1991 Shani Fashions. **$18.00.**

1992 SIZZLING STYLE FASHIONS #5969 contains orange pants, an orange/gold/black lamé skirt, matching jacket, and black gym shoes. **$18.00.**

1993 BEACH STREAK ASHA #3457 features Asha wearing a one-piece swimsuit with pink lamé bottom and pink and black top. This Asha is a favorite with collectors because of her silky hair with highlights and new body. **$22.00.**

1993 BEACH STREAK SHA **#3428** features Shani wearing one-piece gold lamé with bla swimsuit. The Beach Streak girls have silky hair with beautif streaks of color highlights, and new body mold with smaller hi and a slimmer waist that twists an angle. MARKINGS: Back: c 19 MATTEL, INC/ MALAYSIA. **$18.00.**

1992 SHANI CORVETTE #7981 Shani's metallic-looking goldtor Corvette with moving wheels. This one of the most beautiful cars ev made for 11½" fashion dolls. This hard to find. **$50.00.**

1993 SOUL TRAIN SHANI #10289 features Shani and friends wearing ethnic-print hip hop fashions for their dancing debut on the Soul Train television show. In the photo on the box back, Soul Train Shani wears thigh-high golden net stockings, but she comes wearing orange ankle socks with short golden net tops. The 1993 Mattel Girls Toys catalog states that each Soul Train doll comes with glitter hair lotion, but Mattel packaged stick-on star-shaped jewels with these dolls instead. All four dolls wear the same basic Kente-cloth caps with golden bands. **$20.00.**

1993 BEACH STREAK NICHELLE #3456 wears a one-piece blue and black lamé swimsuit. **$18.00.**

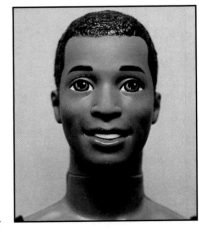

1992 SHANI BEACH DAZZLE PLUS 2 FASHIONS #5882 is a Sears exclusive set which packages Beach Dazzle Shani with two of her Sizzling Style Fashions: **#5968** (black gown with gold lamé coat) and **#5969** (orange pants with orange and black jacket and skirt) in a white catalog mailer box. The outfits inside the box are in plastic bags. This is hard to find. **$50.00.**

1993 BEACH STREAK JAMAL #3802 has shaved his moustache and come to the beach wearing a black body tank suit and sandals. He now uses the straight-arm Ken doll body. MARKINGS: Back: c MATTEL INC/ 1968/ MALAYSIA. **$18.00.**

1993 SOUL TRAIN NICHELLE #102
is shown on the box wearing
bustier with long yellow fingerle
gloves. The doll released wears
long-sleeve Kente-print shi
$20.00.

1993 SOUL TRAIN ASHA #10291 is
shown on the back of her box
wearing a sleeveless bodice with
long, pink fingerless gloves and
thigh-high black boots; the doll
actually produced wears a long-
sleeve one-piece jumper with
short black ankle boots over red
socks with short golden net tops.
$25.00.

1994 JEWEL & GLITTER SHANI #11215
is an international market exclusive
featuring Shani wearing an orange
skirt and jacket that reverse to yellow,
her outfit also includes a gold lamé
top and orange pumps. The extra
play feature with Jewel & Glitter Shani
is decorating both sides of the
reversible fashion, shoes, and even
Shani's body with Tulip ColorPoint
fabric paint and sequins. In the U.S.,
the fashion, paint, and sequins only
were sold as a boxed Jewel & Glitter
Barbie fashion; that fashion's packaging showed Shani modeling the fashion! **$28.00.**

1993 SOUL TRAIN JAMAL #1028
wears leathery blue shorts, lor
matching jacket with Kente-pri
sleeves to match his cap, yello
tank top, and leathery black boo
with golden laces. He uses th
bent-arm Ken doll body. **$20.00.**

258

1994 SUN JEWEL SHANI #10958 is Shani's lone appearance in the same series as Barbie doll in the U.S. She has blue-green eyes and wears a neon orange two-piece swimsuit top covered with clear diamonds, although the photo on the box back shows her with green diamonds and earrings. Green stick-on jewels in the shapes of diamonds, hearts, stars, and triangles are included. **$12.00.**

1994 SUN JEWEL SHANI #10958 was available later in the year with green, turquoise, yellow, and pink stick-on jewels. This is the more commonly found version. This is the last Shani produced. **$10.00.**

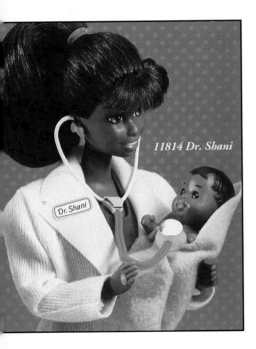

11814 Dr. Shani

994 DR. SHANI #11814 was featured in he Mattel Girls Toys 94 catalog. She is hown wearing a white doctor's coat with r. Shani name tag and stethoscope, as he checks a baby's heartbeat. Dr. Shani vas not released; instead, a black Dr. Bar-ie took her place. Black Dr. Barbie uses he 1988 Christie head mold, although Dr. hani as shown in the catalog has the hani head mold.

1994 ASHA #12676 is the first in Toys 'R' Us' African American Col-lection. Her box states, "Asha means life in Swahili. She looks as vibrant as life itself, wearing her jacket and skirt in a vivid fabric that replicates the brilliant kente cloth of West Africa...the fabric of African royalty....Asha wears her 'kente cloth' to symbolize her pride in her African American heritage and culture." Surprisingly, this Asha uses Shani's head mold, skin tone, and hair texture. The earli-est boxes on the market do not have the new warning box on the lower left front of the box. **$35.00.**

259

1995 ASHA #13532 is the second edition in the African-American Collection. She wears an orange flared skirt with purple dots, golden sheen wrap, and kente-cloth borders and head wrap. She has golden hoop earrings. **$28.00.**

1996 ASHA #12045 is the third edition in the Africa American Collection. She wears a shimmery one-pie gown that flares at the bottom, a matching hea band, and an oversized bow at her waist. **$30.00.**

Shani's Legacy

Shani introduced a great number of collectors to the beau ty and uniqueness of the African-American culture. It is amazir that even today Mattel simply uses Caucasian head molds fro Kelly, Stacie, Tommy, and Skipper to make black versions them or their friends; this practice began in 1966 with blac Francie and continued with 1980 Black Barbie. But the Shani lir has shown that black vinyl alone does not make a truly repre sentative African-American doll, and Mattel has responded t using the Shani, Asha, Nichelle, and Jamal head molds on increasing number of African-American dolls. Listed are the Ba bie family dolls with head molds borrowed from the Sha series of dolls, along with some representative photos.

1996 SPARKLE BEACH CHRISTIE #14355 (Shani's head). **$10.0(**

1997 HULA HAIR BARBIE African American #17031 (Asha's head). **$15.00.**

1997 IN THE LIMELIGHT BARBIE #17031 (Nichelle's head). **$85.00.**

1997 BIG BROTHER KEN African-American #17588 (Jamal's head). **$14.00.**

Not shown:

1994 KENYAN BARBIE #11181 (Nichelle's head). **$25.00.**

1996 GHANIAN BARBIE #15303 (Shani's head). **$22.00.**

1996 SHOPPING CHIC BARBIE African-American #15801 (Asha's head). **$85.00.**

1996 STARLIGHT DANCE BARBIE African-American #15819 (Nichelle's head). **$62.00.**

1997 ROMANTIC INTERLUDE BARBIE African-American #17137 (Nichelle's head). **$65.00.**

1997 RUBY RADIANCE BARBIE #15520 (Nichelle's head). **$95.00.**

1997 SPLASH 'N COLOR STEVEN #16175 (Jamal's head). **$8.00.**

Singapore Girl

Exclusively offered by Singapore Airlines, Singapore Girl is dressed in the outfit of a Singapore Airlines stewardess. Two versions of Singapore Girl are available; the first version from 1992 is packaged in a brown box. The 1994 release, which is more common, is in a hot pink box. The back of their boxes have the "Genuine Barbie" logo, and Mattel Canada released a POG milkcap with her picture and the name Barbie, so she should be considered a Barbie doll.

Mattel Canada's **SINGAPORE GIR**
POG milkcap

1992 SINGAPORE GIRL (no stock number) wears a navy blue print blouse and matching sarong, panties, and sandals. She comes with a brush and doll stand. Singapore Girl uses the Oriental Barbie head mold with short, curly black hair and dull makeup with light pink lipstick. This first issue is hard to find. **$120.00.**

1994 SINGAPORE GIRL (no stock number) was reissued in a hot pink box. The dress is basically the same, but this second Singapore Girl has vivid makeup and red lips. This version was widely available. **$50.00.**

Peppermint Rose

The land of Peppermint Rose is where adorable animals help beautiful dolls make floral and candy perfumes. 10" Peppermint Rose and her three girlfriends are the human characters in this line, helped by three Candy Blossoms plush friends and three Sweet Spray animals/atomizers.

MARKINGS: All of the Peppermint Rose series dolls use the Lady Lovelylocks' head mold with Skipper doll's body. Back of head: c 1986 TCFC, Back: c MATTEL INC 1987/MALAYSIA.

1993 PEPPERMINT ROSE #0791 wears a white satin skirt with rose floral design and matching sleeves, pink bodice with attached cloth rose, peppermint-striped overskirt, white bloomers, pink earrings, pink flat shoes, and a large pink hat with a rose on the brim. Two bottles containing scented perfume concentrate and a rose floral bottle cap are included. When water is added to the bottles, peppermint and rose scented perfume are created. **$20.00.**

1993 LEMON KISS LILY #0792 is Peppermint Rose's strawberblonde friend with violet eyes. She wears a white satin skirt decorated with lilies, pink bodice with sheer white sleeves and a lilac at the waist, sheer white overskirt with yellow dots, lilac bloomers, yellow earrings, lilac colored flat shoes, and a lilac hat with a lily on the brim. Her two perfume bottles make Lemon Kiss and lily perfumes. **$20.00.**

263

1993 MERRY MINT VIOLET #0794 is Peppermint Rose's black friend with violet eyes. She wears a mint satin dress with short white satin overskirt decorated with violets, violet bodysuit with matching sleeves and a violet at the waist, white bloomers, mint earrings, mint flat shoes, and a straw-color hat with a violet on the brim. Her two perfume bottles produce Merry Mint and violet perfumes. **$20.00.**

1993 VANILLA DAISY #0793 is Peppermint Rose's redheaded, brown-eyed friend, wearing a white satin skirt with hearts design, lacy short overskirt with a daisy at the waist, white bodysuit with lacy collar, white-dotted sheer bloomers, pink heart design necklace and earrings, white flat shoes, and a white hat with a daisy on the brim. Her two perfume bottles make vanilla or daisy perfumes. **$20.00.**

1993 BUBBLEGUM DAISY #1222 is one of three Sweet Spray Atomizers, adorable animal friends with two perfume bottles to make candy and flower perfumes. Bubblegum Daisy is white with daisy-print ears. The enclosed perfume bottles make bubblegum and daisy perfumes. **$12.00.**

1993 LEMON KISS BLOSSOM #1221 is a purple animal atomizer with perfume bottles that make Lemon Kiss and lily perfumes. **$12.00.**

1993 PEPPERMINT POSY #1220 is a pink animal atomizer with posies covering its ears. Peppermint Posy has two perfume bottles to make peppermint and posy perfumes. **$12.00.**

1993 COCONUT CARNATION #1226 is the plush white animal who hides behind its ears until hugged; then he blossoms with coconut and carnation perfumes. **$18.00.**

1993 BUBBLEGUM VIOLET #1225 is the first of three large, soft plush animals with floral undersides of their ears, feet, and tummy. When they are hugged, the perfume flower on their heads blooms. Inside the flowers are two solid perfumes — one with a floral scent and the other with a candy scent. Purple Bubblegum Violet holds bubblegum and violet perfumes in the flower on its head. **$18.00.**

1993 LOLLIPOP POSY #1224 is the pink plush animal with posy and lollipop perfumes. **$18.00.**

Erte

On the 100th anniversary of Erte's art and the debut of the Broadway show *Stardust*, which features 45 of Erte's costume designs, Mattel created 13½" fine bisque porcelain dolls from two of Erte's original designs. Erte, credited with creating the Art Deco movement, designed *Harper's Bazaar* magazine covers for 22 years. Mattel's Erte dolls, with their glamour and sophistication, are among the most beautifully dressed fashion dolls. The only complaint collectors might have about the Erte dolls is that they are not poseable — their heads, arms, and legs are not jointed, making them more like fine statues.

1994 STARDUST by Erte features Mattel interpretation of the lead costume from the *Stardust* Broadway musical, worn on 13½" fine bisque porcelain doll attached to an epoxy base. She wears a slim floor length black gown covered with thousands of hand-stitched beads, sequins and golden accents; her flowing white wrap is adorned with golden stars in front and back. Her brown hair is worn in chignon beneath a golden headpiece of nine shooting stars. **$450.00.**

1996 STARDUST Second Edition by Erte features the doll in a gorgeous floor-length black velvet gown adorned with rhinestones both in the front and on her flowing train. She has a matching beaded cloak from which tassles of shimmering beads dangle, and a dazzling fan headpiece sits atop her brown hair. She is affixed to an epoxy base. **$525.00.**

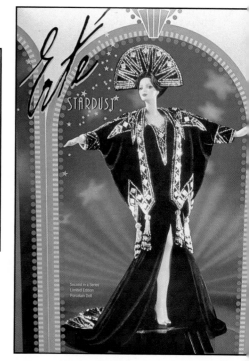

Family Corners

Family Corners is a clever series which allows children to make their own doll families by pairing one of the five females with one of the five males. The instruction sheet asks, "Who will marry whom? You decide! There is no right or wrong choice — any combination makes a family!" This is a very 1990s concept since the dolls encompass Caucasian, Hispanic, African-American, and Asian-American races, allowing a child with parents of two races to pair the dolls accordingly. Each girl in the series comes with a casual outfit, a doll house with four room scenes, and a wedding gown with veil. Each boy has a casual outfit, baby, chapel, nursery room scenes to add onto the bride's house, tuxedo, and stickers. The rhyme on the box explains the Family

Corners concept best: "Match a pretty girl with a handsome guy. It's true love, now don't be shy. Dress them in a tux and a wedding gown...They're the happiest couple in town! Next a chapel wedding for the bride and groom, then send them off on their honeymoon. Now move them into their family home...Add special stickers to make it their own! The time has

come for a sweet surprise...A dear little baby with love in her eyes! This bundle of joy needs a nursery...Add it to your 'house' quick as 1, 2, 3! How great to be part of a family, where we all live together so happily!"

MARKINGS: The girls are 6½" tall with molded-on shoes. Even though they each have a new, different head mold, Becky, Nichelle, and Trista have the same markings on the backs of their heads: c 1994 M. I. Lacey and Melody use the same head mold, marked on back c 1994 MI. All girls' backs are marked only CHINA.

The boys are 6¾" tall with molded-on shoes. Nicholas has no head markings, since his hair is too long. Joey and Ryan have the same head mold, marked c 1994 M.I. Derek and Kurt have different head molds, but the same markings c 1994 M.I. All boys are marked only CHINA on their backs.

All babies are 2" tall and use the same head mold marked c 1994 M.I.; their bodies are marked CHINA.

1995 BECKY #12652 is a blonde girl with blue eyes. Her story says "Hi, I'm Becky. Visit my house and meet my adorable puppies. I'll cook you some yummy food. I hope the man I marry loves to eat!" **$12.00.**

1995 LACEY #12653 is a Hispanic girl with brown hair and brown eyes. Her story says, "I'm an artist. I paint pictures for the books Trista writes. We're a great team! The man of my dream is smart but fun too!" **$12.00.**

267

1995 MELODY #12654 is a redhead with green eyes. Her story says, "I like a little glamour in my life. And sculpting! I'm sculpting a statue of my dog. I'll only marry someone my dog likes too!" **$12.00.**

1995 NICHELLE #12655 is an African-American with crimped black hair and brown eyes. Her story says, "Nichelle is my name, sewing's my game! I design all my clothes, plus cute outfits for my pets. I'll sew for my husband too — when I meet him!" **$12.00.**

1995 TRISTA #12656 an Asian-America with black hair an brown eyes. Her stor says, "I love cats an computers. I need husband who love pets and wants lot of them! I write sto ries for children o my computer." **$12.0**

1995 DEREK #12662 is an Asian-American with black hair and brown eyes. His story says, "I need a wife who loves kids — and dancing. I'm a pretty good dancer myself, but in the daytime, you'll find me at the beach!" Derek's baby has brown eyes, black hair worn in two pigtails, and a blue dress. Derek is the only Family Corner doll who is hard to find. **$18.00.**

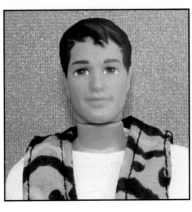

995 **JOEY #12659** is a ispanic with brown air and brown eyes. s story says, "I like orts cars and cycling d a good game of ess. I'm looking for a fe who likes romantic ndlelight dinners for o." Joey's baby has own hair and brown es and wears a blue aysuit. **$12.00.**

1995 KURT #12661 is an African-American with short black hair and brown eyes. His story relates, "I like hot jazz and cool cloth-es...and beach volley-ball with my buddies, Derek and Ryan. I want a wife and a family too." Kurt's baby has black hair worn in pig-tails and brown eyes; it wears a two-piece white play-suit. **$12.00.**

269

1995 NICHOLAS #12658
has blonde hair and blue eyes. His story says, "I'm Nicholas but my nickname is Nick. Get it? Nick-name. My wife will need a good sense of humor. I like surfing and playing guitar." Nick's baby has blonde hair and blue eyes and a white and pink dress. **$12.00.**

1995 RYAN #12660
has brown hair and blue eyes. His story reveals, "Running's my favorite sport. Basketball, tennis, even ping pong — any game will do. I'm looking for a wife who likes sports too." His baby has reddish brown hair and blue eyes and wears a white playsuit. **$12.00.**

Tenko and the Guardians of the Magic

Based on the children's television series, **Tenko and the Guardians of the Magic** features the great magician Tenko, who "travels the world performing her amazing shows of magic, illusions, and daring feats." With her are her faithful friends, the Guardians of the Magic, who assist with her performances and in her ultimate goal...finding and protecting the Magic Starfire Gems. Mattel's 6½" doll line includes three versions of Princess Tenko in different, themed outfits, companions Ali and Shonti, nemesis Jana, and two animals — a leopard and a horse. In 1997 the six dolls were re-released in a few areas with two bonus gems in a keep-sake bag. Mattel made prototypes of 11½" dolls, including mock packaging, but these were never released on the market.

MARKINGS: The Princess Tenko dolls have new head molds, marked c 95 SABAN. Ali uses the Family Corners Becky head mold, marked c 1994 M.I. Jana uses the Family Corners Lacey head mold, marked c 1994 MI. Shonti uses the Family Corners Nichelle head mold, marked c 1994 M.I. All girls have only CHINA on their backs.

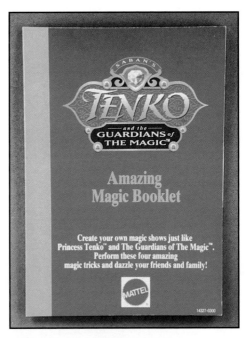

1996 PRINCESS TENKO GOLDEN LION FASHION #14323 features black haired, brown-eyed Tenko with gold eyeshadow wearing a yellow catsuit and Golden Lion fashion with pink plastic chest plate. When her headdress is on and her gem is attached to the chest plate, her lion super powers are released. The chestplate and magic gems attach to the doll's body because they contain magnets. A box and rope are included with instructions on how to perform a magic rope trick. **$12.00.**

271

1996 PRINCESS TENKO ROSE EAGLE FASHION #14325 features Tenko with lavender eyeshadow wearing a fuchsia catsuit with Rose Eagle fashion with pink plastic chestplate. When her headdress is on and her gem is attached, her eagle super powers are released. A magic box trick is included. **$12.00.**

1996 PRINCESS TENKO SAPPHIRE SEA DOLPHIN FASHION #14324 features Tenko with blue eyeshadow wearing a blue catsuit under her Sapphire Sea Dolphin fashion with pink plastic chestplate. When her outfit and gem are magically attached, her dolphin super powers are released. A magic gem trick is included. **$12.00.**

1996 ALI GUARDIAN OF THE MAGIC #14327 is the violet eyed blonde Guardian of the Magic who is like a little sister to Tenko. Alison Chambers' magic gem gives her wrist shields and waist beads super powers when the gem is magically attached to her plastic yellow chestplate. She wears a purple catsuit and has a golden headdress. The Amazing Magic Booklet included with Ali, Jana, and Shona feature magic tricks children can do with household items such as disappearing coin, magic spool, money magic, and string tricks. **$12.00.**

1996 JANA DARK TWIN #14331 is the red-haired, green-eyed adversary of Tenko and twin of Jason Dark (not produced). Jana seeks the Magic Starfire Gems to strengthen her evil magic. If she succeeds in finding them, she will rule all time, space, and the world. She wears an orange catsuit with orange plastic bodice and mask headdress. The Magic Starfire Gem attaches to her outfit to release her evil powers. **$12.00.**

1996 SHONTI ANIMAL TRAIN-ER #14333 is Tenko's black friend with brown eyes. She wears a blue catsuit with blue cape and white chestplate. Shonti Baraka is Tenko's faithful friend and animal trainer with the ability to talk to all creatures. She attached the Magic Starfire Gem to her outfit to cause all animals to become her allies. She has a white animal trainer headdress with blue feathers. **$12.00.**

1996 NINJARA SNOW LEOPARD #14334 is Princess Tenko's beautiful green-eyed snow leopard. The Magic Starfire Gem transforms Ninjara into a powerful protector. Ninjara has a white furry headdress and a silver chain collar with jewel. This is the same leopard used with Princess of Power's Clawdeen. MARKINGS: Inside leg: c Mattel, Inc. 1985/ CHINA. **$14.00.**

273

1996 PEARL RIDER HORSE #11435 is Princess Tenko's white horse that grows wings when the Magic Starfire Gem is placed on its head. Pearl Rider has a winged saddle. **$14.00.**

1997 PRINCESS TENKO ROSE EAGLE FASHION #14325 includes the same bonus offer of two extra gems in a purple keepsake bag. **$20.00.**

1997 PRINCESS TENKO GOLDEN LION FASHION #14323 was re-release in a few locations in 1997 with a bonus offer. Included in the packag were two extra gems in a purple keepsake bag. A yellow banner abo the doll's head announces, BONUS! 2 extra gems in a keepsake bag! Th other five dolls in this series were repackaged with this offer. The dolls with the bonus offer are hard to find. **$20.00.**

1996 PRINCESS TENKO AND ROSE EAGLE FASHION & JANA DARK TWIN #14829 is a two-pack containing the two regular dolls repackaged in this white catalog box exclu-

sive to J. C. Penney. **$24.00.**

1997 PRINCESS TENKO SAPPHIRE SEA DOLPHIN FASHION #14324 includes the bonus gems and purple keepsake bag. **$20.00.**

1997 ALI GUARDIAN OF THE MAGIC #14327 also features the bonus offer of two extra gems in a purple keepsake bag. **$20.00.**

1997 JANA DARK TWIN #14331 contains the bonus gems and purple keepsake bag. **$20.00.**

1997 SHONTI ANIMAL TRAINER #14333 contains the bonus gems and keepsake bag. **$20.00.**

Barbie Dolls

Barbie Dolls on Parade

A representative look at the Barbie dolls from 1967 to present who best reflect the fashions, trends, and innovations of the day.

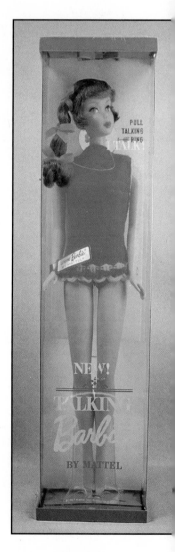

1967 NEW BARBIE TEEN-AGE FASHION MODEL #1190, called a Standard Barbie, features Barbie doll's first newly designed face and body, giving her a more youthful appearance. **$550.00.**

1968 TWIST 'N TURN BARBIE #1160 with light brown hair has rooted eyelashes and a Twist 'N Turn waist, features the Standard Barbie lack. **$575.00.**

1968 TALKING BARBIE #111 with Chocolate Bon Bon ha features the first time a Bar bie doll talked! She has a pul string at the back of he neck, and her box top an posin' stand form a seat fo her. **$325.00.**

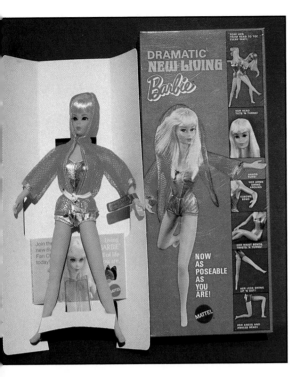

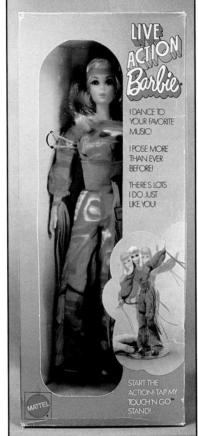

1970 DRAMATIC NEW LIVING BARBIE #1116 with ~~ash~~ blonde hair has jointed wrists, bendable ~~elbows~~, swivel waist, tilting and turning head, ~~swinging~~ arms, legs that swing up and out, and ~~bendable~~ knees. **$195.00.**

1971 LIVE ACTION BARBIE #1155 is associated with Woodstock by many collectors and is one of the best period pieces in Barbie doll's history. **$175.00.**

1970 TWIST 'N TURN BAR-BIE #1160 with light brown hair has a different hairstyle — a flip! **$550.00.**

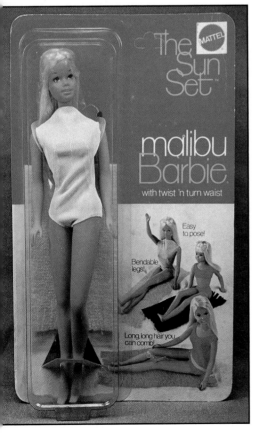

1971 SUN SET MALIBU BARBIE #1067 begins an ongoing series of Malibu swimwear dolls that still continues today, even though the place name Malibu has been dropped. She has tan skin and uses her British friend Stacey's head mold. **$60.00.**

1972 THE ORIGINAL BARBIE #3210 was commissioned by the Montgomery Ward store on the occasion of its 100th anniversary. Supposed to be The Original Barbie of 1959, her rounded eyebrows, blue eyes, and tan skin make her more like a 1961 Barbie doll. **$650.00.**

1972 TALKING BUSY BARBIE #1195 combines two great innovations in one doll. She has opening and closing hands thanks to her movable thumb, and she is also a pull-string talker. Add the hot early 1970s fashion that she wears, and a classic is born. **$325.00.**

1972 WALK LIVELY STEFFIE #1183 is shown here because so many dolls have used her head mold, including Barbie, Miss America, Stacie, and African-American Mrs. Heart. **$250.00.**

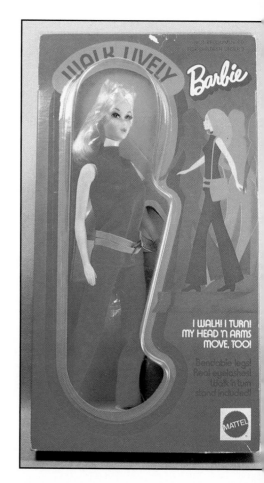

1972 WALK LIVELY BARBIE #1182 is able to walk with a Walk 'N Turn stand that causes her arms and legs to move back and forth as her head turns from side to side. **$275.00.**

1973 QUICK CURL BAR-BIE #4220 has tiny wires rooted with her hair to give it extra styleability. **$85.00.**

73 BARBIE GET-UPS 'N GO #7700 features a busy ctor's professional wardrobe for Barbie, including r medical school diploma, surgeon's outfit, doc- r's coat, x-ray, and telephone. This is the first fash- n to portray Barbie doll as a doctor. In the 1960s e was a nurse. **$60.00.**

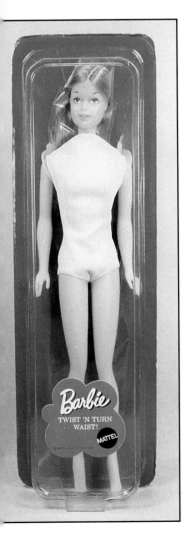

1973 TWIST 'N TURN BARBIE #8587 is a rare doll sold in Europe who has titian hair and pale skin. She wears Sun Set Malibu Barbie doll's swim-suit and the Stacey head mold. **$200.00.**

1974 BARBIE'S SWEET 16 #7796 features Barbie with a shag hair-cut dressed in her Sweet 16 party dress. Mattel used Barbie doll's patent date, 1958, as her birth year, making 1974 her six-teenth birthday. **$125.00.**

1975 GOLD MEDAL BARBIE #7233 features Barbie wearing her official Olympic outfit with gold medal. This was Barbie doll's first association with the Olympic games. **$65.00.**

1975 HAWAIIAN BARBIE #7470 features the first Barbie doll made in an ethnic version. She has the Steffie head, tan skin, and black hair. **$65.00.**

1976 BEAUTIFUL BRIDE BARBIE #9599 is a department store special featuring Barbie doll with rooted eyelashes wearing a wedding gown. She is the last doll to use the 1967 Barbie head mold with rooted eyelashes. **$200.00.**

1977 SUPERSTAR BARBIE #9720 features a newly designed smiling head mold and new permanently bent arms for glamorous modeling poseability. She is the first Barbie doll in a decade to have earrings. **$70.00.**

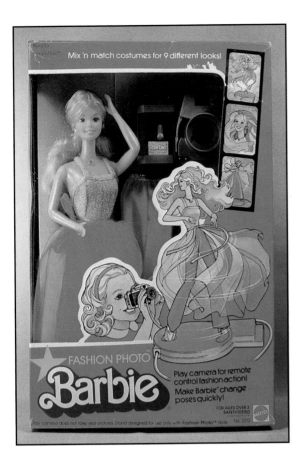

1978 FASHION PHOTO BARBIE #2210 has real modeling action activated by the child's play camera. **$55.00.**

1977 SUPERSIZE BARBIE #9828 is the first 18" Barbie doll. **$165.00.**

1979 KISSING BARBIE #2597 features a new, puckered-up lips head mold; when the panel in her back is pressed, she tilts her head back and makes a kissing sound. **$45.00.**

1980 BLACK BARBIE #1293 is the first African-American Barbie doll on the market. **$75.00.**

1979 PRETTY CHANGES BARBIE #2598 contains wigs for this short-haired Barbie doll, a hair-play feature not used since in the U.S. **$40.00.**

1979 SUN LOVIN' MALIBU BARBIE #1067 is the doll with the peek-a-boo tan! She has painted tan lines to show off her dark suntan. **$25.00.**

1980 HISPANIC BARBIE #1292 is the first Hispanic Barbie doll on the market. **$60.00.**

980 ITALIAN BARBIE #1602 features a ew head mold and an authentic Italian costume. She has long been a vorite of the International arbie/Dolls of the World series, which ebuted in 1980. **$185.00.**

1980 ROLLER SKATING BARBIE #1880 is queen of the roller scene. **$45.00.**

1981 GOLDEN DREAM BARBIE #1874 has the billion dollar look. This first edition features an unusual upswept hairstyle. **$45.00.**

1980 ROYAL BARBIE #1601 is a second doll introduced in 1980 to launch the International Barbie collection. She borrows her scepter from Miss America. **$185.00.**

1981 ORIENTAL BARBIE #3262 is the first Asian Barbie doll. **$135.00.**

1981 WESTERN BARBIE #1757 has a winking eye that closes with the touch of a button on her back. **$30.00.**

1982 MAGIC CURL BARBIE #385 has curly, big permed hair — trademark look of the early 1980. **$35.00.**

1983 FASHION CLASSICS FUN AT MCDONALD'S #4274 features Barbie doll's work uniform at the popular restaurant. **$25.00.**

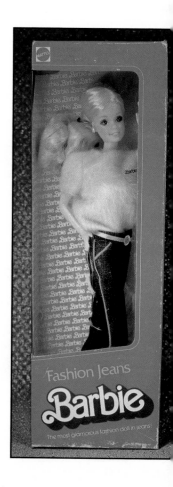

1982 FASHION JEANS BARBIE #5315 wears the Barbie name on her sweater, boots, and designer jeans. **$32.00.**

1983 TWIRLY CURLS BARBIE #5579 has extra-long hair to style with her Twirly Curler, a hair braider. **$25.00.**

1984 CRYSTAL BARBIE #4859 is an unofficial 25th anniversary Barbie doll wearing a ruffled ballgown that is one of her most beautiful. **$30.00.**

1984 GREAT SHAPE BARBIE #7025 epitomizes the workout craze of the early 1980s. **$25.00.**

1985 DAY-TO-NIGHT BARBIE #7944 wears a pink business suit that reverses to evening wear. **$40.00.**

Barbie Dolls

1986 ASTRONAUT BARBIE #2449 is the first Barbie doll sold wearing an astronaut uniform. **$70.00.**

1987 FEELI GROOVY BARB #3421 is the fir doll to featur the designer name on th package. **$225.0**

1986 ROCKER BARBIE #1140 features Barbie doll in her most outrageous career to date — a rock musician! A free cassette tape containing the band's songs is included. **$45.00.**

1988 BARBIE AND THE SENSATIONS BARBIE #4931 is the first Barbie doll dressed in 1950s inspired fashions, including saddle shoes, 50s sunglasses, and a going steady ring on a cord around her neck. **$40.00.**

1988 DOCTOR BARBIE #3850 is the first Barbie doll sold as a physician. Of course, her uniform becomes an evening gown. **$45.00.**

1989 ARMY BARBIE #3966 is the first in a series of Barbie dolls dressed in authentic uniforms of the four branches of armed services. **$45.00.**

988 HAPPY HOLIDAYS BARBIE #1703 is the first doll in the annual Happy Holidays Barbie eries. **$750.00.**

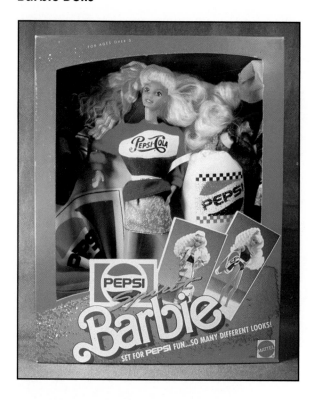

1989 PEPSI SPIRIT BARBIE #4869 has the name Pepsi on five items in her ensemble — on her shirt, belt, jacket, blanket, and beach bag (Toys 'R' Us Exclusive). **$75.00.**

1989 PINK JUBILEE BARBIE is the official 30th anniversary Barbie doll, given to 1,200 guests at a gala on February 13, 1989 – the 30th anniversary of her debut at Toy Fair in 1959. **$2,000.00**

1989 DISNEY CHARACTER BARBIE #4385 is the first Barbie doll to wear Disney fashions, including a Mickey Mouse ears hat and Minnie Mouse tee shirt (Children's Palace Exclusive). **$65.00.**

1989 UNICEF BARBIE #4782 is the first Barbie doll to be made in four ethnic versions, each wearing identical outfits. **$30.00.**

1990 FLIGHT TIME BARBIE GIFT SET #9584 features Barbie doll as a pilot; in the 1960s she was always a stewardess. **$35.00.**

1990 FRIENDSHIP BARBIE #5506 from Germany was released in celebration of the reunification of Germany. **$50.00.**

1991 AMERICAN BEAUTY QUEEN BARBIE #3137 features Barbie as a beauty pageant contestant, not affiliated with the Miss America pageant. **$35.00.**

1990 SUMMIT BARBIE #7029 commemorates the first Barbie Summit of 1990 in which children from 30 countries gathered to discuss world issues. **$40.00.**

1992 BARBIE FOR PRESIDENT GIFT SET #3722 marks Barbie doll's only bid for the presidency (Toys 'R' Us exclusive). **$50.00.**

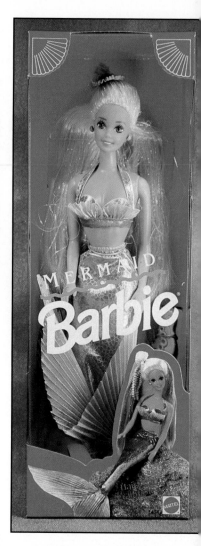

1992 MERMAID BARBIE #143 was on sale at the same tim Tyco's Little Mermaid line wa available. Like Ariel, Barbie has removable fish tail. **$30.00.**

1992 ROLLERBLADE BARBI #2214 wears skates that flicke and flash, causing safety cor cerns that prompted Mattel t offer non-sparking replace ments. Just as roller skatin was a craze of the 1980s rollerblading has become trend of the 1990s. **$40.00.**

1992 RAPPIN' ROCKIN' BARBIE #3248 personifies the early 1990s with her black leather look and working boom box. She has a new, more youthful head mold introduced with Teen Talk Barbie. **$50.00.**

1992 SPARKLE EYES BARBIE #2482, called the prettiest Barbie ever, has blue rhinestone eyes — a feature later used on Disney's Special Sparkles dolls. **$28.00.**

1992 SNAP 'N PLAY BARBIE #3550 wears plastic, snap-on clothing as used previously on the Guardian Goddesses and Spectra dolls. **$20.00.**

1993 LITTLE DEBBIE SNACK CAKES COLLECTOR'S EDITION BARBIE #10123 is the first Barbie doll to be made in the likeness of a company mascot. **$65.00.**

1992 TEEN TALK BARBIE #5745 introduces a new, fuller, youthful face representative of a teenager. Not since the 1970s has a Barbie doll been called a teenager on her packaging. She says four random phrases, one of which— "Math class is tough" — garnered national attention. **$35.00.**

1993 NATIVE AMERICAN BARBIE #1753 is the first Barbie doll representing a Native American, although not the first Native American doll produced by Mattel. **$50.00.**

1993 POLICE OFFICER BARBIE #10688 is featured in a police officer's uniform with extra fashion for the awards ball (Toys 'R' Us exclusive). **$55.00.**

1993 TROLL BARBIE #102 wears tiny trolls on her clothin — another 1960s trend revis ed. **$20.00.**

1994 BEDTIME BARBIE #11079 is the first soft-bodied Barbie doll whose eyes close with warm water. This feature is used on Sleeping Beauty. **$20.00.**

1994 GYMNAST BARBIE #12127 has a new, poseable bend and move body. **$20.00.**

1994 SUPER TALK BARBIE #12290 says 100,000 phrases by randomly combining pre-recorded phrases into new sentences. **$30.00.**

1994 TOOTH FAIRY BARBIE #11645 features Barbie doll in the role of the Tooth Fairy; she even has a pouch for the child's tooth (Wal-mart exclusive). **$25.00.**

1994 35TH ANNIVERSARY BARBIE KEEPSAKE COLLECTION #11591 includes a vinyl reproduction of the original 1959 Barbie doll with two reproductions of rare 1959 fashions. **$125.00.**

1995 MATTEL GOLDEN ANNIVERSARY BARBIE #14479 is a porcelain doll commemorating Mattel's fiftieth anniversary in a red velvet gown with golden flounce. **$495.00.**

1995 POG FUN BARBIE #13239 represents the POG milkcap collecting craze (Toys 'R' Us exclusive). **$16.00.**

1996 GRADUATION BARBIE #15003
is the first Barbie doll sold as a
graduate. **$24.00.**

1997 SIXTIES FUN BARBIE #17693 wears
a trendy mini dress with lace-up boots,
net stockings, and cap (Wholesale Clubs
exclusive). **$25.00.**

**1997 HONG KONG COMMEMORA-
TIVE EDITION CHINESE EMPRESS
BARBIE #16708** was sold in Hong
Kong with a commemorative gold
coin marking the transfer of Hong
Kong back to China in the summer
of 1997. **$200.00.**

Barbie Dolls

Barbie Doll Family Tree

Barbie
1959

*P.J. is called Barbie doll's cousin on the 1983 Dream Date and
bie and Friends dolls.

Barbie Magazine called the 1991 Kelly, Barbie doll's sister
Todd, Ken doll's brother, but official Mattel catalogs do n

FAMILY

Skipper 1964 –	Tutti 1966 – 1969	Todd 1966 – 1967	Francie 1966 – 1976	Jazzie 1989 – 1993	Stacie 1992 –	**Todd 1991
(little sister)	(tiny sister)	(tiny brother)	(modern cousin)	(cousin)	(sister)	1993 – 1995
		(Tutti's twin)				(Stacie's twin)

*P.J.	Brad	Jamie	Steffie	Kelley	Cara	Curtis
1969 – 1985	1970	1970 – 1972	1972	1973 – 1974	1975 – 1976	1976

Diva	Miko	Whitney	Becky	Belinda	Bopsy	Steven
1986 – 1987	1986 – 1989	1987 – 1989	1988	1988	1988	1988 –

SKIPPER'S FRIENDS

Nichelle	Shani	Jamal	Tara Lynn	Becky	Ricky 1965	Skooter 1965 –1
1991 – 1993	1991 – 1994	1992 – 1993	1993	1997 –		

JAZZIE'S FRIENDS   ### STACIE'S FRIENDS

Chris 1967	Chelsie 1989	Dude 1989	Stacie 1989	**Kelly 1991	Janet	Whitney
(Tutti's friend)				(flower girl)	1994	1994

296

Barbie Doll Family Tree

Kelly 1995 –
(baby sister)

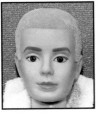
Ken
1961 –

Midge
1963 – 1966, 1988 –

Allan 1964 – 1965
Alan 1991

Casey 1967, 1974
(Francie's friend)

Christie
1968 –

Stacey
1968 – 1970

Todd 1983
(groom)

Tracy 1983
(bride)

Mr. Heart
1985 – 1990

Mrs. Heart
1985 – 1990

Dana
1986 – 1987

Dee Dee
1986 – 1987

Derek
1986 – 1987

Teresa
1988 –

Devon
1989

Kayla
1989, 1994

Nikki
1989

Kira
1990 –

Nia
1990

Asha
1991 – 1993

Fluff
1971

Tiff
1972

Ginger
1976

Scott
1980

Courtney
1989 –

Kevin
1990 – 1995

Nikki
1997

Becky
1996 –

Chelsie
1996 –

Melody
1996 –

Deidre
1997 –

Jenny
1997 –

Marissa
1997 –

Tommy
1997 –

Disney Classics

Mattel Toys began producing dolls based on classic Walt Disney Company animated motion pictures in 1991. Most of the dolls produced since then have been 11½" to 12" tall, using Barbie doll and Ken doll bodies with new heads molded after the Walt Disney Company animated characters they represent. In the first year, Mattel released dolls, fashions, and playsets based on the Walt Disney classic *Cinderella*, as well as dolls and fashions based on the new animated release *Beauty and the Beast*. Prov-

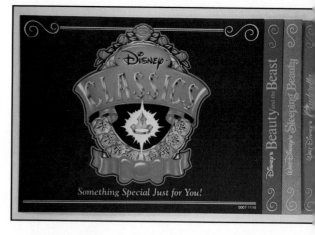

Something Special Just for You!

ing successful, Mattel has continued making dolls based on other Walt Disney Company movies, borrowing from the classic Disney archives as well as from brand new releases. The year 1992 saw adaptations of *Sleeping Beauty* and the newly-released *Aladdin*. In the years since, a multitude of dolls, fashions, and playsets have been released. The Mattel dolls are considered by many collectors to be the definitive examples of classic Disney characters. With the release of the Signature Collection and Great Villains Collection, there has been renewed interest in past Mattel Disney Classics dolls, which have always been of great quality.

MARKINGS: Most Mattel Disney dolls are marked simply c DISNEY on the backs of their heads. The adult female Disney dolls typically use Barbie doll bodies marked c MATTEL, INC. 1966, along with the country of origin. Most adult male Disney dolls use the Ken doll body marked c Mattel, Inc. 1968, along with the country of origin. Notable exceptions will be identified.

Cinderella

Cinderella, the classic Walt Disney animated feature from 1950, offerred Mattel the challenge of producing a doll as beautiful as the animated character. Collectors agree that Mattel's Cinderella doll is superlative, cherished by collectors and children alike.

1991 CINDERELLA #1624 wear a satiny blue ballgown with lon white gloves, hairband, ribbo choker, silvery earrings, an glass slippers. Her ballgow reverses to a white weddin gown with veil. A first-editio Little Little Golden Book wit illustrated adaptation of *Cir derella*, is included, as well a pop-up cardboard animal char acters and a brush. The doll cardboard liner lavishly illus trates the outside of the castle **$40.00.**

1991 PRINCE CHARMING #1625 wears red velvet pants with golden trim, formal white jacket with removable shoulder decorations, gold lamé belt, white socks, and black shoes. He carries a blue pillow with a single glass slipper. A child-size locket, first used with 1988's Perfume Pretty Whitney (Barbie doll's friend) is included, along with two cardboard characters. MARKINGS: Back of head: c DISNEY; Back: c Mattel, Inc. 1968/ MALAYSIA. **$35.00.**

1991 FAIRY GODMOTHER MASK & COSTUME PLAYSET #2419 contains a Fairy Godmother vinyl mask with attached satiny blue cape and pink ribbon, satiny blue dress, blue shoes, a Cinderella paper doll, and cardboard mice characters. The vinyl mask is for use with any 11½" doll. This boxed series of four fashions is very hard to find. These four were re-released on blister cards in 1992; that series is easier to find. **$35.00.**

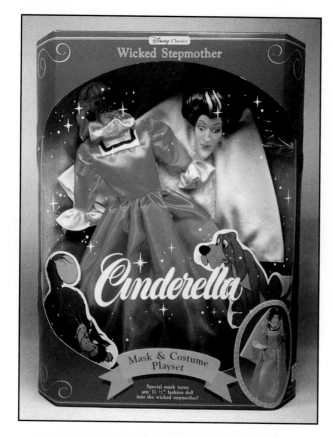

1991 WICKED STEPMOTHER MASK & COS-TUME PLAYSET #2421 contains a Wicked Stepmother vinyl mask with attached lavender shawl, satiny rose-colored gown with lavender cuffs and collar, black shoes, a Cinderella paper doll, and two cardboard characters. **$35.00.**

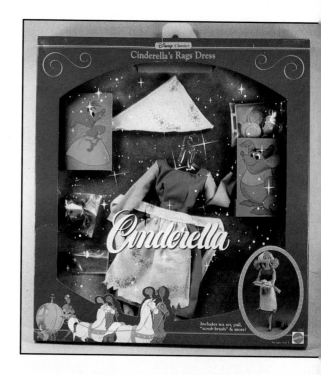

1991 CINDERELLA'S BALLGOWN #1275 is the gown Cinderella hoped to wear to the ball until her jealous stepsisters tore her dress to shreds. The two-piece gown is satiny pink with a white underskirt and removable collar, bows, and skirt. A pink hair ribbon, pink shoes, blue necklace, and two cardboard animal characters are included. **$30.00.**

1991 CINDERELLA'S RAGS DRESS #1347 contains a brown dress with blue sleeves, beige apron with matching scarf, brown flat shoes, brown pail, scrub brush and sponge, blue tray with two teacups and two saucers, and two cardboard mice. **$30.00.**

991 CINDERELLA WEDDING CARRIAGE & HORSE SET 2422 features a white carriage with golden accents ulled by a white horse with golden mane and tail. As the arriage rolls wedding bell jingles are heard. Cinderella's ink pillow reverses to a bridal bouquet. A bridle/plume eadpiece, six removable horseshoes, four satin ribbons, nd a brush are included for the horse. This is a hard to nd set. **$55.00.**

1991 CINDERELLA HORSE #1628 features Cinderella's white horse with shimmery white mane and tail, pink satin saddle and bows, six removable horseshoes, removable bridle, and pink feathery plume. **$24.00.**

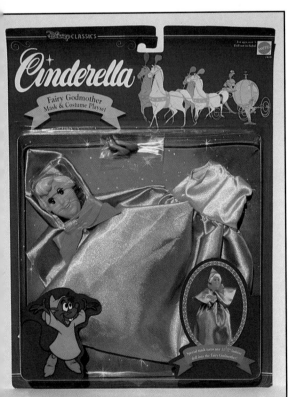

1992 FAIRY GODMOTHER MASK & COSTUME PLAYSET #2419 was reissued in 1992 on a blister card package, as were the other three 1991 fashions. The Cinderella paper doll was not included with any of the 1992 reissues. Only one mouse cardboard character is included in this set. Some minor differences in the fabrics of the four re-released fashions can be noted, such as the dark pink bow on this gown compared to the light pink bow on the earlier 1991 costume. **$25.00.**

991 CINDERELLA MAGICAL BUBBLE BALL-OOM #2416 contains a plastic pink ballroom vith railing and two illustrated backdrops, doll stand/dance mechanism that holds two dolls in olace as they dance around the floor, and a han-dle in the floor which when turned produces bubbles. A silvery crown and pink wand are included for the child. **$60.00.**

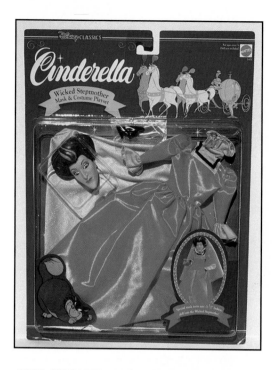

1992 CINDERELLA BALLGOWN #1275 is shown with the blister card packaging. **$20.00.**

1992 WICKED STEPMOTHER MASK & COSTUME PLAYSET #2421 is shown in the blister card packaging. Only one animal character, the cat, is included. **$25.00.**

1992 CINDERELLA RAGS DRESS #1347 is shown with the blister card packaging. **$20.00.**

1992 CINDERELLA GIFT PACK #10370 packages Cinderella doll with her two fashions, Cinderella Ballgown and Cinderella Rags Dress. Each of the items are still in their original packages, but are secured to a large cardboard display. This is a wholesale club exclusive, and it is very hard to find. **$125.00.**

1997 WINTER DREAM CINDERELLA #18505 a K-B Toys exclusive. She wears a satin ivory gown, golden bow and holly — her outfit for the grand holiday ball. **$50.00.**

Beauty and the Beast

Released for Christmas 1991, *Beauty and the Beast* was a new Disney animated film based on the literary classic. *Beauty and the Beast* is widely considered to be one of the best new Disney films in years. Mattel released its Beauty and the Beast dolls just before the movie opened, and they were also well received by collectors.

1991 BELLE #2433 has brown eyes and brown hair with bangs. She wears a lovely gold lamé gown with sheer yellow overskirt and sleeves, fingerless gold lamé gloves, and white shoes. A blue and white French-style village dress is included, along with cardboard characters of Mrs. Potts and Lumiere, and a brush. When Belle's lipstick is applied, she can kiss and leave her kiss print on the Beast's cheek. Belle's lipstick container is the same type as first used with 1979's Kissing Barbie. **$40.00.**

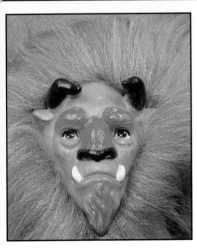

1991 THE BEAST #2436 features The Beast in his human form with ng rooted blonde hair and blue eyes. He wears black knickers with tached white shirt and yellow vest, white socks, and black shoes. A nyl Beast mask with rooted hair is included, along with The Beast's ue jacket with sewn in paws and black pants with cloth legs sewn in. comb, brush, mirror, and two cardboard characters are included. ter editions of The Beast feature the prince with a pinker skin tone nd silkier blonde hair. **$35.00.**

1992 BELLE #2433 was re-released in 1992 with a no-bangs hairstyle, and her lipstick was discontinued. The caption beneath the photo on the box front is altered to delete references to her kiss and the lipstick. **$35.00.**

1991 BELLE DOLL #45536 is an Applause doll manufactured by Matt She wears an iridescent golden gown with sheer panels, yellow finge less gloves, a yellow bow in her hair, and yellow shoes. A brush ar hang tag are included. **$40.00.**

1993 BELLE EN HET BEEST #151514 is a deluxe set from the Netherlands pairing Belle with no bangs, no village dress, and no lipstick with a foreign-language video cassette of *Beauty and the Beast*. This is rare. **$125.00.**

1992 BEAUTY AND THE BEAST GIFT SET #1622 includes Belle with the no-bangs hairstyle wearing a lovely pink ball gown and pink shoes, accompanied by The Beast wearing a blue jacket and black trousers; when The Beast's costume is removed, the human Prince is revealed wearing a one-piece white shirt/black knickers/ white socks outfit with black shoes. A brush is included. **$60.00.**

992 WINTER BELLE #1637 contains Belle with no angs wearing the same pink ballgown and shoes om the Beauty and the Beast Gift Set with the ddition of a dark pink fur-trimmed cape and a nd-held rose. Also included with Winter Belle are rs. Potts and Chip plastic characters, a brush, and Little Little Golden Book. **$60.00.**

1992 DINNER FASHION #3152 contains a lavender dress with pink collar and sleeves, a white apron, and lavender shoes for Belle, along with table settings for four and a cardboard character. **$30.00.**

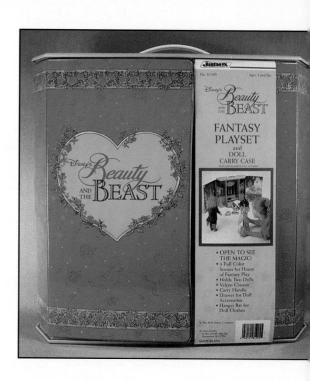

1992 LIBRARY FASHION #3153 contains an iridescent green gown with sheer sleeves and dark green bodice, lime green shoes, a hair ribbon, three books, a cardboard foot stool character, and a pink basket. The two Belle fashions are very hard to find. **$30.00.**

1992 FANTASY PLAY SET AND DOLL CARRY CAS **#81205** is made by Janex but the illustration fe tures Mattel's Beauty and the Beast dolls. The tw doll case features three scenes from the movie, plastic drawer for accessories, and a hanger b for doll clothes. This case is hard to find with th paper panel with UPC still attached. **$35.00.**

1993 BELLE #1647 more common referred to by collec tors (and by the Ma tel catalog) as Villag Belle. She wears blue dress with whit apron and satin tie this outfit is virtuall identical to the extr village dress include with the original Bell dolls. Her hair no appears to have brushed-back bang look. Shoes and hairbow are included **$18.00.**

1993 BEAST #1976 is a plush Beast doll wearing a blue jacket, black trousers, white shirt, and yellow vest. He has gold lamé claws on fingers and toes. **$25.00.**

993 BE OUR GUEST MUSICAL GIFT SET #10477 fea-
ures Belle wearing a blue satin version of her village
ress packaged with a dining table that rotates to the
nusic of *Be Our Guest*. Four enchanted characters
rom the movie, Lumiere, Mrs. Potts, Chip, and
ogsworth are featured atop the table. Silverware, one
hair, and napkins are included. **$55.00.**

1993 MUSICAL TABLE SET #10571 contains two
chairs, the rotating musical table that plays *Be Our
Guest*, Lumiere, Mrs. Potts, Chip, Cogsworth, a nap-
kin, four glasses, four plates, four forks, four
spoons, and four knives. **$30.00.**

1994 THE WEDDING DELUXE GIFT SET #11021 features Belle in a white satin wedding dress with iridescent white bodice, bows, veil, and bouquet with
one rose. A diamond adorns the bodice of her
gown. The bow at the back of Belle's gown con-
ceals a tiny music chip that plays two wedding
melodies when pressed. The Prince wears a white
satin tuxedo with iridescent lapels; a diamond holds
his tie in place. Shoes and a brush are included.
$55.00.

1994 THE WEDDING MUSICAL BELLE #10909 features the doll from the gift set sold individually. **$30.00.**

1994 THE WEDDING PRINCE #10910 features the doll from the gift set sold individually. **$20.00.**

1997 THE ENCHANTED CHRIST-MAS BELLE #17969 is a Block-buster exclusive packaging th small Belle wearing a blue lam gown with Lumiere. **$15.00.**

Tinkerbell

In the 1991 Mattel retailer catalog, a photo of a new 11½" Tinkerbell doll was shown. Tinkerbell uses a SuperStar Barbie body with permanently-bent arms and the Steffie head mold. She has short auburn hair and a short sparkly white fairy costume. The doll was not released. Two years later, Mattel would release a blonde Tinker Bell using the shorter Skipper doll body and head.

Sleeping Beauty

In 1992 Mattel produced two dolls, a mask playset, and one fashion based on the 1959 Walt Disney classic *Sleeping Beauty*. Once again, Mattel's ingenuity provides collectors with a doll with reversible fashion and an added feature: eyes that open and close.

1992 SLEEPING BEAUTY #4567 features lovely Princess Aurora, better known as Sleeping Beauty, wearing a pink gown with rose bodice, iridescent white sleeves and collar, and a golden crown and necklace. When the rose bodice is removed, a blue bodice remains, and the long pink gown reverses to blue. When warm water is applied to her violet eyes, they appear to close, in a few moments they open again, all due to the color-change paint used for her eyes. A Little Little Golden Book, white shoes, brush, applicator, cardboard Flora and Merryweather fairies, and spinning wheel are included. The earliest dolls on the market have light pink bodices, while later dolls wear dark pink bodices. **$35.00.**

309

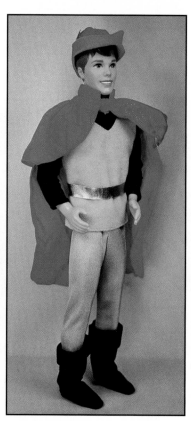

1992 PRINCE PHILLIP #4597 wears gray pants, black flocked boots, blue prince shirt, golden belt, and red cape. A horseman's tan and black shirt and red cap with golden feather are included for a second look. He carries the Shield of Virtue and the Sword of Truth used to defeat Maleficent. Cardboard Fauna fairy and guard pop-up characters are included. **$30.00.**

1992 MALEFICENT MASK & COSTUM **PLAYSET #4613** features a superb designed Maleficent vinyl mask, blac dress with pink panels and purple colla black shoes, and staff. Cardboard guar and crow characters are included. **$28.0C**

1992 PEASANT DRESS #4614 features the blue peasant dre with black lace bodice that was worn by Princess Aurora whe she lived with the fairies in the forest as Briar Rose. Black fl shoes, a basket of berries, black hair ribbon, and cardboa pop-up forest characters are included. **$22.00.**

Aladdin

A wonderful animated feature film of 1992, *Aladdin* provided ample material for Mattel to make years of original Aladdin dolls and toys. Only the original Aladdin and Jasmine dolls, along with several plush toys, were released in time for the movie's release. Always a great bargain, these Disney dolls came with not one but two completely different fashions, and Aladdin sported a color-changing lamp and his pet monkey Abu. The Aladdin and Jasmine characters offer a wider range of play options, so these dolls were sold wearing swimwear for the next two years, a look not especially practical for several other Disney dolls. The *Aladdin* animated television series coincided with more dolls being released.

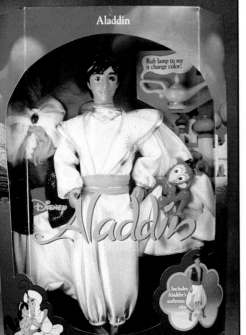

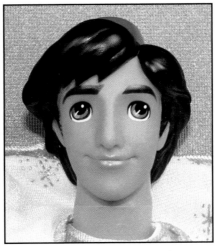 

1992 ALADDIN #2548 wears his white Prince Ali costume and cape, complete with a feathered, jeweled turban. Faithful monkey companion Abu hangs on his arm. His Agrabah street fashion, white baggy pants with purple vest, is included. The first edition Aladdin comes with a color-changing lamp; when it is rubbed, the warmth of the touch causes the lamp to lighten from tan to yellow. Also, a city scene depicting Agrabah is used on the early doll's liner. Some early dolls have the permanently bent arms Ken doll body, but most have the straight arms Ken doll body. **$25.00.**

1992 JASMINE #2557 has long black hair and big brown eyes. She has molded-on golden earrings. Jasmine wears her two-piece blue palace outfit with white slippers, golden necklace, and jeweled headband. Her royal princess wedding costume with iridescent trim is included. **$24.00.**

Disney Classics

1993 TOURIST GENIE #5340. $25.00.

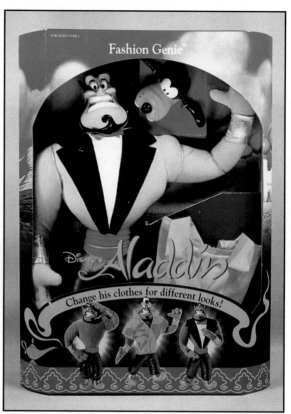

1993   FASH GENIE #10709 tures a plush-b four-fingered G with vinyl head w ing blue lamé pa red belt, gold l boots   and   w bands, and a rem able tuxedo dic An   extra   yel tourist   shirt Goofy hat are inc ed for the Gen first   vacation 10,000 years. **$25**

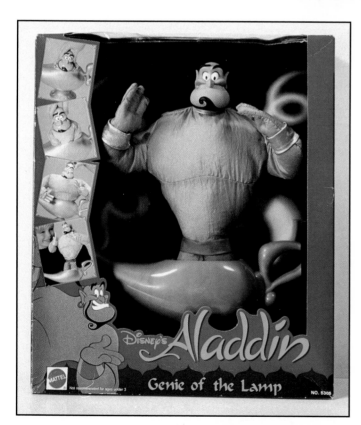

1992 GENIE OF THE LAMP #5305 contains an 11" fabric genie with all vinyl head wearing a red lamé belt, gold lamé wrist bands, and gold lamé boots. A 12" long hollow golden lamp with cover can hold the Genie's entire body. **$25.00.**

1993 JASMINE & RAJAH FRIENDSHIP SET #1058 contains Jasmine wearing yellow harem pants matching top with jewel, iridescent necklace orange bracelet, jeweled headdress with veil, an golden slippers. Her plush friend Rajah the tiger by her side. **$45.00.**

312

993 MAGIC CARPET GIFT SET #10657 features Aladdin wearing light pink baggy pants, gold lamé oots, and a purple jacket, Jasmine wearing purple arem pants, panties, purple top, jeweled head-and, golden necklace, shawl, and golden shoes, nd the plastic magic carpet that plays a melody rom the song *A Whole New World* when the but-on on the bottom of the carpet is pressed. **$42.00.**

1993 JASMINE GIFT PACK #10935 contains the original Jasmine #2557 packaged with her two fashions, Jasmine's Evening Palace Gown and Jasmine's Traveling Coat. The set was exclusive to wholesale clubs and is very hard to find. **$125.00.**

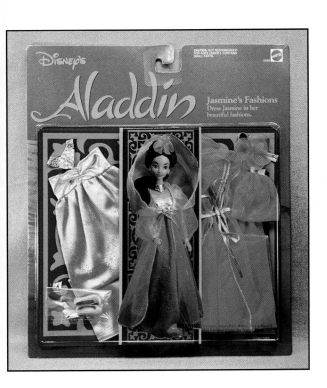

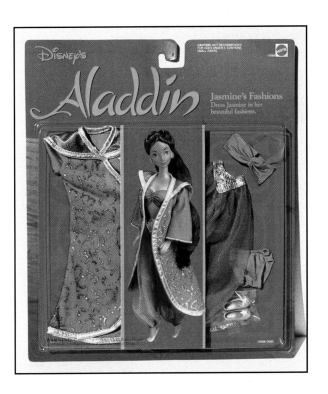

1993 JASMINE'S EVENING PALACE GOWN #10589 contains a pink dress with gold lamé bodice, sheer pink robe with matching hair band, golden neck-lace, and slippers. **$17.00.**

1993 JASMINE'S TRAVELING COAT #10588 con-tains a blue coat with golden designs, sheer blue harem pants with panties, blue bikini top, and golden slippers. **$17.00.**

313

1993 GENIE #10778 is a 14"
plush doll with gold lamé hair
band, bracelets, earring, and
boots. He has a soft felt beard.
$18.00.

1993 JASMINE #10912 is a 14
plush doll with vinyl head an
soft black hair. She wears her pur
ple palace costume with jewele
headband and gold lamé slipper
$20.00.

1993 ALADDIN #10914 is a 14"
plush doll with vinyl head wearing
his Prince Ali white outfit with
jeweled turban. He has gold lamé
boots and a purple lamé cape.
$15.00.

**1994 ARABIAN LIGHTS JAS-
MINE #11750** wears red
pants, gold lamé top with
sheer red sleeves, matching
sheer red overskirt decorated
with glow-in-the-dark stars
and crescent moons, and
attached red jeweled headpiece and earrings that really
light up when the button in
her back is pressed. She uses
the permanently bent arms
SuperStar Barbie body.
$30.00.

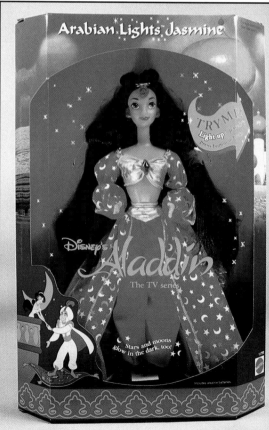

1994 ALADDIN #2548 is shown here with the final packaging used with Aladdin. His box liner is solid purple — the Agrabah city scene is gone. The words above his lamp say "Aladdin's magic lamp," as there is no color-change feature. The gold speckled design has been removed from his purple street vest. **$18.00.**

1994 ALADDIN #2548 is shown here with transitional packaging. His color-change lamp was being changed to a non-color-changing solid yellow lamp late in 1994, so a sticker with "Aladdin's lamp" was placed over the words, "Rub lamp to see it change color!" **$22.00.**

1995 FANTASY HAIR JASMINE #13126 features Jasmine wearing pink pants with purple overskirt, pink top, golden necklace, and pink shoes. A golden-twist braid is included to help style her longest hair ever. Her glittery overskirt can be worn as a cape or veil. **$25.00.**

1994 PALACE WEDDING JASMINE STYLING HEAD #66347 is 7¾" tall including the base. The large styling head features combable, styleable hair, removable earrings, jeweled headband, jeweled necklace, veil, and brush. **$20.00.**

315

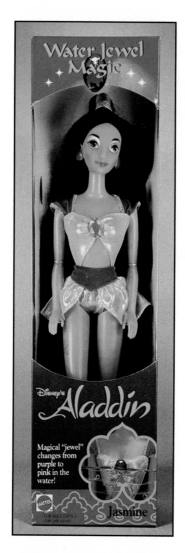

1994 WATER JEWEL MAGIC ALADDIN #11273 features Aladdin wearing purple swim trunks and a purple vest with golden accents. The purple jewel on the gold lamé top of Aladdin's swim trunks changes to pink in warm water. The box states that the jewels on Water Jewel Magic Aladdin and Jasmine dolls will change from passionate purple to true-love pink only if their love is really true! **$15.00.**

1994 WATER JEWEL MAGIC JASMINE #11272 features Jasmine wearing a purple and gold lamé swimsuit with removable skirt and golden hair decoration. The jewel on her bodice changes from purple to pink. **$15.00.**

1994 WATER JEWEL MAGIC GIFT SET #11769 packages Water Jewel Magic Aladdin and Jasmine dolls with the plush Rajah tiger from the Jasmine and Rajah Friendship Set. This set was exclusive to Disneyland/Disneyworld, but some were found at a close-out department store. This set is very hard to find. **$65.00.**

1996 PRINCESS IN PINK JASMINE #16200 is base on the Disney video *Aladdin and the King c Thieves*. She wears pink harem pants with irides cent white waist band and matching top, pink cap golden necklace, and golden slippers. She ha very limited distribution in 1996. **$25.00**

1995 WATER SURPRISE JASMINE #12640 features Jasmine in a shimmery blue two-piece swimsuit with golden hair decoration. The petals of Jasmine's water lily corsage open in warm water to reveal a shiny jewel. The front of her swimsuit changes color in water. **$15.00.**

1996 PALACE WEDDING JASMINE #16199 features Jasmine wearing a white wedding gown with golden accents, jeweled bodice, and white veil. **$20.00.**

995 WATER SURPRISE LADDIN #12641 is based n Disney's *Aladdin the eries* animated television how. Water Surprise laddin wears shimmery lue shorts and vest with jeweled genie lamp anging on a string round his neck. The enie lamp pendant pens to show off a brilant jewel. His swim runks change color in ater. **$15.00.**

1996 PALACE WEDDING GIFT SET #15822 is based on Disney's video *Aladdin and the King of Thieves*. Aladdin wears white baggy pants, a white robe with gold lamé collar and cuff trim, and yellow panel held by a gold lamé belt, and a white hat with plumes. Jasmine wears her white wedding gown. This set was not released.

Snow White and the Seven Dwarfs

Snow White and the Seven Dwarfs is Walt Disney's first full-length animated motion picture, and many will argue it is his best. *Snow White and the Seven Dwarfs* offered Mattel the opportunity to produce both the heroine and her seven companions. A mask playset containing the Queen offers the only other original doll in the Mattel series, leaving collectors, like Snow White, longing for her prince.

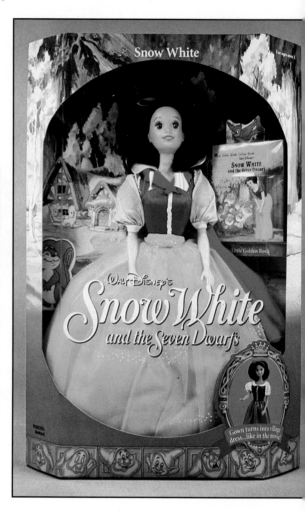

1993 SNOW WHITE #7783 is not considered by many collectors to be the best adaptation of Snow White, who has skin as white as snow, lips as red as a rose, and ebony-black hair. The hair color is correct on this doll, but her lips are pink and her complexion too flesh-tone to be compared to snow. She wears a long yellow gown with blue bodice, red cape, and pink hair ribbon. When the yellow skirt and blue sleeves are removed, her village dress remains. A Little Little Golden Book, white pumps, a brush, and two pop-up forest characters are included. **$20.00.**

1993 BASHFUL #10224 is a 6½" all-vinyl version of Bashful wearing a mustard-yellow top and shoes, purple pants, and blue cap. Each of the seven dwarfs features a different color-change feature; Bashful's cheeks turn red when icy water is applied, returning to normal moments later. MARKINGS: All dwarfs are marked on their backs: c DISNEY/THAILAND. **$15.00.**

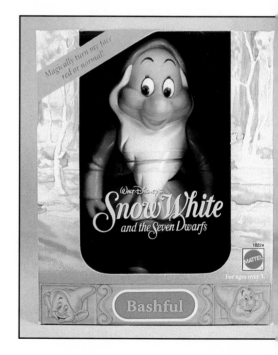

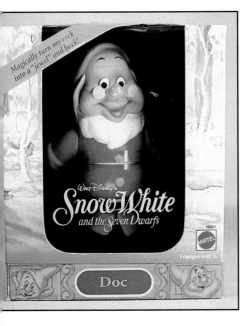

1993 DOPEY #10225 is a favorite with movie-goers and collectors alike. Only 5¼" tall, this all-vinyl Dopey wears a green shirt with lavender shoes and cap. A kiss-print from Snow White appears on Dopey's left cheek when water is applied. **$20.00.**

1993 DOC #10221 is a 6½" all-vinyl doll. Doc wears a coral shirt, orange pants, blue glasses, and yellow shoes and cap. He carries a color-change rock in his right hand which reveals a jewel when water is applied. **$15.00.**

1993 HAPPY #10222 is a 6½" all-vinyl doll wearing a lavender vest over yellow sleeves, yellow shoes and cap, and turquoise pants. Happy carries a scrub brush and soap; his face gets dirty when water is applied. **$15.00.**

1993 GRUMPY #10223 is a 6½" all-vinyl doll with coral coat, lavender pants and cap, and tan shoes. Grumpy's eyebrows raise to a less-grumpy scowl when water is applied. **$15.00.**

1993 SLEEPY #10220 is a 6½" all-vinyl doll wearing a brown coat, blue pants and cap, and lavender shoes. Sleepy's eyes close when water is applied. **$15.00.**

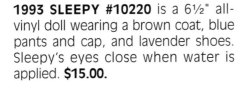

319

1993 SNOW WHITE AND THE SEVEN DWARFS CLASSIC GIFT S[...] #10558 packages all seven dwarfs with color-change feature wi[...] Snow White in the ultimate multiple-doll gift set. This is a har[...] to-find wholesale club exclusive. **$125.00.**

1993 SNEEZY #10226 is a 6½" all-vinyl doll wearing a lavender shirt and shoes, rose pants, and yellow cap. His nose turns red when water is applied. **$15.00.**

1993 DANCE 'N PLAY DELUXE GIFT SET #10559 features Snow White, Dopey, and Sneezy in one of the most memorable scenes from the movie, when Snow White dances with Dopey, who wears a blue cloak while standing on Sneezy's head. The three dolls are the same as those sold individually, with the addition of the blue cloak Dopey is wearing. **$45.00.**

1993 DOPEY & SNEEZY STACKABLE DOLLS #0611 features Dopey wearing the blue cloak while standing on Sneezy's head. **$35.00.**

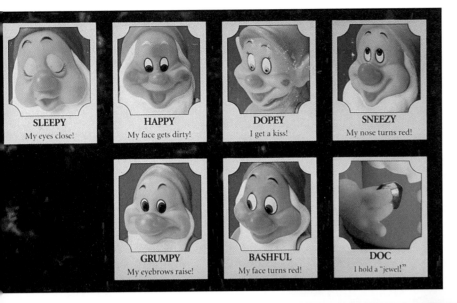

SLEEPY My eyes close!	**HAPPY** My face gets dirty!	**DOPEY** I get a kiss!	**SNEEZY** My nose turns red!
GRUMPY My eyebrows raise!	**BASHFUL** My face turns red!	**DOC** I hold a "jewel!"	

1993 SEVEN DWARFS GIFT SET
#5278 packages all seven individual vinyl dwarfs with color change action together in one large gift set. **$65.00.**

1993 SNOW WHITE AND THE SEVEN DWARFS COLLECTOR DOLL PLAY & CARRY CASE #86205 is a 7¼" deep turquoise case by Janex with compartments for two 11½" dolls and all seven dwarfs. **$25.00.**

Her Magic Mirror!
©The Walt Disney Company

1993 THE QUEEN MASK & COSTUME PLAYSET #7784 features the beautiful Queen vinyl mask with attached black hood and golden crown, purple gown, long black cape with iridescent white collar, purple shoes, and cardboard pop-up characters of the raven and the Magic Mirror. **$15.00.**

1993 SNOW WHITE #17090 is a 16" soft-bodied doll with vinyl head and black yarn hair. She wears a yellow dress with blue bodice and blue and red sleeves and a blue cape with red lining. Inside the heart-shaped pocket on her dress is a brown cloth bunny on a cord. MARKINGS: Back of head: c DISNEY THAILAND. **$20.00.**

1997 HAPPY BIRTHDAY SNOW WHITE #16635 is a Wal-Mart exclusive featuring Snow White wearing pink and blue streamers on her shimmery yellow gown with satiny blue bodice and shiny sleeves. She comes with a birthday cake and party hats for herself and her forest friends, a deer and a rabbit. **$25.00.**

Special Sparkles Collection

In 1994 Mattel released special new versions of classic Walt Disney characters with rhinestone eyes! Mattel made a Sparkle Eyes Barbie in 1992 with blue rhinestone eyes; she was touted as the prettiest Barbie ever. Now that rhinestone-eye feature began appearing on classic Disney beauties.

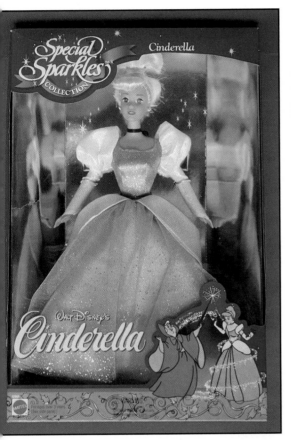

1994 SPECIAL SPARKLES CINDERELLA #12988 features Cinderella in a spectacular rendition of her blue ballgown with shimmery fabric and iridescent sleeves. She has the straight Shani style arms with wrists turned slightly to the sides. She has inset blue rhinestone eyes and a labeled pedastal doll stand. **$65.00.**

994 SPECIAL SPARKLES BELLE 1923 features Belle with green hinestone eyes. She wears a unning gold lamé gown with ngerless gloves and iridescent olden overskirt and sleeves. She as a golden necklace holding a amond, golden hair ribbon, slip, ellow shoes and brush, and hite pedastal doll stand labeled elle. The Mattel 1994 catalog ows Belle, Jasmine, and Snow hite with wrist bracelets bearing e portrait of each; these were ot included. **$50.00.**

1994 SPECIAL SPARKLES JASMINE #11922 is the first 11½" Jasmine doll with removable earrings. She has turquoise rhinestone eyes and wears shimmery turquoise harem pants, short top with golden trim, long sheer robe, golden crown with jewel, metallic golden shoes, and golden ring and earrings. A brush and turquoise pedastal stand labeled Jasmine are included. **$45.00.**

1994 SPECIAL SPARKLES SNOW WHITE #11832 has red lips, black hair, and blue rhinestone eyes. Her out-fit is incredible, with yellow satin skirt covered with sheer gold-flecked overskirt, blue lamé bodice, irides-cent blue and red sleeves, iridescent white collar, and shiny red hair bow. Yellow shoes, a brush, and white pedastal stand labeled Snow White are included. **$40.00.**

1995 SPARKLE EYES CINDERELLA #14789 is a reissued version of 1994 Special Sparkles Cinderella with a new style box. Sparkle Eyes Cinderella wears a blue satin gown with iridescent white sleeves and short overskirt. A black cloth choker is around her neck, and a blue headband is in her hair. She has blue rhinestone eyes. Jewelry, a brush, and shoes are included, but the display stand was discontinued. **$35.00.**

1995 SPARKLE EYES CINDERELLA DELUXE GIFT SET #15211 is a wholesale club gift set that pairs Sparkle Eyes Cinderella with a child-size locket featuring tiny Prince Charming and Cinderella figurines. **$50.00.**

1997 SPARKLE EYES SLEEPING BEAUTY #15808 is a Disney Store exclusive. She has blue rhinestone eyes and wears a

shimmering pink ball gown with shoes and a brush. Even though her head is the same closed-mouth head used for the original 1992 Sleeping Beauty, her markings are altered to DISNEY 1991 on the back of her head. **$30.00.**

325

It's a Small World

A popular ride at Walt Disney World is It's a Small World, which gives riders a world tour of mechanized dolls in costumes and settings appropriate to their part of the world. The dolls sing, *It's a Small World*, *After All*, a tune known by millions. Mattel's name, appropriately enough, is listed as a sponsor of the ride on the outside of the building housing the attraction. An adorable It's a Small World line of six 6" dolls, representing six different countries, was available in scattered locations in 1994. Few collectors of Mattel's Disney dolls are even aware this line exists.

MARKINGS: Each of these dolls uses the Cherry Merry Muffin head and body molds, marked c Mattel, Inc. 1988 on both their heads and backs of their bodies. The dolls have identical boxes with the same assortment number; only the doll and the sticker on the bubble changes from card to card. The lower front of each doll's outfit is stamped "it's a small world (country) c Disney."

1994 AMERICA #10489 has brown skin, brown eyes, and black hair adorned with feathers. America wears a white Native American outfit with cloth boots. **$30.00.**

1994 GERMANY #10489 h blonde braided hair worn buns and blue eyes. S wears a white blouse w black vest, red skirt, wh apron, and red painted- shoes. **$30.00.**

1994 JAPAN #10489 has black hair and brown eyes. She wears a white floral-print kimono with lavender obi and lavender painted-on shoes. **$30.00.**

1994 MEXICO #10489 has brown skin, black hair, and brown eyes. She wears a pink dress with yellow and orange stripes and lace trim. She has pink painted-on shoes. **$30.00.**

1994 MOROCCO #10489 has brown skin, brown eyes, and black hair. She wears fuchsia harem pants with purple panties and matching top. She wears a purple veil with golden band and pink painted-on shoes. **$30.00.**

1994 NIGERIA #10489 h black skin, brown eyes, a curly black hair. She wear kente-cloth gown wi golden collar and brace and painted-on yello shoes. The kente-cloth the same as used with t Soul Train Shani series a Toys 'R' Us' 1994 Asha do **$30.00.**

Disney Store Exclusives

Several notable series of Mattel dolls based on Disney characters or motion pictures were sold exclusively at Disney Stores and at the Disneyland and Walt Disney World theme parks. These include Peter Pan, Mary Poppins, Alice in Wonderland, Davy Crockett, and a pirate.

1993 FLYING PETER PAN #10719 is one of three dolls made in honor of the fortieth anniversary of Disney's 1953 animated feature *Peter Pan*. Flying Peter Pan is 11½" tall with molded orange hair and green cap with feather. He wears green tights, a green top, beige cloth boots, and belt with sheath and knife. Attaching the enclosed 6" string between two points allows the doll to fly when the plastic feather in

his cap is hung on the string. The Peter Pan series' boxes are in English and French, since these dolls were also sold at EuroDisney. Mattel reissued the Peter Pan line for Toys 'R' Us in 1998 with several changes. The Disney Store's boxes have the Disney Exclusive banner on the left side of the boxes, and the writing on the boxes is in both English and French (the boxes are dated 1993.) The Toys 'R' Us dolls have the new warning boxes in the top right corners, and the boxes are in English only (the boxes are dated 1997). The re-issued dolls are valued at **$16.00 each.** MARKINGS: Back of head: c DISNEY; Rear: c MATTEL INC. 1968/ CHINA. **$35.00.**

1993 FLYING TINKER BELL #11762 features blonde-haired, blue-eyed 10" Tinkerbell wearing a neon green bodice with attached skirt and wings, green panties, green slippers, and black hair bow. She has a star-tipped wand. A hair clip attached to a 6" line allows her to fly between two points. She has the Skipper head and body. The Toys 'R' Us re-issue is shown on the right with lemon blonde hair. MARKINGS: Back of head: c MATTEL INC 1987; Back: c MATTEL INC 1987/ MALAYSIA. **$35.00.**

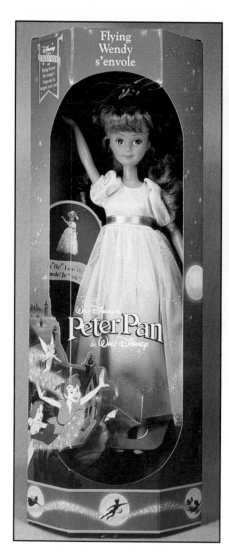

1993 FLYING WEND
#10720 is a 10" brow
haired, blue-eyed g
wearing a blue dre
with hair ribbon ar
dark blue shoes. Whe
her hair clip is attache
to the 6" line, she ca
fly in the same mann
as Tinker Bell. She h
the same head ar
body markings as Flyir
Tinker Bell. The Toys
Us re-issue is shown on the right with a new head mold — the re-issue has th
1995 Pizza Party Skipper head mold, while the original Wendy used the 198
Teen Fun Skipper head mold. **$35.00.**

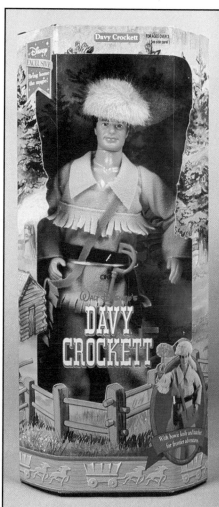

1994 DAVY CROCKETT #10308
commemorates the fortieth
anniversary of the Disneyland *Davy*
Crockett television series, starring
Fess Parker, which debuted in
December 1954. The Davy, Davy
Crockett, King of the Wild Frontier
melody is well-known to a genera-
tion of viewers. Davy Crockett
wears fringed buckskin pants and
shirt, coonskin hat, moccasins, belt
with knife sheath, bag, Bowie
knife, and hatchet. Interestingly,
the Grandpa Heart head mold with
brown — not white — hair is used
for Davy Crockett. MARKINGS: Back
of head: c MATTEL, INC. 1986; Back: c Mattel, Inc. 1968/ MALAYSIA. **$35.00.**

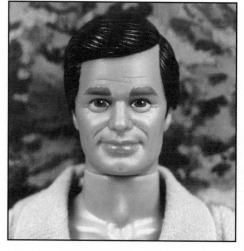

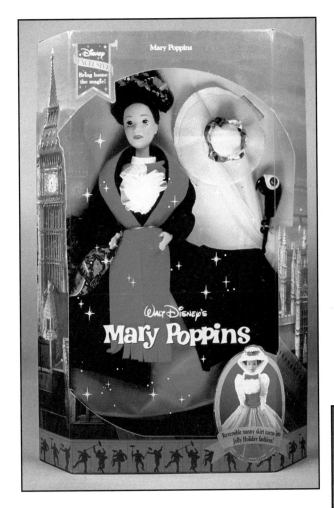

1994 MARY POPPINS #10313 represents the title character from Disney's 1964 motion picture *Mary Poppins*, starring Julie Andrews. This Mary Poppins doll does not attempt to capture Julie Andrews' likeness, borrowing the Sleeping Beauty head mold instead. She comes lavishly dressed in a long red dress over white pantaloons, navy

blue coat with red scarf, white blouse with red midriff and bow, red boots, and black hat with floral brim. She carries a carpet bag and talking parrot umbrella. Her skirt reverses to red with white sheer overskirt; a white hat is included to complete this Jolly Holiday ensemble. **$40.00.**

**1994 PIRATES OF TH
CARIBBEAN CAPTA**
#10258 is based on th
Disney theme pa
attraction Pirates of th
Caribbean. The Capta
has rooted black ha
and beard, with mena
ing brown eyes. H
wears a red coat, bla
pants, tan boots, be
dagger holder, and
black hat with skeletc
and crossbones logo. H
comes with three da
gers and a sword. It
hard to believe, but th
Captain uses The Princ
head mold from Beau
and the Beast. **$35.00.**

1995 ALICE IN WONDERLAND #13537 is based on the Disney 1951 animated feature *Alice in Wonderland*. Alice wears a blue satin skirt, white apron,
white stockings, black hair
bow, and black shoes.
Cardboard pop-up charac-
ters of the Cheshire Cat
and the Caterpillar are
included. Alice has the
Skipper head and body.
MARKINGS: Back of head: c
MATTEL INC 1987; Back: c
MATTEL INC 1987/
MALAYSIA. **$24.00.**

Disney's 6½" Princess Collection

In 1994 Mattel released five 6½" versions of their 11½" Disney princess dolls, along with three 6¾" princes, in a series called the Musical Princess Collection. The dolls were so successful that every year since, a new series of 6½" princesses with different themes has been released, including the 1995 Perfume Princess collection, 1996 Bubble Princess collection, and 1997 Dancing Princess collection. In addition, a number of gift sets and store exclusives have appeared.

MARKINGS: Every 6½" princess has c DISNEY on the back of their heads, and CHINA on their backs. Their heads appear to be reduced-size versions of the 11½" dolls' heads. All dolls have painted, molded-on shoes. All girl dolls are packaged with brushes.

1994 MUSICAL PRINCESS CINDERELLA #11597 features Cinderella wearing a miniature version of her blue ball gown. Musical Princess Cinderella's doll stand plays *Bibbidi-Bobbidi-Boo*. Every year the Cinderella dolls seem to be the bestseller, as they are the first to disappear from stores. **$20.00.**

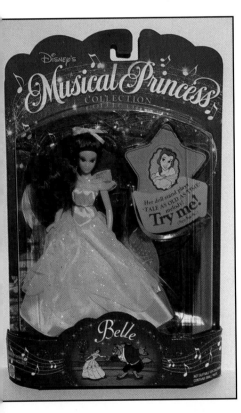

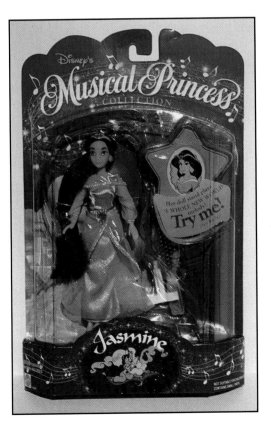

1994 MUSICAL PRINCESS BELLE #11600 features a 6½" Belle wearing a minature version of her yellow ball gown with yellow hair bow. Each Musical Princess has a star-shaped doll stand bearing her portrait; the stand plays the most memorable tune from each movie. The child can wear the stand as a locket with the enclosed ribbon. Musical Princess Belle's stand plays *Tale As Old As Time*. **$20.00.**

1994 MUSICAL PRINCESS JASMINE #11601 features Jasmine wearing her purple royal palace outfit with jeweled headband. Her doll stand plays *A Whole New World*. **$20.00.**

1994 MUSICAL PRINCESS COLLECTION PRINCE CHARMING #11872 wears red pants and white jacket with golden epaulettes. His doll stand plays *A Dream is a Wish*. **$22.00.**

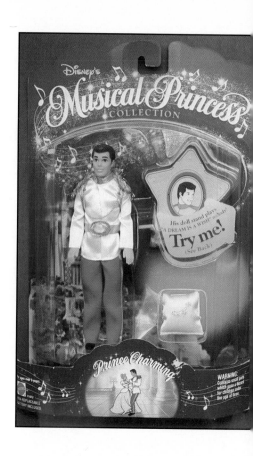

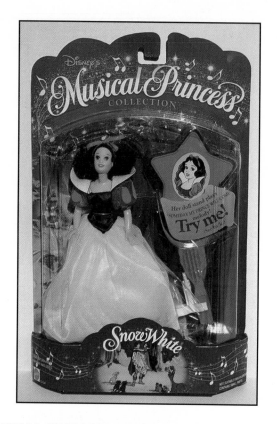

1994 MUSICAL PRINCESS SNOW WHITE #13134 features Snow White wearing her yellow gown with blue bodice, white collar, blue and pink sleeves, and pink hair bow. Her doll stand plays *Someday My Prince Will Come*. **$20.00.**

1994 MUSICAL PRINCESS COLLECTION GIFT SET #11757 combines all five Musical Princesses with muscial doll stands in one large gift set. **$75.00.**

1994 MUSICAL PRINCESS SLEEPING BEAUTY #11598 features Princess Aurora wearing her pink ball gown with golden necklace and crown. Her doll stand plays *Once Upon a Dream*. **$20.00.**

1994 MUSICAL PRINCESS COLLECTION THE BEAST
11870 features The Prince wearing black pants with
white silky shirt and yellow vest. The Beast's vinyl
ead mask, cape, and furry leggings are included to
ansform The Prince into The Beast. His doll stand
lays *Something There That Wasn't There Before*.
22.00.

994 MUSICAL PRINCESS COLLECTION ALADDIN
11871 features 6¾" Aladdin wearing his royal
/hite Prince Ali outfit with golden trim and jeweled
urban. His doll stand plays *Prince Ali*. $22.00.

1994 MUSICAL PRINCESS TALKING CASTLE #11757 is a 15" x
13½" four-room castle with marble floor and opening drawbridge, and special talking areas for each of the five Musical
Princesses; Belle has a library where she says, "I love to read,
don't you?"; Cinderella has a parlor where she says, "My little
friends sewed a lovely gown."; Jasmine has a terrace with flying carpet where she says, "Let's ride the magic carpet!";
Snow White has a dressing room with mirror where she says,
"The Dwarfs are my friends!"; and Sleeping Beauty has a bedroom where she says "I was raised by three fairies." The dolls
say two other phrases each, and the drawbridge opens with a
magical sound. A special dance stand allows one doll and a
prince to really dance. Unfortunately, the castle was never
released. The photo here is from the 1994 Mattel Girls Toys
catalog.

1994 MUSICAL CLASSICS LITTLE MERMA **#13538** is a Disney Store exclusive release for the fifth anniversary of Disney's 198 animated film *The Little Mermaid*. This Mattel's first adaptation of *The Little Me maid*; Tyco Toys produced Disney's The L tle Mermaid dolls previously. She has re hair and green eyes and wears a turquoi fish tail with iridescent fins and iridescen purple bikini top. She uses the Cinderel head mold. Her doll stand plays *Part of Your World*. **$28.00.**

1994 MUSICAL CLASSICS MARY POPPINS #13362 features Mary Poppins wearing a red dress with navy coat, red scarf, and black hat. The illustration on the lower front of her box shows the 11½" doll flying by Big Ben with her umbrella air brushed out; no umbrella is included. The cameo illustration on her doll stand shows a brown-eyed Mar Poppins; the doll stand illustrated on the box back shows a blue-eye Mary Poppins with her hair in a bun and her teeth showing. It plays *Spoonful of Sugar*. **$25.00.**

1994 MUSICAL CLASSICS TINKE BELL #13363 features Tinker Be wearing her neon green outfit wit wings and green cloth slippers ove her molded-on shoes. Her doll stan plays *You Can Fly*. **$25.00.**

1995 PERFUME PRINCESS BELLE #12743 features Belle with green eyes wearing her iridescent green library fashion with green hair ribbon. Each doll in the Perfume Princess Collection has a scent like a flower from a royal garden. The dolls have openings in their backs which are filled with fragrance. When the applicator is dipped into the doll's back, fragrance can be dabbed on the child. Each doll also has a doll stand. Perfume Princess Belle has a bottle of rose fragrance. **$18.00.**

1995 PERFUME PRINCESS CINDERELLA #12746 features Cinderella wearing an iridescent white wedding gown with matching hair band. She has a bottle of gardenia fragrance. **$18.00.**

1995 PERFUME PRINCESS JASMINE #12742 features Jasmine wearing an iridescent turquoise palace costume with golden necklace and jeweled headband. She has a bottle of jasmine fragrance. **$18.00.**

1995 PERFUME PRINCESS SNOW WHITE #12744 features Snow White in an iridescent blue gown with dark blue iridescent lamé bodice, iridescent white sleeves, and pink hair bow. She has a bottle of honeysuckle fragrance. **$18.00.**

1995 PERFUME PRINCESS SLEEPING BEAUTY #12745 wears an iridescent pink version of her Briar Rose fashion with black velvet bodice and black hair ribbon. She has a bottle of lily fragrance. **$18.00.**

1995 PERFUME PRINCESS COLLECTION GIFT SET #14134 packages all five Perfume Princesses with their bottles of fragrance together in one large gift set box. **$68.00.**

1995 PERFUME PRINCESS COLLECTION FAIRY GODMOTHER #12747 is a Disney Store exclusive. She wears an iridescent pink dress and cape with hood. She has a bottle of violet fragrance. **$25.00.**

1996 BUBBLE PRINCESS BELLE #14633 features Belle with green eyes, brown hair with shimmery purple strands, and purple fashion with apron. The Bubble Princess Collection dolls each come with a doll stand filled with bubble solution which can be poured into the openings in the dolls' backs. Using the wand /stopper to dip solution from the doll's back allows the child to blow bubbles. **$16.00.**

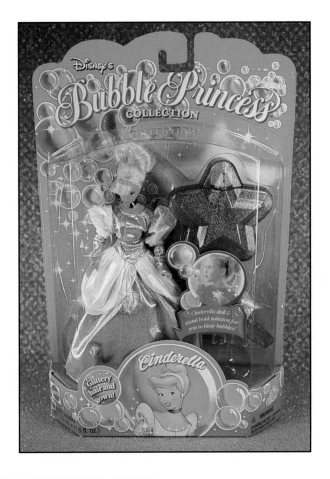

1996 BUBBLE PRINCESS CINDERELLA #14635 features Cinderella with iridescent strands of hair wearing a shiny aqua blue version of her classic ballgown. **$16.00.**

1996 BUBBLE PRINCESS JASMINE
#14637 has black hair with shiny turquoise strands, shiny gold dress with aqua and gold top, golden necklace and jeweled headband. **$16.00.**

1996 BUBBLE PRINCESS SLEEPING BEAUTY #14634 features Princess Aurora with iridescent strands in her hair wearing her pink princess ball gown with golden crown. **$16.00.**

1996 BUBBLE PRINCESS SNOW WHITE #14636 features Snow White with shiny blue strands in her black hair. She wears a shiny golden gown with shiny blue bodice, red cape, and hair ribbon. **$16.00.**

1997 DANCING PRINCESS CINDERELLA #16533 wears her classic blue ballgown with full skirt. She also wears a wrist corsage and blue headband. Her doll stand plays *A Dream is a Wish*; that tune was used with 1994's Musical Prince Charming, while Musical Princess Cinderella's tune was formerly *Bibbidi-Bob-bidi-Boo*. **$16.00.**

997 DANCING PRINCESS BELLE #16532 is he of three dolls in the first edition Dancing rincess Collection, which uses lavender ackaging. Dancing Princess Belle wears a bil-wing yellow ball gown with an iridescent ellow bodice with rose. Each of the Dancing rincess Collection dolls have a musical irntable base which plays music as the child ishes it, causing the doll to spin and dance. ancing Princess Belle's doll stand plays *Tale Old as Time*. **$16.00.**

1997 DANCING PRINCESS BELLE #16532 was re-released late in 1997 with new dark pink and purple packaging; a newly added portrait of Belle next to the doll replaces the hand mirror illustration. The doll and contents are the same; only the packaging differs. **$14.00.**

1997 DANCING PRINCESS CINDERELLA #16533 was re-released late in 1997 with new dark pink and purple packaging; a newly added portrait of Cinderella next to the doll replaces the glass slipper illustration. **$14.00.**

1997 DANCING PRINCESS POCAHONTA **#17394** is one of three new additions to the Dancing Princess Collection, and the first ever 6½" Pocahontas doll. She wears a long fringed off white Native American outfit with decorative beads at the bottom, turquoise fringe at the top, necklace, and feathers in her hair. Her doll stand plays *Colors of the Wind*. **$17.00.**

1997 DANCING PRINCESS JASMINE **#16534** wears a sheer layered gown of turquoise, purple, and blue materials with turquoise jewels at the hem. She has a golden necklace and hair decoration. Her doll stand plays *A Whole New World*. **$16.00.**

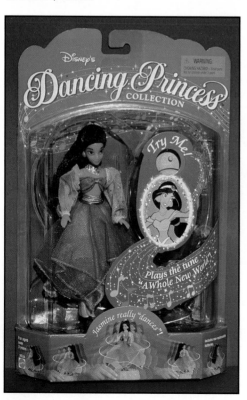

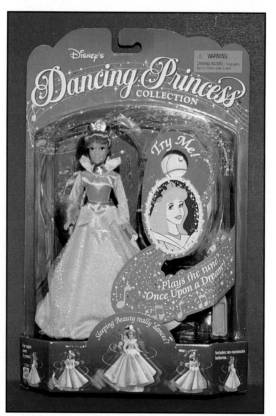

1997 DANCING PRINCESS SLEEPING BEAUT **#17396** features Princess Aurora wearing h pink gown with iridescent collar, shimmer overskirt, silvery necklace, and crown. Her doll stand plays *Once Upon a Dream*. **$14.00.**

1997 DANCING PRINCESS JASMINE #16534 was re-released late in 1997 with new dark pink and purple packaging; a newly added portrait of Jasmine next to the doll replaces the magic lamp illustration. **$14.00.**

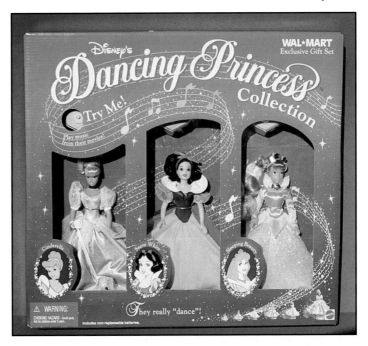

1997 DANCING PRINCESS SNOW WHITE #17395 wears her classic blue and yellow outfit with long red cape and hair bow. Her doll stand plays, *Someday My Prince Will Come*. **$14.00.**

1997 DANCING PRINCESS COLLECTION Wal-Mart Exclusive Gift Set contains Dancing Princess Cinderella, Dancing Princess Snow White, and Dancing Princess Sleeping Beauty with their musical dancing doll stands in one box. **$40.00.**

1997 DANCING PRINCESS ARIEL AND PRINCE ERIC GIFT SET #17855 features Ariel with a newly designed head wearing a pale pink gown with silvery flower and ribbon in her hair, along with Prince Eric, dressed in blue pants, white shirt, blue cape, and golden belt. The dolls dance together on a double-doll turntable base as the tune *A Part of Your World* plays. **$20.00.**

1997 DANCING PRINCESS BELLE & THE BEAST GIFT SET #17839 features Belle wearing a green satin gown with white fur collar and cuffs and molded-on ice skates, along with The Prince wearing black pants, a white shirt, and molded-on ice skates. The Beast's vinyl mask and red cape are included. They skate together on the double-doll stand to the tune *Tale as Old as Time*. **$20.00.**

341

Disney Classics

1997 DANCING PRINCESS CINDERELLA AND PRINCE GIFT SET #18058 features Cinderella wearing her beautiful white wedding gown with veil, along with Prince Charming in his royal outfit of red pants, white jacket with golden epaulettes, and golden belt. As they dance on their double-doll turntable stand, *A Dream Is a Wish* is played. This is a Toys 'R' Us exclusive. **$25.00.**

1997 STOCKING PRINCESS ARIEL #118-208 is one of three Avon 6" Stocking Princess exclusives. Each comes wearing a red Santa hat; t doll is tucked into a red felt stocking ornament with white fur to and each princess' picture is on her stocking. Stocking Princess Ar wears a purple bikini top with turquoise fish tail and red Santa h **$20.00.**

1997 STOCKING PRINCESS BELLE #119-850 wears her yellow b gown and a red Santa hat. Her stocking has her illustration on **$20.00.**

1997 STOCKING PRINCESS CINDERELLA #118-121 wears her blue b gown, cloth black choker, blue hair band, and red Santa hat. Her r felt stocking has her illustration on it. **$20.00.**

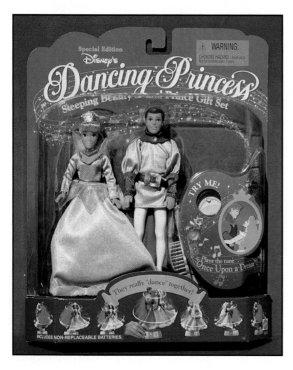

1995 DISNEY BEDTIME PRINCESS COLLECTION. Matt planned to release soft-bodied 11" dolls of favorite Disn princesses. When hugged, each doll's glow-in-the-dark gov plays a melody from her movie. They were never realesed.

1997 DANCING PRINCESS SLEEPING BEAUTY AND PRINCE GIFT S #18059 features Princess Aurora wearing a gown, along with Prin Phillip dressed in gray pants and blue vest with a red cape. This the first 6¾" version of Prince Phillip; he uses the 6¾" Prin Charming head mold. This is a Toys 'R' Us exclusive. **$25.00.**

Pocahontas

Loosely based on the real-life meeting of Native American Pocahontas and colonist John Smith, the 1995 Disney adaptation introduces a new heroine learning to adjust to another culture. Mattel initially produced dolls of Pocahontas, her Native American companions Nakoma and Kocoum, and John Smith. The male Kocoum was discontinued after the first year, but the other three appeared together in a Color Splash swimwear line. The largest number of fashions made to date for a Mattel Disney doll were released, along with a variety of animals, not to mention numerous versions of Pocahontas.

1995 SUN COLORS POCAHONTAS #13328 is shown here in the earliest style box. Pocahontas, who uses a new head mold with black hair and brown eyes, wears a simple beige dress with golden fringe and belt and blue necklace. Leaf designs appear on her dress when exposed to sunlight. She has a pink blanket and wears a compass tied to her left wrist. She was meant to have her bird Flit, which doubles as a child's ring, but they were not ready in time for the movie release, so Mattel attached a card stating, Flit ring not included. To receive yours at NO ADDITIONAL COST, call 1-800-524-TOYS. Dolls appearing later had the Flit ring affixed to the liner. A second feature identifying this doll as a first-edition Pocahontas is the photo sticker on her window; Mattel felt that the color-change feature of the dress needed to be shown, but since the dolls were already sealed in packages, a photo sticker was placed on the box window to illustrate the dress with leaf design. **$30.00.**

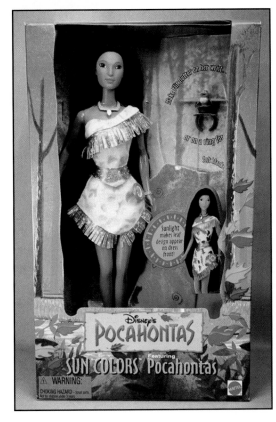

1995 SUN COLORS POCAHONTAS #13328 second edition is shown here. The Flit ring is now included, held to the box liner with clear form-fitting plastic. Instead of the sticker on the box window, a photo cardboard insert shows Pocahontas modeling her dress with leaf designs. **$22.00.**

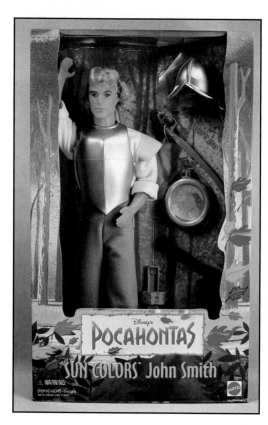

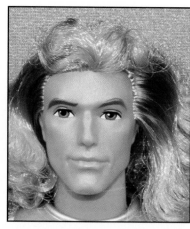

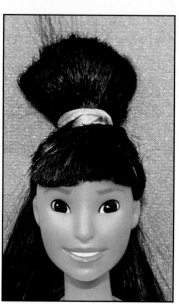

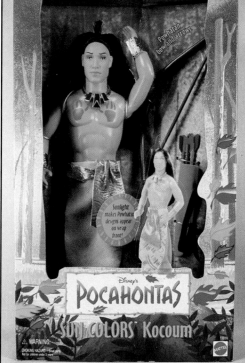

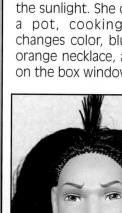

1995 SUN COLORS JOHN SMITH #13329 contains John Smith with rooted blonde hair held in a ponytail and blue eyes. He wears blue pants, beige shirt with gray armor chest plate, and gray cloth boots. He also comes with a helmet, sword, belt with pouch, brush, and child-size compass with ribbon to be worn as a necklace; the compass face is a lenticular picture of Pocahontas with John Smith at one angle, and a compass face at another. John Smith has a new head mold used on a Ken body. **$22.00.**

1995 SUN COLORS NAKOMA #13331 has black hair and brown eyes. She wears a two-piece tan outfit that reveals a butterfly design in the sunlight. She comes with a pot, cooking pit that changes color, blue blanket, orange necklace, and hair bow. The first edition doll with photo sticker on the box window is shown here. **$24.00.**

1995 SUN COLORS KOCOUM #13330 has long black hair with mohawk and brown eyes. He wears a tan wrap with copper belt, arm bands, and necklace. Red bear claw marks are painted on his chest. He has a bow with three arrows and a quiver. **$22.00.**

95 BRAIDED BEAUTY POCAHONTAS #13332 features Pocahontas h knee-length black hair wearing a peach dress with fringe, a cop-

per-color belt, and blue necklace. Her raccoon Meeko serves as a styling tool in this set, as his two paws clasp onto the doll's (or child's) hair and twists and twirls to create braids. A similar design mechanism was used with 1983's Twirly Curls Barbie. A brush and hair accessories including feathers, leaves, a seashell, and a sunflower are included. **$24.00.**

1995 SUN COLORS NAKOMA #13331 second edition is shown here with cardboard photo insert attached to the box liner instead of a photo sticker on the box window. **$20.00.**

995 RIVER ROWING POCAHONTAS #13333 features Pocahontas n a move and bend body with jointed elbows for ease in paddling he plastic canoe in which she and Meeko ride. Pocahontas wears a wo-piece outfit with fringe and a blue necklace. The canoe really oats, and a battery in the canoe moves the paddle in Pocahontas' and. **$40.00.**

1995 SPIRIT OF LOVE GIFT SET #14051 contains Pocahontas wearing a two-piece fringed dress with golden designs and John Smith wearing blue pants, blue vinyl boots, a beige shirt, and belt with satchel. **$50.00.**

1995 BEAD-SO-PRETTY POCAHONTAS #14055 is an 18" doll using the 1977 SuperSize Barbie body. She has black hair and brown eyes and wears a large-scale version of the fashion worn by Sun Colors Pocahontas. A beader, eighteen beads and hair decorations, and a Flit comb are included for the doll's use. **$28.00.**

The prototypes of the Pocahontas doll line all used different head molds from the dolls actually released.

1995 MY FIRST POCAHONTAS #13522 is a 16" soft vinyl doll wearing a one-piece beige dress with pink fringe, blue belt, and blue necklace. A Flit comb is included. **$20.00.**

1995 FLUTTER 'N FLOWER FLIT #13492 features the large hummingbird Flit whose shimmery wings flutter when his feet are pushed. His flower bed is included. This Flit, Run 'n Carry Meeko, and Sleep 'N Eat Percy are the only three plastic animals sold individually designed specifically for use with the 11½" dolls. **$10.00.**

1995 RUN 'N CARRY MEEKO #13491 features the hungry raccoon Meeko, who scampers forward when given a push. He comes with a platter of food. **$10.00.**

1995 SLEEP 'N EAT PERCY #13490 features the pampered bulldog Percy with purple blanket and crown/dog bowl. When his head is pressed, his eyes close. **$10.00.**

1995 POCAHONTAS STYLING HEAD #66520 is 8" tall including plastic base. The Pocahontas Styling Head has long styleable hair with removable earrings, a necklace, comb, mirror, and headband with flower. **$20.00.**

Disney Classics

1995 SWIMMING DRESS 'N PLAY #68452 contains a blue two-piece fashion with blue moccasins, a blue purse, mat, turtle, necklace, comb, fish, and two shells. **$12.00.**

1995 DANCE 'N PLAY #68452 is the first o four deluxe Pocahontas fashions with plastic moc casins and numerous play pieces. All four deluxe fashions have the same stock number. This fashion is a two-piece leaf-print outfit with two drums, tam bourine, squirrel, frog, bracelets, necklace, comb and two morracas. **$12.00.**

1995 WILDERNESS DRESS 'N PLAY #68452 is a one-piece gray and blue fashion with moccasins, two birds, comb, compass necklace, pumpkin, basket of berries, bowl, basket of corn, and basket. **$12.00.**

1995 WINTER DRESS 'N PLAY #68452 features pink dress with pink moccasins, matching purse basket of berries, firewood, bracelets, comb, an two rabbits. **$12.00.**

1995 EARTH DANCE FASHION #68451 is one of four Earth Dance fashions, each with plastic moccasins and a purse. This is a blue two-piece outfit with fringe, blue purse, and blue moccasins. **$8.00.**

1995 EARTH DANCE FASHION #68451 is a green one-piece dress with fringe, green purse, and green moccasins. **$8.00.**

1995 EARTH DANCE FASHION #68451 is a pink one-piece dress with beige fringe, beige purse, and pink moccasins. **$8.00.**

Disney Classics

1995 EARTH DANCE FASHION GIFT SET #68470 is a Disney Store exclusive containing all four Earth Dance fashions with purses and moccasins, with the addition of Flit and Meeko animals and sunflowers. **$40.00.**

1995 EARTH DANCE FASHION #68451 is a tan one-piece fashion with matching purse and peach moccasins. **$8.00.**

1995 POWHATAN VILLAGE PLAY SET #67217 is for use with the 11½" dolls. Included are a hut, drying rack with fish, campfire, berries, four baskets, bushel of corn, apples, wooden pot, wooden bowl, bed, bed spread, tomatoes, and ladle. The background of the box is only a turquoise blue color. **$20.00.**

1995 POCAHONTAS COLLECTOR DOLL CASE #80205 by Janex is vinyl case with divided black plastic tray with room for two dolls. An enclosed diorama features three settings from Pocahontas – the Powhatan village, the interior of a tent, and the river. **$15.00.**

1995 POWHATAN VILLAGE PLAY SET #67217 was re-released in new packaging featuring a forest background depicting John Smith, Pocahontas, and Nakoma in the village. The contents are identical. **$14.00.**

1996 COLOR SPLASH HAIR POCAHONTAS #14864 features Pocahontas wearing a blue and white outfit with leaves decorations and blue necklace. When immersed in warm water, blue and pink streaks appear in her hair. **$14.00.**

1996 COLOR SPLASH HAIR NAKOMA #14867 wears a pink and white two-piece outfit with two butterfly decorations, an orange necklace, and a hair bow. When her hair is immersed in warm water, purple and pink streaks appear in her hair. **$14.00.**

1996 COLOR SPLASH TATTOO JOHN SMITH #14865 wears white pants with a blue belt and a compass around his neck. He has a blue tattoo on his chest that turns purple when warm water is applied. **$14.00.**

Disney Classics

1996 FEATHERS IN THE WIND POCAHONTAS #14920 features Pocahontas wearing a beautiful long cream-colored dress with white frings on the sleeves, bodice, and hem. A copper-colored belt holds a metallic leaf and a collection of feathers. She has two braids in copper bands with feathers, while the rest of her hair cascades to the floor. Flit perches on her arm, and Meeko, wearing a feathered headdress, sits on a log. A doll stand is included. This is a Toys 'R' Us exclusive. **$55.00.**

1996 COLOR SPLASH TATTOO POWHATAN WARRIOR #1486 wears a tan loin cloth and purple belt holding feathers. He has red bear claw tattoos on his chest, which darken when warm water is applied. He has long black hair with a mohawk and warrior facial paint. The doll was not produced, but his picture appears on the back of the Color Splash dolls' boxes. It is not clear whether he is Kocoum, who died in the *Pocahontas* movie, or another Powhatan warrior.

1996 SHINING BRAIDS POCAHONTAS #15416 has ankle length hair and a long blue dress with pink fringe. She wears a blue necklace and has shimmery, poseable braids that hold her hairstyles in place. **$20.00.**

The Hunchback of Notre Dame

If ever a character demonstrates it's what's inside that counts, it's The Hunchback of Notre Dame. The critically-acclaimed animated motion picture from 1996 afforded Mattel the opportunity to immortalize Quasimodo in vinyl. Esmerelda, as a fashion doll, appears the most in this line, joined by Phoebus and Quasimodo, a horse, play set, and six fashions.

1996 MAGIC VIEW QUASIMODO #15313 is a 9" all-vinyl doll with movable arms and waist. Quasimodo wears molded-on clothing, consisting of a green shirt, brown pants, and blue shoes. A brown cloth toolbelt holds four carved dolls representing himself, Esmerelda, Phoebus, and Friar Rollo; a cardboard city scene is included for the tiny dolls. Also included are a tool-chest with tools and a magic lens that allows children to view the city scene as Quasimodo does. MARKINGS: Bottom of left foot: c DISNEY/CHINA. **$15.00.**

1996 ESMERALDA #15311 wears a lavender dress, purple overskirt with golden coins attached, white blouse, sparkly pink head scarf, gold earring, and golden bracelets. She has black hair with blue eyes and comes with a white petticoat with attached bells. She has a fully poseable body, used first with 1994 Gymnast Barbie. MARKINGS: Back: c 1993 MATTEL, INC./ CHINA. **$15.00.**

1996 ESMERALDA DELUXE GIFT SET #16204 features the Esmeralda doll with a Festival of Fools fashion and a Dance Fantasy fashion. This is a wholesale club exclusive. **$50.00.**

1996 GYPSY DANCING ESMERALDA #15314 was repositioned in her box soon after release. The doll now stands up straighter in her box, and the cardboard insert on the left is repositioned. **$17.00.**

1996 GYPSY DANCING ESMERALDA #15314 feature Esmeralda wearing an orange and purple dancing co tume with golden jeweled headband, golden bracelet and a tambourine with music chip that plays music whe pressed. This first edition has the doll positioned lo inside the box. She has straight arms with unbending pla tic legs. **$22.00.**

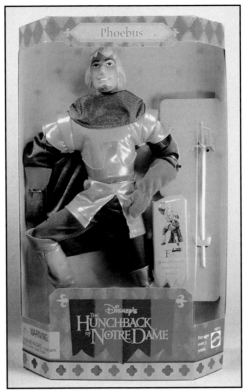

1996 PHOEBUS #15312 features Phoebus wearing a blue-green shirt and cape, golden chest armor and boot tops, brown pants and gloves, and sword. Phoebus uses the Young Sweethearts Michael's body. MARKINGS: Back: c 1975 MATTEL, INC./ CHINA. **$15.00.**

1996 TRUE HEARTS GIFT SET #15315 features Esmeralda dressed in a white blouse, yellow belt, magenta, purple, and green skirt, matching head scarf, earring, and bracelets. She uses a different body from the other two Esmeralda dolls; this body is the bent-arm SuperStar Barbie body. Phoebus is wearing the same outfit as the individual doll **#15312**, except this Phoebus uses the stockier 1968 Ken doll body with straight arms. **$50.00.**

1996 BURGER KING PROMOTIONAL THE HUNCHBACK OF NOTRE DAME HAND PUPPETS were offered when the movie opened in the summer of 1996. Quasimodo, Esmeralda, Phoebus, and Hugo hand puppet dolls were available in plastic bags with the purchase of value meals. Each doll is packaged with a Mattel Toys booklet featuring The Hunchback of Notre Dame toys. **$8.00 each.**

1996 ESMERALDA #42122 is an 8" tall rooted hair doll by Applause wearing an outfit in the style of the 11½" Esmeralda doll. **$15.00.**

1996 ESMERALDA CHARMS 'N BEAUTY STYLING HEAD #66217 is 9" tall including the base. The styling head has only one earring hole, in her left ear, and she comes with 12 charms, a necklace, one earring, a brush, and tiara. **$15.00.**

1996 ESMERALDA #15281 is a 15" soft-bodied doll with vinyl head wearing a larger size version of the outfit worn by the 11½" Esmeralda. **$15.00.**

1996 MAGIC BRAIDS ESMERALDA #16001 is an 18" version of Gypsy Dancing Esmeralda. She uses the 197 SuperSize Barbie body. Ten extra braids, a magic brush and four removable scarves are included. MARKING Back: c 1976 Mattel, Inc./ CHINA. **$30.00.**

96 PRETTY DANCIN' ESMERAL-
. #66235 is a 32" soft-bodied
rsion of the 11½" Esmeralda
ll with removable pink scarf,
ring, bracelets, ankle ring, and
cklace. **$45.00.**

1996 CELESTIAL DREAM FASHION
#66230 is one of three simple fashions
inspired by *The Hunchback of Notre
Dame.* Celestial Dream is a blue gown
with a yellow star design, yellow top,
and orange apron. **$8.00.**

1996 DANCE FANTASY FASHION
#66230 is a magenta skirt, orange
blouse, and purple floral-print apron.
$8.00.

1996 GYPSY MAGIC HORSE #15318 is a
white horse with long white mane and
tail containing golden strands of hair; he
wears gypsy saddle blankets which,
when turned over, reveal a gallant coat-
of-arms. **$25.00.**

357

1996 FESTIVAL OF FOOLS DRESS 'N PLAY #66231
features purple pants with a red shirt, purple wrap,
purple hair band, puppet, flag, wand, horn, necklace, three bracelets, and comb. **$10.00.**

1996 FESTIVAL OF FOOLS FASHION #66230 is
a yellow and green skirt with pink blouse and
blue vest. **$8.00.**

1996 TRUE LOVE DRESS 'N PLAY #66231 features a pink and aqua dress with yellow bodice,
yellow belt, basket of fruit, mandolin, pillow,
pitcher, hand mirror, comb, necklace, goblet,
spice shakers, and tray. **$10.00.**

996 ESMERALDA GYPSY FESTIVAL TENT #66234 contains an orange and ellow tent, table, chair, crate, tray with fruit and bread, jug, basket, two lates, goblet, dagger, and candlestick. **$14.00.**

1997 ESMERALDA #16960 wears an orange swimsuit with magenta sleeves, pink skirt, magenta hair bow, purple belt, and earring. She had extremely limited distribution. **$35.00.**

1996 TRUE LOVE DRESS 'N PLAY #66231 has been found with a brown belt, and the dress in this set has a lighter floral print. **$12.00.**

Hercules

Opening in the summer of 1997, **Hercules** is an enjoyable journey into Greek mythology. While the film received good reviews, Mattel's toy line based on this movie seems too short lived. Even though the film remained in theaters until late summer, retail stores began reducing the prices on their Hercules dolls well before the Christmas shopping season had even begun. The Hercules line is rather small, consisting of just two human characters, Hercules and Megara in several different versions, along with a horse and two fashions.

1997 GOLDEN GLOW HER-CULES #17112 features the muscled champion wearing gold-tone chest armor that turns a bronze color in sunlight, removable cape, blue tank overskirt that reverses from gold tone to bronze color, cloth headband, plastic wrist bands, sword, sandals and hero's medallion worn on his belt. MARKINGS: Back: 1996 Mattel, Inc./ CHINA. **$16.00.**

1997 FASHION SECRETS MEGARA #17149 wears a lavender Grecian gown with overskirt, shawl, sash, hair band, and sandals. Her gown can be worn long or short. Early Megara doll's eyes are looking further to the left than later dolls, whose eyes appear more centered. She uses the Beach Streak Shani body mold, which has smaller hips and waist than Barbie doll bodies. MARKINGS: Back: c 1991 MATTEL, INC/ CHINA. **$16.00.**

1997 LEGEND OF LOVE GIFT SET #17479 contains Hercules wearing gold-tone armor over his blue tank undershirt, blue cape, golden headband, plastic wrist bands, sword, and sandals. Megara wears a long white pleated dress with light blue bodice, iridescent blue cape, headband, and sandals. She is the only Megara doll with earrings. **$40.00.**

1997 POWER FLEX HERCULES #16886 is 15" tall with a rubber latex chest which appears to flex when his arms are pushed down. **$27.00.**

1997 MEGARA #17261 wears a blue tunic with golden belt and bodice trim, a hair band, and sandals. She was only available in select locations for a short time. **$25.00.**

997 MEGARA GIFT SET #18044 packages Fashion Secrets Megara with a Once Upon A Time Locket featuring tiny Hercules and Megara figures with a locket containing a flying Pegasus. This is a wholesale club exclusive. **$45.00.**

1997 GRECIAN FANTASY 'N FUN #69268 features Megara's pink gown with a belt, purse, sandals, lyre, goblet, bowl, fruit, basket, and vase. **$9.00.**

1997 MAGIC WINGS PEGASUS #17254 features the white winged horse with soft blue mane and tail. When tilted skyward, his shimmery wings move for about 20 seconds to simulate flying. **$22.00.**

1997 BABY PEGASUS # 69847 is small plush horse in scale with th dolls. **$9.00.**

1997 PAIN #69847 is in scale wit the dolls. **$9.00.**

1997 PANIC #69847 is in scal with the dolls. **$9.00.**

1997 PHIL #69847 is in scale wit the dolls. **$9.00.**

The Little Mermaid

Disney's 1989 animated feature *The Little Mermaid* was an instant favorite with children, as well as adults. Beautiful songs and an intriguing new villainess, Ursula the Sea Witch, delighted audiences. Tyco Toys had the rights to produce dolls and toys based on this movie. Their 10½" Ariel doll appeared in 1991 with a closed mouth head. The next edition of Tyco's Ariel used a new, smiling head mold with teeth showing. This Ariel became the standard look for the doll for each year their Little Mermad line returned. Mattel got the rights to this Disney character in 1994, producing only a 6½" Musical Classics Little Mermaid then before beginning a new line of dolls in late 1997. Mattel now owns Tyco Toys, so many collectors of Mattel's The Little Mermaid may wish to purshase past examples of the doll from the Tyco line.

1997 ARIEL THE LITTLE MERMAID #17595 is Mattel's first 11¼" vinyl doll representing the Disney character. She has bright red hair and big blue eyes. She wears an iridescent purple bikini top and blue-green lamé fish tail with iridescent fins. She wears a purple bikini bottom under her tail for use as a human. She uses the 1997 Teen Skipper body except Ariel's waist is non-twisting. MARKINGS: Back: c 1995 MATTEL INC/ CHINA. **$14.00.**

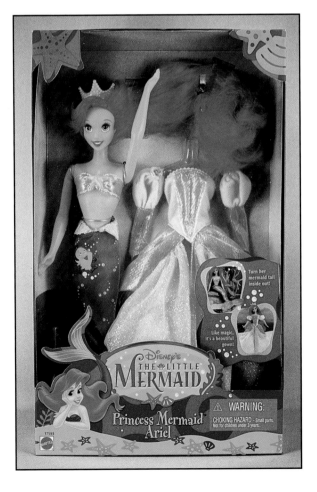

1997 PRINCESS MERMAID ARIEL #17593 has a purple fish tail with illustrations of Flounder the fish and Sebastian the crab and a purple bikini top. When her mermaid tail is turned inside out, it becomes a beautiful pink gown. She has a tiara, earrings, and shoes. **$20.00.**

1997 PRINCE ERIC & MAX GIFT SET #17591 features Prince Eric wearing a white shirt, gray pants, and black boots with his loyal sheepdog Max. A red bandana can be used as Prince Eric's belt or Max's collar. **$18.00.**

1997 SEA PEARL PRINCESS ARIEL #18327 is an Avon exclusive with 7" of long, red hair. Sea Princess Ariel wears a shiny purple two-piece swimsuit and a removable tail with shiny purple fins. She carries a red net purse containing a pearl bracelet with a golden shell charm. **$24.00.**

1997 WEDDING PARTY GIFT SET #17592 contains Ariel wearing a lovely white wedding gown with veil, white earrings, and shoes; Prince Eric wearing a white jacket with sash, blue pants, and black boots; and Flounder and Sebastian carrying wedding bands on a sea shell. **$32.00.**

1997 SWIMMING ARIEL #17562 is several inches taller than the regular Ariel because of the swimming mechanism in her tail. She wears a bikini top and a mermaid tail; she has no legs, as her lower half is a solid skin-tone compartment for holding the battery that operates her tail movement. MARKINGS: Rear: c 1997 Mattel, Inc./ MALAYSIA/ 1.5v. **$25.00.**

1997 MY FIRST ARIEL #17117 is a soft, plush doll with vinyl head and combable hair. She wears a purple bikini top and a mermaid tail that changes into two shimmery gown looks. **$20.00.**

Disney Classics

1997 DRESS 'N PLAY #69291 features Ariel's blue dress with white sleeves, lavender shoes, picnic basket, flowers, and hat. **$9.00.**

1997 DRESS 'N PLAY #69291 features Ariel's pink mermaid tail and top, shell tray, miror, comb, perfum bottle, necklace, and tiara. **$9.00.**

1997 DRESS 'N PLAY #69291 contains Ariel's purple dress with shimmery overskirt, necklace, bouquet of flowers, purse, and blue shoes. **$9.00.**

97 **LITTLE MERMAID BEDROOM SET #65928** contains a sea
~~~ell bed, vanity, chair, bedside table, lamp, comb, necklace, head
~nd, hand mirror, perfume bottle, breakfast tray, photo frame,
~ffee pot, cup, saucer, and lamp stand. **$17.00.**

1998 TROPICAL SPLASH ARIEL #17842 features
Ariel with a non-removable plastic color-
change fin. Her female friends in this line have
the same feature. All use the Ariel head mold.
$15.00.

1998 TROPICAL SPLASH ERIC #18478 features
Eric with a color-change swimsuit. **$15.00.**

1998 TROPICAL SPLASH ARISTA #18696 is Ariel's sister. **$15.00.**

1998 TROPICAL SPLASH ATTINA #18694 is Ariel's sister. **$15.00.**

1998 TROPICAL SPLASH KAYLA #18695 is Ariel's friend. The
name Kayla was used for a friend of Barbie doll in 1989 and
1994. **$15.00.**

101 Dalmatians

Disney's 1961 animated feature *101 Dalmatians* involves a new family of Dalmatians trying to escape the clutches of Cruella de Vil, who wants the puppies for a coat! A live action feature film by the same name featured Glenn Close in the de Vil role. Mattel produced 101 Dalmatians Barbie and 101 Dalmatians Teresa dolls exclusively for Toys 'R' Us..The dolls have a Dalmatian dog each, and a maze on the back of the dolls' boxes features a double-decker bus with London sign, tall, three-story townhouses, Big Ben, and a bridge — the same locale where *101 Dalmatians* takes place.

1997 101 DALMATIANS BARBIE #17248 wears a red tee-shirt, Dalmatian-look vest, skirt, and headband, black boots, socks, and sunglasses. She carries a purse and holds a leash attached to her Dalmatian puppy, which has a golden sequin name tag. The same Dalmatian was first used by Mattel with 1992 Pet Pals Kevin. MARKINGS: Back of doll's head: c 1976 MATTEL, INC.; doll's back: c MATTEL, INC. 1966/ INDONESIA; dog's rear: c 1991 MI/ INDONESIA. **$20.00.**

1997 101 DALMATIANS TERESA #17602 is Barbie doll's Hispanic friend who wears the same Dalmatian-look outfit and has the same Dalmatian dog. MARKINGS: Back of doll's head: c 1990 MATTEL INC.; rest same. **$20.00.**

1997 101 DALMATIANS BARBIE (Black) #17601 wears the same outfit and has the same dog as the white doll. MARKINGS: Back of doll's head: c MATTEL INC. 1987; rest same. **$20.00.**

Princess Stories Collection

Mattel re-released five 11½" Disney dolls in 1997 wearing fashions similar to the earlier editions of 1991 – 1993. The box states "You get 3 times the magic with a pretty princess, a friend, and a Little Little Golden Book." These dolls are very popular with collectors.

1997 BELLE #18193 wears her yellow ball gown with shiny bodice and fingerless gloves, hair bow, and shoes. She comes with a Little Little Golden Book with illustrations from *Beauty and the Beast*, and the enchanted candlestick Lumiere. **$20.00.**

1997 CINDERELLA #18195 wears her classic blue ball gown with iridescent over-skirt and sleeves, black cloth choker, blue head band, pearl earrings, and shoes. She comes with a Little Little Golden Book and her friend Gus the mouse. **$20.00.**

1997 JASMINE #18191 wears her purple royal princess wedding costume with iridescent collar, jeweled headband, and slippers. She comes with a Little Little Golden Book and two individual palace doves, which can be removed from their perch. **$20.00.**

1997 SNOW WHITE #18194 demonstrates what a lovely paint job Mattel's China factory does on doll faces — this Snow White barely resembles the 1993 Snow White made in Malaysia. This new doll is gorgeous with red lips, light skin, and black hair. She wears her classic yellow gown, blue bodice with white collar, red cape, and shoes. She comes with a Little Little Golden Book and a rabbit forest friend. **$22.00.**

1997 SLEEPING BEAUTY #18192 has a new smiling, head mold with teeth showing; the original 1992 Sleeping Beauty has a closed mouth and color-change eyes — the 1997 doll does not have this feature. She wears her pink Princess Aurora gown with iridescent bodice, golden necklace and crown, and shoes. She comes with a Little Little Golden Book and the tiny Merryweather fairy, who saved Princess Aurora from death when she pricked her finger on a spinning wheel on her sixteenth birthday, making her sleep until true love's kiss broke the spell. Merryweather is marked c DISNEY/ c MATTEL INC/ 1992/ CHINA; she first appeared in a tiny Disney play set from 1993. **$20.00.**

Disney Collector Series

Mattel realized that the adult doll collector market might welcome a high-quality Disney doll collection featuring dolls dressed in the finest quality fabrics. While most of Mattel's Disney dolls are already of superb quality, price constraints prohibited more expensive dress materials and accessories; after all, the Disney Classics series of dolls is designed for children (even though collectors love them!). The first Disney Collector Series by Mattel, The Signature Collection, features a series of Disney dolls wearing their classic signature fashions from classic Disney animated films. Doll stands are included with each collector series doll.

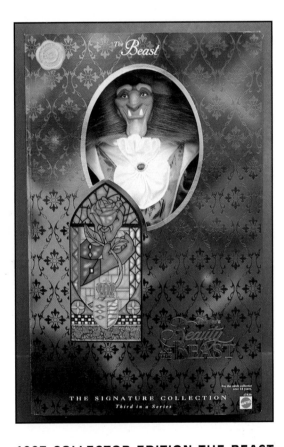

996 COLLECTOR EDITION BELLE #16089 features Belle wearing her billowing golden ball gown with golden lace bodice, osettes, crystal rhinestones, gold lamé fingerless gloves, rnate earrings and hair decoration, and shoes. A prototype f this doll sold at Walt Disney World's one-of-a-kind auction or thousands of dollars in 1995. **$70.00.**

1997 COLLECTOR EDITION THE BEAST #17826 is 13½" tall. He wears a formal royal blue and gold tuxedo with metallic jacquard vest. A blue tone ruffle pin is affixed to his shirt. The Beast has vinyl feet and hands, combable hair, and small horns. **$70.00.**

1997 COLLECTOR EDITION SNOW WHITE #17761 commemorates the sixtieth anniversary of the original release of *Snow White and the Seven Dwarfs* in 1938. It is hard to imagine a better Snow White doll than this — her lips are as red as a rose, her hair is black as ebony, and her skin is white as snow. This spectacular doll wears her signature yellow satin charmeuse gown with royal blue brocade bodice, a lacy white petticoat, white satin collar, golden braid trim, shoes with bows, and a red bow in her upturned black hair. A tiny bird friend perches on her hand. **$75.00.**

Great Villains Collection

Occasionally frightening but always outrageous, Disney's villains are often as memorable as the movie's hero and heroine. When Disney's 1964 animated picture *101 Dalmatians* was made into a live-action movie in 1996, Cruella de Vil was marvelously portrayed by Glenn Close, affording Mattel the perfect doll with which to launch this series.

1996 POWER IN PINSTRIPES CRUELLA DE VIL 16295 features the doll made in Glenn Close's likeness, wearing a form-fitting black suit, accented with glittery pinstripes, white lapels, black pantyhose, extravagant faux fur stole and muff, black hat with veil, and spiked black heels. Her accessories include a signature cigarette holder and sunglasses. The doll's hair is rooted with black hair on her right and white hair on her left. **$70.00.**

1997 RUTHLESS IN RED CRUELLA DE VIL

#17576 features the devilish dog-napping diva wearing a crimson pillbox hat, oversize red and black faux fur coat, slick scarlet pants, red cable sweater, and necklace. Her accessories include a bracelet, cigarette holder, and sunglasses. **$65.00.**

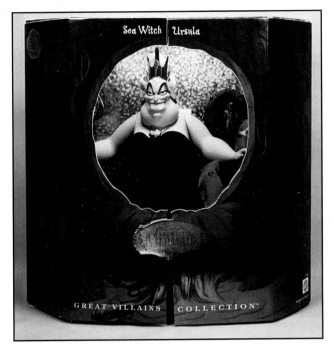

1997 SEA WITCH URSULA #17575 features a perfect vinyl rendition of Ursula with rooted white hair and lavender skin wearing a flocked black gown with purple tentacles accented with sequins. She wears a golden crown and necklace, and her accessories include a golden staff and a tiny shrimp. **$85.00.**

Disney Collector Series

Holiday Princess

The Happy Holidays series of Barbie dolls are among the most collected Barbie dolls made, so it is not surprising that a similar series would be introduced featuring Disney dolls. The first Holiday Princess doll appeared in 1996. Each doll in the series has a holiday ornament featuring the princess' portrait.

1996 HOLIDAY PRINCESS CINDERELLA #16090 wears a white satin gown with faux fur collar and trim, sparkly sheer overskirt with metallic snowflakes, silver lamé bows on her gloves and dress, silver lamé hair band, silvery cloth choker, and silver jewelry. A snowflake ornament featuring her portrait is included. **$50.00.**

1997 HOLIDAY PRINCESS BELLE #16710 is featured in the new Disney video, *The Enchanted Christmas*. Belle wears a rich burgundy velvet gown with gold lamé trim and hair bow. Her ornament features her portrait. **$45.00.**

Film Premiere Edition

Since Ariel did not wear elegant, sequinned swimwear in *The Little Mermaid* movie, she does not technically qualify as a candidate for the Signature Collection, so this Film Premiere Edition series features Disney dolls in fanciful costumes.

1997 FILM PREMIERE EDITION ARIEL #17827 features The Little Mermaid wearing a pleated iridescent collar, waist accent, and tail fin; her blue green tail and purple top with sheer sleeves are adorned with faux pearls, sequins, and starfish. Ariel wears a starfish and pearl tiara in her red hair. This Ariel uses the 1991-dated Shani body. **$70.00.**

Wedding Collection

Toys 'R' Us released its first exclusive Disney Wedding doll in 1995, Wedding Cinderella, wearing an elegant wedding gown. A second wedding doll joined the series in 1997, followed by a third in 1998.

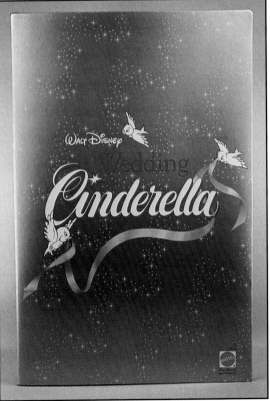

1995 WEDDING CINDERELLA #14232 commemorates the forty-fifth anniversary of the movie's release in 1950. *Cinderella* won three Academy Awards, and since then has been re-released five times. Wedding Cinderella wears a shiny full gown with iridescent overlay and bodice. She wears a veil held with three white roses. She wears an elegant pearlescent necklace and earrings, fingerless white gloves, and she carries a rose bouquet. **$70.00.**

1997 WEDDING SLEEPING BEAUTY #18057 features the new Sleeping Beauty smiling head mold with teeth showing. She wears a white brocade gown, accented with satin and faux pearls. **$50.00.**

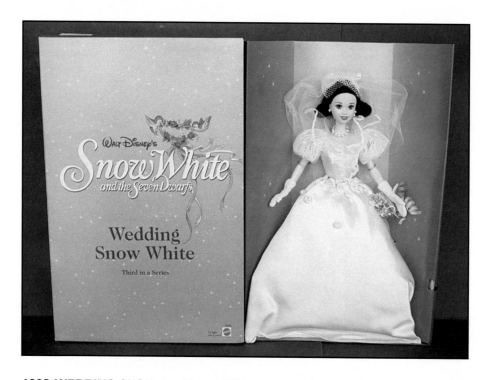

1998 WEDDING SNOW WHITE #18958 wears an ivory satin gown with tulle veil. She is third in Toys 'R' Us Wedding Collection. **$44.00.**

One of a Kind

My thanks to Suzanne Seagalbaum for these photos.

DEMI MOORE. At the annual Dream Halloween auction, on October 25, 1997, one-of-a-kind dolls were auctioned to raise funds for the Children Affected by AIDS Foundation; CAAF offers financial support to non-profit organizations that help children affected by AIDS. The highest bid of the evening belonged to this Demi Moore doll designed by Patricia Chan with facial sculpting by Hussein Abbo. The Demi Moore doll, a superb likeness of the actress (and doll collector), wears a silk dress adorned with 25,000 Austrian crystals. **$19,000.00.** Courtesy of Mattel, Inc.

ENGLAND'S ROSE. A beautiful doll commemorating Princess Diana, England's Rose, designed by Debbie Chang and Cynthia Miller, wears a satin gown with a white rose and golden leaf crown. At the 1997 Dream Halloween, England's Rose brought **$10.000.00.** Courtesy of Mattel, Inc.

HOLLY WOODY. Star of Toy Story, Woody wears a gold lamé shirt with a tie adorned with Swarovski crystals. This one-of-a-kind doll designed by Lisa Temming for the 1997 Dream Halloween auction sold for **$11,000.00.** Courtesy of Mattel, Inc.

CRUELLA'S HALLOWEEN MASQUERADE. Designed by Lisa Temming, Cruella's Halloween Masquerade features the character Cruella de Vil from *101 Dalmatians* in a black gown with a feathered mask and cigarette holder. **$3,000.00.**

Index

Index

Index

Index

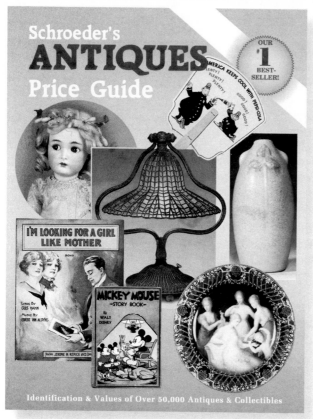